Psychological Consultation in the Schools

Psychological Consultation in the Schools

A Catalyst for Learning

Ruth G. Newman

Basic Books, Inc., Publishers
NEW YORK/LONDON

To my children
Jeffrey and Brooke
and to the memory of my husband
James R. Newman
with love and pride in them for their understanding

Foreword

William C. Morse

Professor of Education
The University of Michigan

Education is fast becoming the world's largest enterprise, if indeed it is not already. And yet, when it comes to seeking answers to the many problems, educators appear to embrace easily practices and panaceas gratuitously offered by outside specialists. Since everyone has been to school, everyone thinks that he is an expert. Seldom do outside specialists take time to study the system itself to see what is really needed. Seldom do they "live in" to test their proposals.

Nowhere is this cure by remote control more patent than in the offers of advice to schools when they are faced with pu pils who cannot manage to conform. Admonitions to understand come in one ear, while solutions by repression come in the other. In fact, the relationship between the schools and the experts in human behavior often turns rancid because of the unreality of the so-called assistance. Indeed, the same issues come to the fore wherever we work with disturbed children in an action setting—school, camp, day care, or other institution.

But things are changing. Some psychologists, social workers, and psychiatrists are taking their cues from the reality of the school situation itself. Not many perhaps, but some. And the reality of a difficult school induces humility and sympathy from these conscientious workers.

Dr. Newman is one of these leaders. She brings to the situation an extensive background of clinical training, clinical practice, and research. But more than that, she and her co-workers have had long-term, deep involvement with the public-school establishment. Their activities with teachers have extended over many years. And the activities do not consist merely of teaching teachers: These workers have gone directly to the teachers' work space in the schools. The test of new concepts is in whether or not they can be made to function in the actual setting for which they are intended. The crucible of practice is the place to test and to perfect theory. This is the professional account one finds in this volume.

Since the approach is reality-bound, it will not always satisfy. School difficulties with discipline increase by the day, both in magnitude and in intensity. It is a symptom of the culture we have produced. In many classrooms, and indeed in whole schools or areas, the anxiety of teachers and administrators has reached high pitch. An incident causes someone to push the panic button for control no matter what the side-effects. We are often ready to settle for surface compliance rather than hygienic management which teaches through the confrontation of the problem. Those looking for instant solutions will not be pleased with this book, for it offers no psychological "Mr. Clean." In place of palliatives it offers only hard work. The solution to helping distraught children is to be found in our attitudes, our purposes, and our skills. In short, we must change if we are to help pupils change. There is no attempt to gloss over this critical and, to some people, disquieting fact. There are others who see the same need for change, and they solve it by blame. This produces in some educators a counter-hostility, in others guilt. Seldom does this approach produce the needed alteration in the educational process. Herein lies the positive approach of this book. No time is taken to drag us through abstract discussions of what is wrong. It is only too evident as we read the analyses presented. The stress here is on how we can move off dead center. Certainly, it will be hard work, but no one says that compounding the mistakes as we do now is easy. We are working hard in ineffective ways. Can we face the situation in such a way as to deploy our same energy in creative, long-term, problem-alleviating action? The examples speak louder than adages. We can.

The keystone to bringing about this new style of work with children is consultation. But the very nature of the consultation is itself a far cry from a visit by the on-the-line worker to hear messages in the expert's office—whether the "office" is distant or on the grounds. Here, consultation is concerned with handling the child's behavior, and it takes place "where the action is." In fact, as we learn, the concept of Life Space Interviewing was born in the action setting. At the same time it becomes clear that no pattern of adult-child interaction alone is enough. Most often there is something awry in the total situation as well as in communication, and no intervention of this type will be enough. It is this combination of interpersonal and milieu forces which must be appreciated. Yet it is often the ferment started in working with individual children or with groups which can generate a real solution or the start toward one. This book makes it evident that there is no substitute for money to purchase the birthrights of children, in special services or enriched experience. The economy of scarcity has got to go. What the consultation depicted in this book does is to provide a way to reduce current fragmentation and ineptness through psychological understanding. The consultation alone cannot supply the help: It depends upon working through others. But by looking both toward inner and outer difficulties children face, we see the connection between what we do of the moment and the social changes we must induce over the long pull.

If there is one basic asset in this type of consultation, it is flexibility. When one leaves the defining perimeters of the professional office, new things begin happening. This is the story of social psychiatry of which we hear so much today. If one tries to help no matter what, there is nothing constant but the helping methodology. What one does depends upon how one can help. The flexibility in technique runs all the way from testing and research to advice and oblique conversation. All the old "thou shalts" give way to this flexibility. The consultant role may mean serving as an expert in one situation and passive non-direction in another. Consultation content ranges from case conferences to grading practices and over-all educational philosophy. Neither is this consultation method a one-age-level approach: Examples extend from preschool through high school and to other agencies as well. The immediate target for consultation might be the teacher, child care worker, principal, or specialist. This is in-service education with a vengeance.

To read this book is to live years of professional work in a few hours. It is a fatiguing, draining experience. But then, that is the nature of life on the line. Will you believe what is written here? Only if you have been around. The tone is frank and speaks not always of successes. But these consultants really do choose the hard situations for the tests. Essentially it is the saga of humanizing the school and other agencies, through finding ways to make group and individual interventions serve to help children in trying situations.

Teachers will identify immediately with the types of conditions described. The transfer value will be evident. Those administrators who are responsible for the social fabric created by schools and agencies will find ideas for making a more hygienic life space for children in their care. The many specialists in and out of the school hierarchy will have the direction clearly pointed and a tactic outlined. Given the immensity of the task which can overwhelm and produce despair, we all need such an account as this to define where and how to begin the quiet revolution of a new approach.

January 1967

Acknowledgments

The concern for children and youth and the problems of those who teach and work with them that are expressed in this book have been developed over the years, in large part, through working with and learning from Dr. Fritz Redl. It was with his help that the consultation program described was launched and carried out. But before the program began, I spent five years in happy proximity to him, his thinking, and his varied approaches. I am deeply in his debt for his gifts of insights, ideas, and understandings.

For this book to have been written at all meant hard labor in writing, editing, and proofreading by Marjorie Keith and Claire Bloomberg, to whom I am most grateful. I want also to thank Joan Tilley for her patience in reading my impossible handwriting and in typing draft after draft of the manuscript. I am most grateful to my husband, James R. Newman, before his untimely death, for his painstaking reading of the manuscript and his advice.

Without the interest, cooperation, and efforts of planning of Dr. Irene Hypps—who at the time of the work on the project was Assistant Superintendent of Schools in charge of the Department of Pupil Appraisal—the consultation programs could never have come into being. I herewith acknowledge my debt. I am also grateful to Dr. Carl Hansen, Superintendent of Schools of the District of Columbia, and to Mrs. Aileen Davis, now Superintendent of Pupil Personnel Services, for their cooperation. I would like to mention the fine work of Mr. Howard Kitchener, M. S. W., and Mrs. Ruth Emerson during the first two years of the project, and that of Mrs. Miriam Jaegerman during the early stages of this book. I am deeply appreciative of the interest, support, and work of Dr. William Morse, and I am happy that he chose to write a foreword for it.

Without the help and information given by many teachers, principals, counselors, and school psychologists, as well as by our teacher diarists not within the school system studied, the book could not have been written.

Ruth G. Newman

Contents

Author's Note

The schools and the people described in this
book are real. However, in every case names have been concealed and where possible the identity of schools has also been
concealed. Where personal material has been given, the au-
thor has gone to great lengths to conceal identifying information, sometimes changing the sex of individuals where sex
was not an important feature of the case, sometimes changing
features of the relationships and the places mentioned. The
effort has been to keep as strictly to the significant facts as
possible and yet to protect the privacy of individuals. Where
readers may believe they recognize an individual, they are
probably mistaken. Other than naming the city of Washington, D.C., and the superintendents in charge of education or
divisions of the school administration, no proper names, other
than those of the consultants themselves, have been used.

Psychological Consultation
in the Schools

1

Introduction:
The Schools in Need

While we support the idea of public education today and require that every child in our enormously expanding population attend school until the age of sixteen, we must also recognize that many of our school children are badly served by a system of practices geared to other times and other conditions. Our schools are in trouble. Teachers and pupils are in trouble. This volume presents an attempt to deal with the massive problems which confront our schools. These are not educational problems as such; they are concerned, rather, with the conditions which make education possible. That is, the climate for learning.

It has become clear to everyone who has worked in schools that the traditional methods of "trouble shooting" are not adequate. Actually they often do no more than aspirin tablets for a pneumonia victim—they temporarily lessen the pain or fever but do little to combat the virus. In the traditional approach, each crisis is dealt with as it arises. Not only does the diagnosis of a single case take months, with the result that treatment is delayed, but in the time between a call for help and the rendering of assistance, the child and the teacher are often caught in a mutually damaging deadlock. Equally often the child is removed to harry another teacher, and continues to hamper his own and his classmates' ability to function well. Not only has the treatment of single cases been a sadly deficient approach; it has defeated and frustrated the school professionals who have been forced to use it in the face of growing odds and increasing hopelessness.

This book reports on a method of consultation that grew out of a small, intensive clinical study. Though in its original form it was unrelated to consultation for schools, it came to be seen that much of the information gained would serve as a useful basis for helping school staffs deal with emotional problems in various school settings.

Background of the Method

The subjects of the clinical study, conducted from 1955 to 1960, were a carefully selected group of extremely disturbed, hyper-aggressive children in residence at the National Institute of Mental Health at the Child Research Branch under the direction of Dr. Fritz Redl. At first the children lived in a locked ward and attended an especially designed school on the ward; eventually they were moved, through various stages, to the public schools. They were given total milieu treatment, were cared for and studied by psychiatrists, psychologists, teachers, group workers, nurses, social workers, occupational therapists, and sociologists. All the insights contributed by these disciplines were explored, as well as the impact that the children-patients had on the staff members who worked with them. The children's inner dynamics and outer behavior, their learning patterns, their living style and their uses of the variety of activities they participated in, from school to play, from sleep to fantasy, from meals to fights, were examined. The knowledge gained from dealing with their problems (which represented the kind most bothersome to teachers and schools) was translated into means for helping teachers deal with aggressive, acting-out behavior even in cases in which the underlying pathology might not be so severe as in our children. Both in medicine and in psychiatry the knowledge gained by working with the very sick is often found applicable to those who are mostly well. So through our experience with these children, a program that could be useful to hundreds of pupils and their teachers was developed.

Even more important for the development of a consultation method, we learned much about what teachers needed, to be able to cope effectively with both troubled and more normal children so that both could develop within the same class. This experience made us intensely aware of the multiple pressures on school staff that make the fulfillment of their professional tasks more difficult. We developed some leads about what pitfalls to watch out for, what methods could actually help and which could not, and under what conditions children would accept help. In many ways our information supports the theory and techniques and experience of Caplan's Consultation methods; in some ways it differs.

The Experiment

With this experience behind us, we decided to try consultation methods in a variety of schools, developing our method jointly with many staffs to find the best ways of working together. Our bias is psychodynamic and interdisciplinary. Despite our tenets the method is not unique. It is by no means the only method of consultation with school staffs; nor do we wish to be exclusive; on the contrary, we trust it adds to existing methods.

Our method, though flexible enough to be modified according to the individuality of the school and the age levels of the students, is based on certain principles of a psychodynamic approach to learning. It is centered on the relationships of consultant to staff members, and of staff members to the children they serve and to the schools that employ them. The method, we have discovered, can be applied through consultants outside the school, as we have done, or it can be developed inside the school if qualified internal staff members are trained to use it.

Our method differs from "crisis consultation," for we are available for *continuous and regular consultation* not limited to the explosion of a crisis in a single child, teacher, or administrator. We have borrowed from psychoanalysis, clinical psychology, and social casework. We believe that continuing relationships and familiarity form the basis for trust, and that only with such trust, skillfully worked with, can one open up new pathways of behavior and the new understandings that make possible desired changes of a lasting nature. We are convinced that without familiarity and continuing support, during quiet as well as crisis periods, backsliding and subsequent despair too easily occur. In addition, we have become increasingly sure that although individual, one-to-one consultant contacts are sometimes essential, small group work is equally important. School staffs lead fragmented professional lives, and what communication there is is often faulty, concealing more than it reveals. Therefore we feel there should be more emphasis on working with groups— applying knowledge of group behavior—in consultations with school staffs.

Our method differs also from those weekly seminars given school staffs by outside consultants: We believe that *on-the-spot* consultation offers greater possibilities for mutual understanding and for long-term growth. Whether or not our method is used, we do know that the needs of school staffs are great and the concept of community psychiatry so new and urgently required that patient and imaginative care must be taken to put effective programs into action.

Our Experiences

The best way to explain our method is to report what actually happened in our experiences as psycho-education consultants at various schools—high, junior high, elementary school, nursery school, day care, and residential treatment centers—in or near Washington, D.C.

Washington is a unique city, taxed but unrepresented. It is growing rapidly and has a large, mobile population of both the upper middle class and the poor (largely Negro). But its needs are those typical throughout the nation, rather than unique ones. We have, of course, concealed the identity of schools and of individuals, though we have tried to communicate the quality of the experience. We feel that the problems reported will be found in every urban community and can be useful as a guide to the kind of hazards and satisfactions to be found in creating a consultation program.

For the major part of our consultation, the five public schools were chosen from the Washington Public School System with the permission and cooperation of Superintendent of Schools Dr. Carl Hansen. Although consultation in any urban area will have similar problems, some special features of the local scene should be pointed out. Washington's population covers the whole range of economic, social, and cultural levels from highly privileged to severely deprived. The schools have not only had integration problems of the usual nature; they have special "integration" problems related to the constant moving in and out of the city characteristic of the capital. The only major industry is government and, among the privileged and underprivileged alike, there is constant mobility and few roots. Among the poorer groups there are many families who have moved North and either stay in the city briefly or move from neighborhood to neighborhood, depending on whether they have jobs. The schools have a four-track system, wherein children are placed on the basis of I.Q. and teachers' recommendations. This system has been under much criticism and is being modified. The makeup of various special classes is often a patchwork quilt of mixed diagnosis, mixed behavior, and mixed levels of school functioning. Some schools have 100 per cent Negro attendance; a very few are nearly 100 per cent white. This is not only because of de facto segregation, but because Negroes make up about 80 per cent of the total population. Thus the "minority" group is in fact the majority group in this city's schools.

Washington's community affairs, including its school system, are controlled by a committee of Congress which often determines the school budget according to the individual politics of its members. This situation makes it harder for a program to get consistent support. Not only does the Superintendent of Schools have to please the population of the city his schools serve, and the various people from other states and countries temporarily residing in the capital; he also has to please a Congressional committee whose warring personal and political interests often have little relevance to the needs of the residents. At a time when the government is carrying on huge nationwide community projects, Washington, as the capital, is very much in the public eye. The pressure can be frightening and frustrating to school officials, especially when few other areas are aware of Washington's special problems.

The school system's acceptance of us was, reasonably enough, contingent upon the understanding that, while we were there to learn, we should not be in the way. A current project, in which principals were being trained in methods of consultation that preceded us, made our advent more easily acceptable.*

Selection of Schools

The high school we chose was a large one in a deteriorated urban area where crime and poverty abound. It was known for its high delinquency and low academic achievement rates. The dynamic and imaginative principal who had just taken it over was aware of the low morale of staff and students and asked if we would choose her school to be included in our consultation project. She was starting several new programs, such as a work-study program, remedial and tutorial help by a group of volunteer women, and a first attempt to include an honors track in this school. She wanted help for herself and for groups of teachers and students who were involved in these projects.

Similarly, we chose a junior high school in an equally poor

* School Project on Consultation Skills, Irene Hypps, Ph.D., Stanley Jacobson, Washington School of Psychiatry, Washington, D.C.

area which had special problems because of the section's extraordinarily high mobility rate, as well as because it included more than the usual share of special classes for the emotionally disturbed and the slow learner. When we first went there —it was the first year of our consultation experience in this school system—the community still contained population remnants of the days when it was a fairly stable, lower-middle-class neighborhood. But it was changing rapidly to a much lower level of income and stability, although it bordered on one of the most fashionable, high-rent areas in the city. Many of the parents had recently come up from the South and were trying to find places for themselves in a city already bursting at the seams.

We have emphasized one elementary school in which we consulted, because the interaction between staff and consultant was particularly dramatic and active. It, too, was situated in an area making the transition from white middle class to Negro middle and lower middle class. And it was pervaded with that drive characteristic of the middle class, but especially strong among those newly arrived, often at great psychic cost: parental insistence on high achievement levels for their children no matter how inappropriate to a child's needs. Excerpts are included from two other elementary schools—one a fairly stable lower-middle-class school, the other a school known throughout the system as the dumping ground for all special cases of whatever nature.

We dipped down in age level, out of the organized school system, to report on our consultation with a cooperative nursery school. We did this for a number of reasons: (1) because it was the only strictly upper-middle-class group we worked with; (2) because of the special task of the teachers, who need to work with the participating parents as much as with the children; (3) because the public at large, as well as Boards of Education, have become aware—via Head Start Programs— of the importance and goals of pre-school experience and how it can aid later education; and (4) because the cooperative, in which the parent participates as a teacher-aide, has proved valuable in exploring whether the use of non-professional aides is worth considering by organized school systems. The complications that arise from this last point are worth particular attention. Such participation occurred not only in pre-school education and day-care facilities but also in schools initiated by parents for the mentally retarded, the emotionally disturbed, the physically handicapped, where such children have been left without opportunities for education unless parents provided it. Consultation in this special setting had its unique flavor and uses.

Also outside the school system, but with severe problems requiring consultation, was the combined day-care and residential treatment center for emotionally disturbed children which we cover in this book. Here the anxiety generated within the staff by the emotional illness of the children set up tremendous intra-staff tensions. I have discovered that, to a degree, the problems exhibited here—arising from lack of funds, transitional organization, high staff turnover, low salaries, and conflicting philosophies of treatment—are common to many day-care treatment centers and residential centers. We felt it essential to include samples from this story because some clues concerning the special needs for consultation in such a setting should be given; because the special education classes within schools have similar problems (but in isolation, which is often harder to bear); and finally because, as is true for all psychology, we learn much about the normal from seeing the inner workings of the abnormal. Similarly, we learn much from how a teaching staff handles the disturbed child, for similar patterns arise, less perceptibly but just as surely, in handling the ordinary child who has moments of emotional distress.

We hope by reporting these experiences to indicate the differences in psycho-education consultation in a variety of settings. In many cases the demands on the consultant were different, and consequently a different kind of training for the consultants was necessary. In the last chapter we will indicate the qualifications most useful to this kind of consultative work. Suffice it to say here that, given a focus of psychodynamic understanding, the more varied the background, interests, and point of view of the consultant the better.

There were five active consultants on our project staff, including myself. All were trained in psychodynamics, all had had considerable personal psychotherapy. One was a psychiatric social worker trained to work with schools; one was a lawyer turned remedial teacher; one had been a nursery-school director, therapeutic teacher, and trainer of teachers, I had been a teacher, a remedial teacher, a clinical psychologist, a director of a treatment school, and a trainer of teachers. Dr. Redl and I supervised the consultants and they supervised me.

As well as appreciating the differences between consultation in the various settings, we hope the reader will see what this kind of consultation has in common in all the settings.

When one has had experience in consultation work with schools, one finds that many agencies in the area wish to do similar work. A city's Board of Health and Mental Hygiene Clinics may wish to help out in schools as a preventative as well as a diagnostic and curative measure. People in such agencies are finding mental health consultation to schools a useful tool when adapted to fit their needs. They are eager to learn a method in which they can train their psychiatric residents, social workers, and psychologists in this particular aspect of community psychiatry.

Much as we would like to, we cannot give a recipe for setting up such a consultation service, but we can give guidelines. We hope this book will help those who wish to inaugurate or modify existing psycho-education consultation, either from outside the school as we did, or from inside the school as we are now engaged in training people to do (see Chapter 7).

Conclusion

How our method differs from or is similar to others seeking to grapple with school problems is less important than the fact that multiple services are needed to help school staffs. A method with a chance of producing useful changes of a lasting kind should not be merely a panic response to the periodic community game of "blame the schools." Such indignation is too often like a paper fire—fast to light, bright to the eyes, easy to extinguish, and quick to be forgotten. To be effective, a method must take into account things as they are, without being resigned to them, and be *aware* of what needs to be changed. Practitioners of the method need the foresight and the ability to handle the difficulties that follow change before lasting benefits can result.

To create an effective method, one must be aware of human fears and insecurities and must build in ways for professional egos to survive, if not to thrive, while the pressure of everyday problems continues. One has to be realistically aware of what must be done to fulfill more deep-seated needs in a school than the individual disturbances of any one child—considering the growth of population, the limited number of trained personnel, and urgent pleas from teachers who must deal with all things at all times.

We are convinced that our method is a process worth trying, worth modifying according to the specific community needs and problems. We are aware that various aspects of our consultation method, as well as the whole Gestalt, need far more testing, questioning, and refined evaluating. But from our experience we firmly believe that whatever method of consultation is tried, for it to be successful over the long run, it must include a concept of continual, on-the-spot service by trained people, sufficiently flexible to change procedures, though not principles, as the personnel or conditions of a school demand.

In the Appendix the reader will find two diaries of first

year teachers working in schools where consultation of the kind we have described was nonexistent. These diaries were written for us as part of our research material. They date from before Bel Kaufman's *Up the Down Staircase* or *The School Children* by Mary Frances Greene and Orletta Ryan. The striking similarity of the experiences and these books derives from the desperation of teachers working within highly bureaucratic institutions. Unfortunately, the conditions described in books and diaries are all too common. We believe that good consultation can alleviate many of the "impossibilities" described. We have indicated by our notes where and how consultation might have helped these teachers and might permit other talented and enthusiastic educators to continue in the teaching profession rather than to resign in despair or continue with apathy or a sense of inevitable defeat. We have learned that consultation can be a primary source of effective in-service training. Also, in the Appendix we include more detailed information about the Life Space Interview as it applies to schools.

2

Consultation in the Elementary School

Clements Elementary School

(This section was written by Claire Bloomberg, who was a consultant at this school.)

The principal of Clements Elementary School was eager for consultation, and because of its particular social and economic background, the school was of special interest to us. Like Hoover, another elementary school where we acted as consultants, its pupils were drawn largely from the middle and lower middle classes, but it had a far greater ratio of Negro students. Lincoln, a third elementary school where we worked, was considered the dumping ground for many slow-learning or ill-adjusted pupils and had a great number of special classes. We gave a year's consultation to a fourth elementary school, outside of the school system, because of our desire to make geographical comparisons, but as this school was not in the area where we concentrated, we will mention it only insofar as it brings up problems to consultation not dissimilar to those presented in the three other schools. Since Clements, of all the elementary schools, contained most of the problems common to all the others, we report it here in more detail and will present only short excerpts from our experience at Hoover which illustrate special features of consultation. We will give slightly more space to the atmosphere and problems of consultation at Lincoln, a school for special cases.

Background

The neighborhood of Clements, formerly exclusively white, was composed largely of middle-class Negro families, although there had recently been an influx of poor Negroes. The poor families were doubling up in order to afford housing in this neighborhood. The heads of the families were mostly government clerks and teachers, but there was a small percentage of doctors and other higher-paid professionals at one end of the economic scale and of manual laborers and unskilled workers at the other. The school district also contained a small nucleus of white families who had remained in the area and who had, for the most part, joined with the Negro families to establish a chapter of Neighbors Incorporated, an organization devoted to the refutation of some of the myths concerning Negro occupancy of a new neighborhood, particularly the one which maintains that property values necessarily decline with the influx of a Negro population. Their efforts were successful in that the houses remained attractive and well kept, but the number of white families was too small to enable them to keep the school genuinely integrated. During the year 1962–1963, when I worked there as a consultant, the student population was almost entirely Negro.

The staff of the school was composed of both white and Negro teachers. Most of the whites were older teachers who had remained when the neighborhood changed, and the Negroes were mostly younger newcomers to the school. The principal, a Negro, was a competent and conscientious woman who had been brought in from another neighborhood when her white predecessor had retired. Serving the 1,000 pupils of the school were thirty-two teachers, three of whom were men—a happy and rare situation in an elementary school. The school was neat and well kept, with spacious playground space. It was made up of two buildings connected by a passageway. The older part of the school is about thirty years old, and a new part, added as the neighborhood population increased, about two years old.

As soon as one became acquainted with the neighborhood it was clear that, in nearly all the families in which two parents lived together, each held more than one job. Children were left in the care of aunts or grandparents or friends during the day. By talking to staff members and getting to know some of the parents, I saw, as the year progressed, that the parents were determined that the terrible poverty they had known in their youth should not be the lot of their children. It was remarkable in this school community how the children of even the poorest families were well dressed, extremely clean and neat, and had toys and playthings at home. It is easy for an outsider long established in the middle class to understand this fierce upward push on the part of the parents, but it is very hard to show them the unhappy effects of this drive on their children. So much was the specter of poverty to be avoided, so strong was the emphasis on providing material comforts, that they often didn't or couldn't afford to see the loss in warmth and relaxed contacts. Instead, the children saw the tension that crept into the harried, overworked lives of their parents and saw this kind of life as the model for adulthood. The results were far more devastating than the parents knew. Education was seen as the ladder to eventual success. This belief is an asset to a school staff and contains much truth, but it means tremendous pressure on the children to achieve good grades, and this in turn creates stress and behavior symptoms for many of them.

Preliminary Visits

Although I was not to start my regular consultation until the beginning of a new school year in September, I made several visits to Clements during the preceding spring. I wanted to become familiar with the school, the children, and the teachers so that I would not appear as a total stranger in the fall.

On my first visit, while I was trying to get the feel of the school and the neighborhood, the only staff member I talked to was the principal. I explained the background and objectives of our project and told her about myself. I stressed that I was not a psychologist, but I outlined the extensive experience I have had with both normal and disturbed children. I emphasized the fact that my major interest had been with very young children and that we were interested, in our research, in working with the kindergarten and the first and second grades in this school in order to find out about the onset and prevention of problems of behavior and learning. The principal, Mrs. Tate, seemed disappointed at this restriction, but agreed to go along.

She asked if I would be available for in-service training, such as meetings with her faculty or with area-wide second-grade teachers. I replied that I would certainly meet with her teachers at her request. In order not to seem to take back help as soon as it was offered, I said I was personally interested in the area-wide training of second-grade teachers, and if there was enough of my time available, I would be glad to work with her on that, although it could not be a regularly scheduled activity of mine as part of my weekly visits to her school. I told her I would not actually be working there until the fall, but that I would appreciate being allowed to come to the school once a week for a month that spring to observe the children in their classes, the schedules, and school routines, so that I could get the feel of things. She was pleased with this idea and especially happy when I said I would not come around after the end of May because I knew, from my interviewing, that teachers resent anything extraneous to their regular duties during the closing weeks of school. Mrs. Tate said she would send around a bulletin explaining what I would be doing, and she gave me a list of those teachers with whom I would be concerned. She mentioned a child in the first grade, whom she described as bright but nonconforming, and said I would certainly want to observe him. I found that, even before work began, the concern with the problems and management of certain children was so pressing that it had to be brought out.

As I thanked Mrs. Tate for the time she had spent with me, I told her that on subsequent visits I would always check in with her first. To this she replied that, if she should happen not to be in her office when I arrived, I should just go ahead and wander around and see what I wanted to see.

On my three subsequent visits to the school that spring, I visited all the classes I would be concerned with the following fall. In addition to two kindergartens, four first grades and four second grades, there were a junior primary and a basic primary. The pupils in the junior primary were mostly six-year-olds who had had a year in kindergarten but were considered too immature or too slow to go on to first-grade work. Some were reading at pre-primer level, but others were still on the so-called reading readiness workbook. The pupils in the basic primary were older, up to about ten years of age, and were extremely slow. The teacher had divided them into groups on about five levels of functioning.

All the teachers were expecting me and all were cordial. It was clear that there were a few who felt no need for special help, others who would seek it, and still others who would be unwilling or unable to use it, at least at the beginning of the project. At this time I was somewhat bothered by the feeling that while the principal welcomed help for her teachers, she might be too busy or too personally reserved to want to become very much involved. I noted this in my report of my second visit and again after the third visit.

Consultation

When the school year began I stayed away from Clements for a few weeks, since it is our policy to wait until children and teachers have had a chance to settle down into the year. According to plan, once I began my visits, I was present one day a week for consultation with any teacher of the kindergarten, junior primary, basic primary, first or second grade who wanted to see me. I saw the principal every week except for a few days when she had to be out of the building. Exclusive of my time with the principal, I had 147 conferences with teachers in 32 visiting days. Late in the year, when a counselor was assigned to the school, I began to have weekly conferences with her.

In the beginning of the year, as in the other schools in which we worked, conferences with the principal and teachers centered on discussions of the problems of individual children and what could be done to help them. Some children the principal asked me to observe, others were brought to my attention by teachers, and there were others whom I spotted while in the process of observing some other child in a particular classroom. Though Mrs. Tate, the principal, was always welcoming and obviously glad to have extra help with problems, she was by nature reserved, and it took time for us to be together with ease. It has often struck me how important it is to consider the pace of a relationship in any clinically focused work. Aside from the matter of pace, there were outside influences that blocked our getting together. Mrs. Tate had the usual mountain of duties of any principal. Besides, she was an officer in a school-connected organization where she had to be on hand and, like other principals, was often called out of the building to meetings called by the superintendent's office. From rereading my weekly reports it is clear that what really began to break down the reserve between Mrs. Tate and me was the fact that I didn't confine myself solely to conferences, but allowed her and the teachers to use me in many other ways. Shortly after I began working, a social adjustment teacher was added to the staff, and Mrs. Tate asked me to work with the new teacher to help her understand her pupils and work out a schedule and curriculum for them.

Special Help

I was uneasy at first about this assignment of help to the special class, since it was outside the original plan to work only with the younger grades. On discussing it with the project directors, we all felt that one of the main tenets of our method was that we were there to do what was needed, and consequently this kind of flexibility was warranted. Mrs. Tate very much appreciated my work with the new teacher, since she knew that I was spending a lot of extra time trying to find appropriate material and techniques for helping the teacher with emotionally disturbed children.

There were other ways in which I operated outside the strict bounds of "consultation." One day when I was observing a child in the first grade, the father of another child suddenly appeared in the room and demanded an immediate conference. Since the teacher had been trying to get this man to visit the school, and she knew he had to take time from his work to get there, she very much wanted to see him. What was she to do with her class? Seeing her conflict, I offered to take the class until she finished her conference, and she gratefully accepted. When Mrs. Tate heard about this, she told me she thought I was "a jewel." This was the beginning of genuine confidence in my good will and effectiveness. It may well be that those consultants whose training and background derive from teaching rather than psychology or social work are looked at by principals, and even teachers, more suspiciously than those who come with the halo of an additional degree, and that the breakdown of suspicion is more easily attained if the consultants demonstrate their own ability to cope as well as to help.

Demonstrations

This was not the only first-aid intervention. There are always emergencies in a large school, and there were other occasions when I took over classes for short periods of time, always at the teacher's request. There were several times when, in response to a teacher's request, I sat down with an individual child in a classroom and helped him get started on his work. The first time this happened was when one boy, whose group was doing desk work, was disrupting the class during the time the teacher was trying to conduct a reading lesson with another group. The teacher shot me an entreating glance, we exchanged some sign language, and I sat down and helped the boy get started. The child's response to individual attention was immediate and rewarding and served to demonstrate something to the teacher, though that had not been my original purpose; I merely wanted to help out in a sticky situation. After this incident, I worked with individuals on several other occasions, usually having arranged with the teacher to do so and always with the idea of demonstrating ways in which a particular child's needs might be met. As a result of these incidents, and of my weekly visits to the social adjustment class, I became for many of the children a familiar face in the school. They came to tell me of happenings at home when I saw them at recess or in halls.

One time, the social adjustment teacher and I had arranged to try a technique, the Life Space Interview, the next time a particular boy acted up in the classroom. We had discussed it with the principal and were going to try it as a demonstration, with the idea of eventually training someone on the staff to be available to children in crises in the future. Briefly, one of the many uses of the technique, which was of particular moment in this case, was to take a child who signaled that he was unable to maintain himself in the classroom, give him a respite from a classroom, and offer him a relationship with one adult who was his for the moment of stress. This firm but sympathetic adult would try by words or other means to help him discover why he had to leave and to give him a chance to let off steam, or sit quietly and silently, or otherwise occupy himself until he could regroup himself, so to speak, and return to class without lecture, scolding, or disapproval by the teacher. Because of lack of personnel to carry it through, we were never able to work out the use of the technique in a way to establish it in the school as part of crisis management. This is sad, because those schools which built it in have found it remarkably useful. (The technique is outlined in Appendix B of this book.)

Parent Conferences

I arrived at school one day to find that I had been scheduled for a conference with a parent. I had seen my role as one of helping teachers think through and prepare for parent conferences, but not that of holding such conferences myself. I had not made this clear either to the principal or the teachers, and though I later did so, I did not feel I should refuse to see this parent, particularly since she had had to make many arrangements to get to school on that day. The teacher of the child in question was ill and temporarily out of school. There was not even a chance to bring her in on the conference, so I did the next best thing. While holding the conference, I told the mother I wanted to brief the teacher on what we had discussed, and with her permission, took copious notes, which I went over with the teacher when she returned. There were several follow-up conferences between the teacher and the mother after this, and I was in a good position to serve the teacher as a pre-conference consultant. It worked well.

On other occasions I did sit in on conferences with parents at the teacher's request, but always made sure that the teacher led the conference. I asked occasional questions or tried to change direction when it seemed wise, but I did this only when I thought it might demonstrate something that would be useful to the teacher in future conferences, and always we talked over my interventions afterward.

Sometimes I was drawn into parent conferences simply because I happened to be on the spot during a crisis. This happened with the mother of a boy who was going through the tortures of a school phobia: "At this point," my notes read, "in walked the boy and his mother. She had brought him to school, but he was now refusing to stay, and she was obviously a wreck over it. The secretary suggested that since Mrs. Tate was not there, perhaps the mother could talk to me. I hesitated a moment, but the poor woman was so upset, and I had been so much interested in the boy, that I said O.K., and we went into the nurse's room to talk. The boy came with us, but when I told him I needed to talk to his mother alone, he agreed to sit outside the door and wait for her without any trouble. When we were alone the mother poured out her heart. The father died when the boy was fifteen months old. He is the youngest of five children; the oldest has had psychotherapy because of a deep depression after his father died, and his mother took him to a clinic for eight months. She tried to keep the family together by doing day work, since she didn't want to be on relief. When a new man came along who was good with her kids, she married him to give them a father. When I asked her what methods of discipline she used, she said, 'Beating, but the doctor told me that doesn't do any good so we have stopped it.' Though she described a good relationship between her son and his stepfather, there were many indications to me that the boy is jealous of his new father and not at all sure that his mother won't disappear as did the dead father, or that this new father won't rob him of his mother. The mother, as is always true in school phobias, is deeply involved in the problem of the child, and I felt this was a case where she would have to have professional help both for herself and her child. In this emergency I contented myself with hearing her out and giving her some on-the-spot relief of anxiety. When she asked me if she should insist on his staying at school that day, I said I didn't think it would be a good idea right now because I was quite sure she wouldn't be able to carry through with it, and also because I wanted to tell Mrs. Tate about the whole case and enlist her support in backing up the mother when she was able to leave the boy at school."

Relationship with the Principal

All these ways in which I involved myself with the school were appreciated by Mrs. Tate, with the result that our relationship grew easier and easier as the year progressed. When, toward the end of the year, a school counselor was assigned to her, she asked me to see this new staff member regularly and brief her about the boys in the social adjustment class and the other children in the school who might need special help. When I first came to the school I had asked Mrs. Tate to arrange for me to speak to the teachers with whom I would work and to explain what I would be doing. She now asked me to meet with the whole faculty and do the same thing, with a special invitation to broaden my remarks to include material concerning attitudes toward children with problems.

On my own initiative I made contact with special service personnel in the school system, with outside clinics, and with individual psychologists to arrange for referral of several children who needed it. By the time the end of the year approached, I felt free enough to write out a list of the children I had observed or discussed with their teachers, with my suggestions for placement in the following year. I included their needs for special handling and a description of the kind of teacher I felt might best work with them. Mrs. Tate was most receptive, and later told me she was incorporating my suggestions wherever staff and budget made it possible. This is an interesting indication of how well we had got on, Mrs. Tate and I, for many principals might have been defensive about recommendations for placement. If she and I had not done so well together and talked so openly, I never would have risked such a move.

The majority of my time was spent in consultation with teachers. There were thirteen teachers for whom I was supposed to be available for regular consultation; five more were added at one time or another, either because they were teaching children who were candidates for the social adjustment class, or because they had especially troublesome children in the classroom. Of the eighteen, fourteen used my services during the course of the school year, some of them almost continuously, and some only when an emergency arose. At the beginning of the year, only a few asked for consultation, and I spent a good deal of time with these few, toning down their expectations of magic. I had to repeat over and over again that it was necessary to observe a child many times to get the feeling of his difficulties, and that I would need the help of the teacher's day-to-day observations in our mutual effort to arrive at some plan of dealing with him. We have found that in all schools it takes a few months to become sufficiently acquainted for a consultant to be used in the best way. This "expectation of magic" I speak of is a human enough desire for the expert to come up with instant answers. Though most people know this cannot be done, it is still difficult to counter the need with tact and without losing the support of those who want magic answers so greatly. The first official day at Clements, when I made the rounds in order to get acquainted with all the teachers who might need me, I was confronted with this kind of expectation. Mr. Jacobs, a young man in his twenties, who had not taught in this system before, was then teaching a basic class at Clements. He didn't know anything about me, but immediately began to point out problems when he heard what I was there for. He got out his records on Johnny, his worst acting-out problem, and handed them to me. Even while I was reading them he was enumerating all his other problems in the classroom. After I had had a chance to observe Johnny for about five minutes, he came over and whispered to me, asking what I had been able to see about the problem and what I'd found out. I said I'd need a lot more time to observe, to go over the records, to talk to him, before we could arrive at any idea of the background of Johnny's problem and how to handle him. Mr. Jacobs represented many of the most welcoming teachers who, out of eagerness for help, implicitly demanded that the mental health consultant solve all problems and happily wanted to transfer them to "the expert" and be done with them.

Yet these expectations are understandable when one considers how many times these teachers had been disappointed by "experts" who would test a child or observe him and then leave them with some vague recommendation for more love and attention. And here was a consultant who for one day a week would stay put. Knowing this, I went out of my way whenever possible to make specific recommendations for classroom handling. Gradually, as I spent time in the lunchroom chatting with the teachers and getting to know them, and as the word got around that I could be trusted to make suggestions, to help a child with his work, or to demonstrate new techniques with a group, more teachers asked for consultation. By the end of the year, there were only three teachers who had never used my services and one other who only allowed me to observe a boy in her class at the principal's request. One of these four was a newcomer to the school; she had been teaching for many years and said many times that she had "no problems" with her group. I felt her defensiveness had something to do with her newness in the school and ought to be respected. I had observed the other three in the spring of the preceding year as a preliminary to my presence in the school; all three were strong teachers who had minimal trouble maintaining order. It would seem to be the maintenance of order that gives a teacher security, although maintenance of order alone does not always signify the healthiest management. One of them had talked to me about her worry that there wasn't absolute quiet in her room, and my response had been that I felt the slight noise in her room was a "good noise" of children happily and busily at work. This was true; this woman obviously loved to teach, always had a smile on her face, and the children enjoyed her. All these teachers were pleasant and chatty with me in the lunchroom, and if they were afraid of my position as "expert" it never showed in any surface animosity.

Type of Teacher Request

Though I was often called in to help a teacher deal with a child who was disrupting her class, I was gratified to note that just as often the teacher was concerned because a child didn't speak up, seemed afraid, or was functioning below his capacity. There is no question in my mind that these teachers had been trained in a way that made them able to recognize problems in children—problems of withdrawal and underfunctioning as well as problems of over-aggressiveness. Their need was for help in dealing with these problems once they were recognized. They wanted to know how to handle the child in school and how to involve his parents in helping him.

The questions they asked about classroom handling, the things they tried to do, and the things they didn't think of trying, made me see that although they had been taught certain techniques for handling difficult children, their great need was for help in translating this academic knowledge into practice. One thing that struck me over and over again was the fact that they just didn't think in terms of using the group to help the individual—this despite the fact that several of them were taking postgraduate courses in group dynamics. There is an all too prevalent attitude among teachers that one helps the individual at the expense of the group, or vice versa. They were invariably surprised when I made suggestions about using the group, or a clique, or an individual within the group, to help a child in trouble. They usually received the suggestion with enthusiasm, but often were afraid to try to put it into practice. Wherever possible, I demonstrated what I was talking about. This was not often possible because my suggestions involved day-to-day handling, and I simply couldn't demonstrate in one visit. In these cases I sometimes tried role-playing; more often I outlined a plan, being as specific as possible.

I found at Clements, as we had found elsewhere, that many of the teachers felt quite at a loss as to how to go about enlisting the help and support of parents in dealing with their children. It would appear that they had not been given training in techniques of interviewing. This lack left them foundering —how to begin a conference, how to get across the points they wanted to make, how to find out what goes on at home. Overlaid on this uncertainty was an attitude of defensiveness in relation to parents—this despite (or perhaps because of) the fact that many of these teachers were parents themselves. Here again they saw the situation in terms of a dichotomy: either the teacher won or the parent won. To help a teacher see how a conference with a parent could be used as a vehicle for working together with a common view in mind, the welfare of the child, was a neat trick and often not successful. Even when I could get the point across intellectually, I felt an undercurrent of hostility, competition, and passing of judgments which was hard to tackle and bring to awareness. Part of the embattled attitude, I discovered, was the feeling that if a teacher failed to make a parent see what was wrong, then she had failed in her duty to the child. Again and again, drawing on my own experience as a parent, and trying to draw parallels in the teacher's life, I stressed how hard it is to face up to one's *own* child's difficulties. I talked about setting goals that could be reached, and said that it was tremendously good if even one small point was gotten across in the first conference which could be followed up in further conferences. I tried to enlist the teacher's sympathy with the parent's point of view or troubles in order to water down the effects of that favorite game we all play, "Let's Blame Mamma."

Several factors may interfere with a teacher's ability to feel for the parents of her pupils. Sometimes the teacher and parent compete for the affections of the child (whether consciously or not). Sometimes the parent is defensive and aloof because a teacher stands for authority in her mind, and she is unable to free herself from this child stereotype and relate to the teacher in the present as one adult to another. In such a case, the teacher understandably responds to suspicion and hostility with resentment and impatience. This happens all the more readily because some teachers still see themselves as they saw their own teachers in childhood and behave in the authoritarian manner which they believe to be suited to their role, rather than what is actually native to themselves. Moreover, just as the parent may relate to the teacher in terms of a childhood image, so many teachers see the parents as they had experienced their own parents. In this event, the parent is seen as a stereotype of parents, and these ghostly parent figures hover in the background and interfere with free communication.

The teachers tried not to "preach," but it is hard to refrain from in this culture if one is a teacher. It is more difficult if one is a middle-class Negro teacher whose aspirations for her pupils, like those of the parents, are directed toward the immediate acquisition of middle-class values, attitudes, and behavior.

Teacher Work Load

The teachers tried very hard to work on those areas we had discussed in consultation, in relation both to pupils and to parents. This was true even though the decisions we had made together sometimes added time-consuming duties to the load they already carried. And it was quite a load! Although a great deal has been written about the multifarious duties of the classroom teacher in addition to the actual teaching day, it needs to be respected until the situation can be changed. There is the statistical and clerical work, P.T.A. meetings, home preparation, extracurricular committee work, and forms to be filled out if a teacher wishes to refer a child for special services. These duties meant that there was no small period during the day when a teacher could rest and quietly think. Many teachers complained of this, pointing out how little time was available to them, who were supposed to teach children how to think, to do any real thinking themselves. This was true at Clements and it is a common difficulty. I have heard of school systems, far removed from the one where we worked, in which teachers are literally not allowed to take time to go to the bathroom except at lunchtime. The only way to solve the time problem for these authority-minded professionals, usually over-conscientious and compulsive, would seem to be an edict from the School Board requiring them to have morning and afternoon coffee breaks like those provided for secretaries in the business world.

There is beginning to be some awareness of the elementary-school teacher's need for a few quiet moments to herself during the school day. School administrators have always known about the need, but have been powerless to do anything about it. Now, as the anti-poverty program is getting under way, and as attention is focused on freeing the teacher from strain in order that she may be more competent on the job, school boards are becoming alert to these problems. One way in which some systems have tried to alleviate strain is by using volunteers to help with non-teaching duties in the classroom, and this might well come to include training volunteers to take over the class for a short time to give the teacher a rest. At Clements it would have been accepted as a godsend.

Besides the daily grind, there are periods of additional strain and tension which are part of every school system and certainly showed up at Clements, as well as the other schools where we consulted. One of these was "report-card time." These times of reckoning for the children were equally trying for the teachers, and they often desperately asked for immediate consultation right after reports came out. They found themselves the targets of the gripes and disappointments and projected fears of parents. Many conferences were held with disgruntled parents, and the teachers often found themselves hard put to it to stick to their guns in the face of parental anger. They were lucky in that they had a principal who backed them up and encouraged them to be firm in their honestly held estimates of a child's progress.

I saw this kind of tension grow many times at Clements, most dramatically in the case of one teacher who had twins in her second grade. These twins were the daughters of a woman who taught in another school in the same system. Mrs. Holly, the second-grade teacher at Clements, had graded them differently on their report cards, because she felt their work was quite different. The mother was outraged, because she felt this was psychologically bad for her daughters, and she demanded that she be allowed to see the teacher over the weekend. Mrs. Holly had approached me in the hall when I was on my way to a conference with another teacher and poured out her fears that she would be criticized for the way she had graded the girls, particularly since the mother was also a teacher and was rather influential in the system. At this point I had assured her that from what I had seen of her principal she had nothing to fear from the parent. This turned out to be the case. In referring to the matter in our conference a week after the incident, Mrs. Tate said, "This is Mrs. Holly's honestly held opinion. She must be free to grade children as she thinks they deserve to be graded, and I will back her up in our conference with the parent, no matter how influential she is."

Another time of agony and great tension was the day when the teachers knew that supervisors would be in the school, but did not know when they would be visited. This is part of the school system as it works; it is one of the tenets of our consultative method that we take the schools as we find them and do nor try to change them. Though I could do nothing to change supervisory practices, I did talk to several teachers and try to help them face the irritation, anxiety, and conflicts they felt on supervisory days. Before I left the school I suggested to Mrs. Tate that perhaps it would be possible to have a staff meeting at the beginning of the school year to which the supervisors would be invited. At that time it should be reassuring to have them tell the teachers they understand that they are under tension and probably not doing their best when supervised—an elementary fact many teachers just don't believe. In addition, meeting these supervisors and finding them human beings instead of gods who sit in judgment might be helpful. It could also be an opportunity for the supervisors to learn to know those whom they supervise in a more personal, less threatening, situation.

The Consultant's Schedule

A résumé of my records of several days during the course of the year may give a picture both of the underlying pattern of my work and of the variations, expected and unexpected.

A day early in the school year: I went first to the principal's office and we had a brief discussion of an incident that had occurred at the P.T.A. meeting the previous evening. She then told me that the new social adjustment teacher was there and asked me to spend some time with her that morning. After I was introduced to the new teacher, I explained that I had promised to visit a few teachers that morning and would return as soon as I could. I found that the two teachers I wanted to see were having assembly, so I left notes asking them to meet me at lunchtime in the teachers' room. The new teacher and I talked for two hours about her plans for her group, what she knew about the youngsters, what I knew about them, methods of classroom management, and the choice of appropriate materials and curriculum. When I went down to the teachers' room, one of the second-grade teachers asked me to join a group of them at the cafeteria of the adjoining high school. When I explained I had made appointments during the lunch hour, she said she was sorry and then expressed her relief at being able to transfer one of her boys (probably both brain-damaged and emotionally disturbed) to the new social adjustment teacher. I found that one of the teachers I had planned to meet had gone out to lunch and the other was on playground duty until 12:30, so I made conversation for a while with the lone teacher in the room. Soon the junior primary teacher, whom I was expecting, came in. We discussed a child in her room whom I had observed the week before, and she expressed concern about another youngster who was neither an academic nor a behavior problem but who "seems withdrawn, has strange eyes, and goes to pieces when called on to recite." She asked me to observe him that afternoon. Next I stopped in at the basic primary class to ask the teacher about a boy she had had last year who was now in the social adjustment class, since I had told the new teacher I would get as much information about him as I could from his former teacher. It was then about two o'clock, and I went to one of the kindergarten classes, as I knew it was recess time and I could talk with the teacher about a child who was "driving her crazy" with his disruptive behavior. We discussed the child's behavior, her contact with his parents, what clues she might glean from observing his relations with the other children until next week (when I would see her again), and I expressed my sympathy with her having to deal with him in a group of thirty-four. It was then nearly time for the grade-level meeting of the teachers with whom I was working, so I went to the room where it was to be held, found the principal there, and we had a few minutes to discuss some of the things I had been doing. I had been asked to speak for a few minutes at the start of this meeting; since I was scheduled to talk to the whole staff the following month, I didn't go into the background or research purposes of the project, but emphasized what we might hope to accomplish together—not by applying magic formulas but by learning more about a child by pooling know-how from our respective fields.

At a later date: I arrived to find a message from the principal—she would be out all morning but would be back to meet with me by 1:30. I found that a teacher who I thought was supposed to be present at a conference between me and a parent of one of her pupils was out of school that day, and tried to reach her by phone. When this failed I went to observe a child in the second grade at the request of his teacher, then back to the phone again. This time I reached the teacher, who said the parent had not showed up for an appointment with the school psychologist the week before, that she had sent a note to say she was available any time the parent wanted a conference, and that she hadn't heard from her and so did not expect her for the conference that day. (This is a good illustration of the fragmentation of communication among people in a particular school who are dealing with any one child and/or his parents.)

At this point the parent in question walked into the lunchroom, obviously expecting to have a conference. When I told her the teacher was absent she looked terribly disappointed and told me about the difficulties she had had in making arrangements to leave her job in order to come to school. This is the conference mentioned earlier in this chapter (page 20). The mother launched into an account of her troubles with her child. She had burst into tears the week before when the teacher had called to tell her that her boy had misbehaved in the lunchroom. It came out in the conference that she had felt severely criticized by the teacher. I asked her a few questions about her life at home, about the other children in the family, about her job, and she poured out a story of family difficulties that made me see that the teacher's call had been the last straw in a very trying situation and had made this mother feel she was failing everywhere. I was impressed with this woman, with her insight and her desire to do the right thing with her children, and I was very supportive. I pointed out the strains upon her, the fact that she was actually handling her little boy quite well, that children often misbehaved for one reason or another, and helped her see that she had overreacted to the phone call. When she left she thanked me and said she would keep in touch with the teacher after I had briefed her about our conference.

On my way to a conference with the social adjustment teacher I was stopped in the hall by another teacher who asked if she might talk to me right away. I said I had a few minutes and she poured forth a story of a disgruntled parent who was demanding to see her and the principal immediately.

I went next to the social adjustment class, where the children were in an uproar and the teacher looked strained and tense. I helped her physically restrain two boys, since it was clear no conference was possible at the moment. When the lunch bell rang I arranged to see her later in the afternoon, as I had a luncheon appointment with another teacher. I kept this appointment, then returned to the social adjustment class after lunch.

On my return I was confronted with one of those situations which arise from time to time in any school and which demand no special training or techniques in order to handle them, because what is needed is just plain common humanity. The boys were in an uproar again, and Mrs. May asked me to take one of them to another teacher's room. I tried to do this, and was having a hard time with it, when I heard the principal's voice at the other end of the corridor. Since I was getting nowhere with the boy, I returned to Mrs. May's room to find her near tears, white-faced, and struggling for control. I thought one of the boys had hit her since she was obviously in pain, but it turned out she had caught her hand in the door. At this point the principal walked in with two of the boys who had run out of the room. I explained the situation to the principal and left to get some ice for Mrs. May's hand. When I returned with the ice Mrs. May was in control of herself, and was telling the principal in a quiet voice what had happened.

The principal removed the two boys from the room, but she looked disapproving of Mrs. May. After she left, Mrs. May told me she thought she might be pregnant, that she didn't want to tell the principal until she was sure, that she was preoccupied with wondering whether she was pregnant, and that she felt absolutely unable to control the social adjustment group at this point and was ready to quit. I suggested that it was hard to live with uncertainty, and that the first thing to do was to get to a doctor for a pregnancy test so that she would know for sure one way or another. Since she was new to the city, she asked me to find out where she could have such a test, and I said I would. She also asked me to arrange a conference with the principal for her after school that day, and I did this.

It was now time for my conference with the principal, and I made my way to her office. I found her upset about the climate of the social adjustment class and somewhat disappointed in Mrs. May's handling of it. I pointed out the difficulties of handling disturbed boys, each of whom was functioning on a different academic level, in a group. When she was still somewhat critical of Mrs. May, I told her the problems Mrs. May was presently having with these boys who really didn't fit together in a group, and then, being sure from Mrs. May's communications that this was no breach of confidence, decided to tell her about Mrs. May's possible pregnancy and her uncertainty about it. She softened a great deal at this point and agreed to see Mrs. May after school and talk the whole matter over. Then we talked of a few other matters, including my idea of training someone in the school to use the Life Space Interview technique. She thought this might be a good idea.

A day in early spring: When I arrived I was told that the principal had been called out to an emergency meeting at the superintendent's office, but had left a message for me that she would be back at noon. After the secretary had briefed me on the week's events, I visited two classrooms. The problems included a seven-year-old who had been threatening the other boys with a razor if they wouldn't indulge in sex play, a chronically "sulky" boy, and a dreamy, non-participating child who had just been placed in a foster home, having spent the better part of his life in the city orphanage. At this point I received a message that the principal was looking for me. She had left her meeting, to which she would have to return, in order to have forty-five minutes with me. We made good use of the time. I reported on the testing of a severely disturbed boy, for whom we had arranged therapy, and we agreed on what should be told his teachers relevant to classroom handling at this time. The principal suggested that she and I have a joint conference with the "sulky" boy's parents; she had had contacts with them and with an older brother. I told her I had talked with the brain-damaged boy's doctor, who felt he was doing well with his present teacher and that nothing should be expected of him academically for the time being. After the principal left I went to one of the kindergartens to observe for myself, at the teacher's request, the great improvement in what had been one of her most troublesome youngsters. On my way to another classroom I found a very upset little boy sitting on a radiator in the hall. He told me he was waiting until school was over to "get the kid" who had hit him at lunchtime—he had an ugly looking open cut under his eye. I persuaded him to come with me to his own room; his teacher was much concerned and went off with him to find the culprit. It was now three o'clock and time for my weekly seminar with the high school boys who were working with some of the youngsters from the social adjustment class.

A Series of Consultations about One Child

To show specifically how consultation progressed throughout one case, I have chosen a series of conferences with a new kindergarten teacher, Mrs. Paul.

Mrs. Paul had been a playground director prior to coming to Clements. She is a good-looking woman in her early thirties, married, with children of her own. Being new to the job, she felt insecure, particularly about her ability to maintain order in her class of thirty-four five-year-olds. As a result of this, and of her natural orderliness and conscientiousness, she was conducting her class in an overly strict, rigid way when I first observed her. This observation came about at her request; she had approached me the week before on the playground and asked if I would come and observe a boy in her class who was "driving her crazy." He was indeed disruptive. My notes from this first observation read:

"John is a really sad sack. He is always doing something to

call attention to himself both from the teacher and the children, and he seems to be rejected by both. In a jumping dance they were doing, he had to jump higher than anyone else and then land on someone's feet or knock over a desk. When another boy was put at the head of the line, he kept trying to usurp his place, made grabbing gestures at some of the others, only to be pushed off with a vengeance. All in all, a most lonely little boy who needs friends badly and doesn't know how to make them."

On this first visit I asked Mrs. Paul to let me see John's record, went over it, and spent the rest of the time observing. When I left I made a date to see her and talk to her about him the following week at lunchtime. Mrs. Paul forgot about our conference and went out to lunch, so I went to see her in class during the afternoon. At this time she told me what she knew of John's family. He is the youngest child in a family that includes many older children. The father is listed as "retired"; he presently drives a taxi. He calls for John at school and seems to the teacher to be more dutiful than loving. She also told me that she had heard from other teachers that the mother spoiled this child because "he is darker than the rest of the children and she wants to make it up to him." She reported that she had had to punish him that morning because he had hit another teacher and then went on to detail his other misdeeds in class. I expressed my sympathy and then asked her, both for clarification and because I thought it would help her to see where she stood in relation to him, what her legal rights were here. Did she have to keep the child in class? She said immediately that she thought a child that young could be excluded if he disrupted the class, but that she couldn't do that in good conscience until she gave it a try—perhaps his behavior was her fault, perhaps she was handling him badly. I suggested that she watch him during the coming week, particularly his attempts to make friends, to see how he goes about it and how he defeats himself, and that she think of possible ways to help him make a place in the group. I emphasized that we weren't looking for "faults" here, but for ways of helping both her and the child with a difficult situation. This must have made her feel more comfortable with me, because before I left she proceeded to tell me something about herself and her family.

When I came into her classroom the following week, Mrs. Paul held up in disgust a few mangled pieces of paper, and explained that these were John's attempts at making a lantern out of paper. She showed me the other children's finished lanterns, and then it was time to go out on the playground. There I took the opportunity to talk to her, found that John was still disruptive and that she was at her wit's end with him. Instead of pointing up her expectation of high performance from an immature and unhappy boy, I told her what I had seen before we came outside: John had made a friend for a few minutes by stirring up trouble between two boys and then coming to the aid of one of them. I pointed out what a desperate maneuver this was and stressed again his need of friends. When she still couldn't get beyond her disgust with him, I offered to help him make a lantern when we went back inside, thinking this might demonstrate something about the way he needed to be handled. She was most grateful for this suggestion, and I proceeded to carry it out. I went up to John and said I knew he would feel bad when all the other children left with their lanterns and he had none to take home. Would he like me to help him make one? His response was immediate and pathetic. His whole face lit up and he eagerly said, "Yes." I asked him if he knew how to make the lantern, and he proceeded to do it immediately and perfectly, while I just sat there beside him. Then he put his lantern on the teacher's desk next to those of the other children and went over quietly to join the group who were listening to a story. From time to time he would tiptoe to the desk to touch his lantern, and the teacher, reacting to his pride in it, stopped the story to say, "You are very proud of that, John, aren't you?"

Any encouragement I might have felt about this development was quickly dissipated when I entered the classroom the
following week. The class was in an uproar. There was Hal-
loween all over the place, the principal had just been in to
observe, and there was a mother in the room on some business connected with library books. I was about to withdraw
so as not to complicate matters further for Mrs. Paul when
she grabbed me and said "Please don't leave. John has been
in a snit all day, he is full of tales about a family fight, has
been in trouble over and over again, and is now in the bathroom. I didn't send him in, he took himself there, and I can't
get him to come out—maybe you can." My notes for that day
tell what ensued: "I opened the bathroom door and there was
John, huddled on the floor with his head cradled on his arms,
looking completely forlorn. How long he had been there I
don't know and didn't ask, because Mrs. Paul seems to feel
at once so guilty and so angry with this child. I just sat down
on the floor next to him, put my arms around him, and said,
'Tell me about it, John.' He launched into a long account of a
big fight at the breakfast table, with his mother and father
mad at him and his older sister because they wouldn't eat
their cereal, and the milk was sour. They were also mad at
his older sister because she didn't do any work, and he, John,
did his work. He has two bedrooms to keep clean, he
shouldn't have to do any work today but the bug man was coming and he had to clean them up. Mixed in with all this was a
tale about his father burning him with a cigarette. By gentle
questioning I elicited the fact that this had happened on another day when the father had to go to the dentist and had
taken John along. John knew rationally that the burn had
been an accident, but in his present state the burning and his
father's anger of the morning were all one—he showed me
the scar. All the time this was going on he was racked by internal sobs; he wouldn't let himself actually cry. At one point
I reminded him that I was the lady who had helped him with
his lantern the week before and he corrected me. 'You didn't

help me. You just sat next to me and I did the work.' I said
he was quite right, he had done a good job all by himself and
I bet he did a good job of cleaning the bedrooms, too. I asked
if he didn't want to go out and hear the story, and he said no,
so I held him for about five minutes more without saying anything. Then I said I thought he would feel better about it if
he went back outside, that I would go with him and sit next
to him, and he came along. Twice during the story John
talked out loud to me. When I whispered in his ear that he
was interrupting the story and he should save it until later,
he felt this as rejection and pulled away, but not so far that I
couldn't reach him to pat him, and he didn't pull away when
I did. Finally, I whispered to him that I had to leave, but
would be back next week, and got up to go. Mrs. Paul interrupted her story to come outside and ask me what had happened, and when I told her, tears came to her eyes. I looked
at her and said, 'I know, he makes me feel that way, too.' She
asked if he had mentioned how he felt about her, and I said
he hadn't and promised to come back and talk to her about
the whole thing at lunchtime."

During the lunch conference it was apparent that Mrs. Paul
was in great conflict about John. She appreciated his suffering
and wished she could help him, but at the same time his dis-
ruptiveness and demands for attention were making it impossible for her to conduct her class, and making her angry.
We talked about this two-way feeling, and I kept reminding
her that she had a large class to deal with, was new on the job,
and shouldn't feel so guilty about it. I asked then if she had
thought about using a child in the group to help John, and
went on to suggest how this could be done. I outlined a plan
whereby she could get one of her most stable children enlisted as a friend to John, to sit next to him at story time and
have a signal with him to remind him not to interrupt. She
smiled when I said this and pointed to a textbook on group
dynamics she had with her. She was currently taking a course
in the subject, but had not thought of using the group to help

John. She seemed most enthusiastic about using such tech-niques, and the conference broke up on a note of hope for her. From this time on, Mrs. Paul backed and filled in her re-lationship with John, according to her feelings of encourage-ment and hope or guilt and despair about him. These feelings were reflected in her relationship with me, as the following brief descriptions show:

November 6. Mrs. Paul tried to use another child to help John, but this failed. She feels he is somewhat better, mostly because she has been tough with him. I noted that "any at-tempt to use the group to help John will have to fail until Mrs. Paul is really convinced that John can conform—other-wise her feelings of despair about him will be transmitted to the other children."

November 13. Mrs. Paul told me at lunchtime that John was much better in class. When he hit another child in the hall, Mrs. Paul had winked at the teacher of the other child and taken John's part in the battle, pretending it was not his fault. She said, "Poor little kid, I had to take his side some-time." I felt this supporting of the child at the wrong time for the right reason was perhaps the result of a feeling that I was lined up with John against her and indicated an attempt to please me, which was not the point. I regretted this and felt it was perhaps my fault, that I had become too involved with John and his problems, and resolved to try and keep the re-lationship on a more casual plane and attempt to show Mrs. Paul that I could identify with her and her problems.

November 20. Because of my resolve, I didn't visit Mrs. Paul's room during the morning. As a result she came up to me at lunchtime and asked if I had deserted her and John. She said he had been a mess again, and I agreed to come and observe again the next week.

November 28. Observation in Mrs. Paul's room: "John is quite a changed boy—he is playing with the others, goes out of his way not to bump into the block buildings of others, lis-tens quietly during story time. Mrs. Paul goes out of her way to give him a chance to respond to questions about the story, which he does correctly in a loud, clear voice. He ignores me for the first fifteen minutes of observation, then goes to his desk and gets his lunch bag, from which he draws a cookie and offers it to me. It is as if he senses my feeling that I mustn't be too involved with him, but knows and appreciates the fact that I have something to do with the improved relationship between him and his teacher. I am not so sure what has happened."

December 5. "John is busily working. Mrs. Paul reports that he is much better, though he has acted up several times during the past week. When he does act up he removes himself to the bathroom for a while but then returns to the group, sometimes still angry, and tries to control her with the anger. I get the impression she has been very well able to handle this—refusing to be controlled by the anger, but letting him know it is all right to remove himself if he needs to. I remarked that he didn't seem to be bothering her as he had at first, and she replied that she had been new to the job and worried about establishing herself as a teacher."

This was the last consecutively scheduled consultation with Mrs. Paul about John, though we continued to chat about his progress in the lunch room. From time to time Mrs. Paul would stop me in the hall and talk about her family, or about herself.

On January 28, when I had occasion to observe another child in her class, Mrs. Paul had a long discussion with me about her teaching. She was concerned that perhaps she was too rigid and too tough with her kindergarten children, and we explored together the ways in which scheduling provided a framework of security for some children, and the ways in which a teacher could be flexible within that framework. On February 25, Mrs. Paul interrupted a conference with another teacher in the lunch room to tell me that John was doing so well she wanted me to come and see him in her class that afternoon. Since I wasn't free then, I made arrangements to come the following week. After that observation I recorded in my notes:

"I stopped in Mrs. Paul's room to see my old friend John, and what a joy it was! He is a big shot in the class, liked by the kids and teacher. He raised his hand for everything and recited well. When he forgot something he didn't go into a fit, but just waited and found out the right answer. He waved gaily and intimately to me when I entered, but he obviously didn't need me. Mrs. Paul is so proud of him and what she has done with him. I congratulated her on this, and she said she couldn't have done it without my help, so we had a mutual back-rubbing session. This is all great, but I think it is a bit overdone. This child is now too compliant, too much teacher's pet, and what will happen with another teacher next year, and what he is pushing down, I don't know. I wish I were going to be around to see."

Clearly, consultation had been of help to Mrs. Paul, even though we had both made mistakes along the way. The fact that she had perhaps gone too far in helping John become a big wheel in the group was a natural human reaction after all the guilt and self-questioning she went through about him in the beginning of the year.

The whole course of consultation with Mrs. Paul points up the pressing need of new teachers for help and support as they start their careers. The function of a consultant is to help a new teacher to trust herself, to see what is happening with individual children, to know how to tailor her classroom activities to help them along with the group, and above all, to get comfortable in her teaching role. There is never really enough time to follow through as thoroughly as one would like. There is no question in my mind that consultation about a particular child should go on for more than just a year if one is to be optimally helpful to him and his teachers. Here is my final comment to this effect in my notes about John: "John has learned how to get along in a classroom, and how to accommodate himself to the personality of one teacher. It is quite probable that he will have further difficulties with different teachers, and I made it clear to Mrs. Paul that she could perhaps help his new teacher by passing on any insights she has about him."

There were many other series of consultations with teachers about individual children and about other problems. However, one unique result of consultation with teachers and principal grew out of a major crisis during the school year.

An Experiment—A Plan and How It Came About through Consultation

Mrs. May, the social adjustment teacher, was about to leave the school to have her baby. This caused conflict and turmoil for Mrs. Tate, Mrs. May, and, indeed, affected the whole school. Though the school had the salary to pay a social adjustment teacher at the beginning of the year, there had been no such teacher available. There were six severely disturbed and disruptive boys in the school who needed special placement, and the principal and I had had many conferences to try to work out ways of containing them in school. About the middle of October Mrs. May had been hired, and a social adjustment class had been set up for these troublesome boys. We had worked together long and hard. Now she found she would have to leave, since she was a temporary teacher and school rules forbade her remaining on the job after the fourth month of pregnancy. Once again we were faced with the problem of the placement of these boys, and a three-way conference was called to see what we could do to help them.

My feelings at the conference were somewhat mixed. Mrs. May was a sensitive and intelligent woman, and I hated to see her leave. On the other hand, though she had tried valiantly, it was becoming clearer and clearer that these six boys did not mix well. They had been acting as catalytic agent for each other's acting out rather than a reinforcement for improvement. When a school is large enough, the school budget provides for a social adjustment class within the confines of that one school building, regardless of the pathology of the children and their individual needs. I had felt from the beginning that our inability to select the members of the class on the basis of good grouping was a terrible handicap, but since our consultative method stresses not trying to change what can't be changed and meeting the needs of the schools as we find them, I had tried to do what I could to help within the existing situation.

Though the boys had not been functioning together as a group, each one had established a good relationship on a one-to-one basis with Mrs. May, and it was clear that this relationship was sustaining and helping the child to make some progress. I suggested during the conference that Mrs. May continue to tutor the boys on an individual basis in a special room, but that they be placed immediately in regular classrooms, with carefully selected teachers. During the time that Mrs. May remained in the school, she would give them special assignments on their academic level, which they would work on in the regular classroom. In addition, she would use her room as a sort of cooling-off place to which the boys might come when they could not sustain the pressures of being in the larger class. Mrs. Tate and Mrs. May thought this a good idea and proceeded to plan how it might be carried through. The thing that continued to bother me was that after Mrs. May left, the boys would still need the kind of one-to-one relationship she had been providing. I thought of all the "big brother" types of projects I had heard or read about, and then I had an idea. There was a high school adjacent to Clements—why not try to use the high school pupils as helpers to our younger boys? It seemed to me that the very fact that the high school pupils were not yet adult would work in our favor. The younger boys reacted with defiance toward adults, whom they saw as conveyors of the culture in which they found themselves so lost and unacceptable. Adolescents would be old enough to be respected and admired, but not so old that they couldn't be trusted and accepted friends.

Mrs. Tate liked the idea right away and undertook to call the principal of the high school and enlist his support. In response to her request, he circulated a school bulletin asking for volunteers to work with our boys, and the response was immediate and gratifying.

Just before the Christmas holidays we had our first orientation meeting for the volunteers, at which we had eight boys who were willing to work with troubled elementary school children. Seven of them were seniors and one a sophomore. Later in the year this sophomore brought over another volunteer, a girl who was a friend of his, and who arrived just at the point when we very much needed a girl to work with a particular boy in the school. As had been expected, this group was made up of those who were outstandingly successful in school plus those who had problems of their own. The successful ones were the larger group, and the few who were troubled were only mildly so, mostly because of academic problems, and proved to be quite able to identify with the younger boys and help them. All of those who volunteered had been either members of the school band or friends of those who were members. Consequently, they were used to working together and brought into the group an easy familiarity which included a lot of joking and horseplay. The volunteer group was half white and half Negro; the younger boys with whom they worked were all Negro.

At the orientation meeting I explained the plan to them. They were ostensibly there to help the younger boys with homework, but the really important thing was the need for a one-to-one relationship of trust as a prerequisite to any progress the younger boys might make. Any academic work they did with their young charges was to be supervised by the child's homeroom teacher. They would come to Clements as often as time allowed, either during free periods, lunchtime, or after school. I cautioned them against signing up for more time than they could spare, underlining the fact that any future withdrawal on their part would be felt by the younger boys as just one more place where they themselves had failed, rather than that the older boys had failed them.

Mrs. Tate had arranged to have the respective homeroom teachers at the meeting, and the younger candidates for help were waiting in another room. I proceeded to give a thumbnail sketch of each boy, including his classroom behavior, academic difficulties, and as much of his home background as seemed consistent with confidentiality. As each high school volunteer heard the description of a child who appealed to him, he raised his hand and was taken by the homeroom teacher to meet his new charge and to make arrangements to come and visit him at Clements. When all had been paired off, I went on with the description of the plan, stressing that the most important part of the work would be the relationship with the younger child. I set up a weekly seminar at which the older boys could bring up any problems they had as they went along. The meeting ended with cookies and soft drinks, which turned out to be a very good move with adolescents who were always hungry, particularly after school (to say nothing of the symbolic message that they too, as well as the younger boys, would be psychologically fed). We arranged to meet the following week for our first seminar, and I made a mental note that refreshments must always be part of the meetings.

The seminars got under way just after the Christmas holidays and continued until the end of May, at which time the seniors became so busy with exams and graduation that we had to stop. All in all, there were twenty-two hours of seminar work with the group during the year. Space does not permit a detailed description of our sessions, but a few of the topics which arose during the year can be listed here:

1. The process of maturing in an individual. One of the high school boys said that he didn't see that the child with whom he worked was so very much in need of help. It was true he was unable to share attention and affection, but that seemed a natural thing. This triggered a long discussion of the need to be able to share as part of everyday life, during

the course of which I was able to bring out that it is not possible to share without the basic experience of the kind of one-to-one attention and affection we were trying to provide.

2. The belittling effect of having everything made easy. This arose because one of the elementary school boys had a mother who never demanded that he live up to his potential, never made him face the consequences of his refusal to work and, in fact, had sent him to North Carolina to avoid his having to repeat a grade at Clements. When this child tried to make Fred, his "big brother," react to him in the same way, Fred knew that this would not be helpful, and firmly let him know that he expected the child to do his best. He was afraid afterward that perhaps he had demanded too much, so he brought the subject up for discussion. Other boys in the group then gave examples of having felt belittled when too little was expected of them, and Fred was reinforced in following through on his intuitive handling of the child.

3. The question of separation and what it means to a young child. This first arose when Mrs. May left and several of the younger boys acted out their feelings about her leaving. Later in the year one of the young boys anxiously asked when his high school boy would have to stop coming. As the end of the year approached and the seniors had to cut down on visits because of exams and graduation, all the younger boys reacted adversely in one way or another. I equated these reactions to the feelings of the older boys as they faced the end of high school, going to work, or leaving home for college or jobs. The response to this was instant and the discussion which followed clearly showed how the feelings of the older boys had enabled them to identify with the younger ones.

4. The curative value of a relationship. This was discussed many times in relation to the work of our one girl, Carolyn, with Bertie. He was a shy, withdrawn boy who had caused no trouble in the classroom, but was indulging in sex play with other boys in the lavatory. His mother had been in a mental institution, and we felt he needed a warm relation-

ship with a female. Almost from the first he acted out with Carolyn his feelings toward women, shying away from her, then becoming openly hostile, and at the same time beginning to hit the girls in his class. When Carolyn was too accepting of his acting out and invited him to hit her, I pointed out the need to accept his feelings at the same time that she stopped the hitting in order to prevent the buildup of guilt. As the end of the year approached he began to act out all his fears of separation from Carolyn, and there was much discussion of how to help him with this.

Not all the time was spent in serious discussions; there were many occasions for other satisfactions, including humor. The older boys reported how the younger ones called them on the phone at home, or called to them across the street. Homeroom teachers reported how the elementary school boys talked about their "big brothers" either in the classroom or at home. The identification with the younger boys was clear from expressions of resentment by the older boys when they thought a teacher had mishandled their young charge or failed to teach him well. As the year ended, several of them spontaneously tried to make summer plans for the young boys to go to camp where they would be counselors. One tried to arrange music lessons for his younger boy, who had begun to show a real interest in the violin. Carolyn had a plan to keep in touch with Bertie through weekly postcards. There were many occasions for laughter, as when Richard, who had shied away from any arithmetic with Gordon, because of his own block in mathematics, admitted sheepishly that he and Gordon were doing arithmetic after all, and Gordon, who was good with figures, had inadvertently shown him a few things. The most spectacular satisfaction came on April 24 when the whole group received an award from B'nai Brith for community service.

To help me evaluate the project I had final interviews with all the participants of the seminar. All said they would repeat the experiment again if given the chance. They felt they had learned things about themselves that would help them in their later lives, particularly when they became parents. Some felt they had learned things that would help them in later job choices. Carolyn in particular, who had been sure she wanted to be a veterinarian, now wasn't sure—she felt she might like to work with children. All had experienced satisfaction in doing something for others. Two expressed appreciation for the relaxed and easy atmosphere of the seminars and the respect shown for their intuitive judgments.

It is difficult to evaluate the effects of the project on the elementary school boys. They were so disturbed to start with, and they came from backgrounds that were so difficult to change, that no claims for lasting gains can be made for any of them. In addition, the project started late in the year and finished by the end of May, so that there wasn't a great deal of time in which to work with them. All of them did remain in school and made the difficult adjustment to the large classroom situation. Two showed marked improvement in work habits and some academic gain. One showed no change, and one, though he didn't deteriorate in the classroom, felt downgraded by being singled out for help. All the rest felt that having an older person come over to see them was a status symbol and bragged about it in the classroom. We learned a lot about the pairing off of younger and older participants, and how to avoid some of the errors in a later experiment. The best evaluation of the whole project lies in the fact that Mrs. Tate conducted another such project without my services the following year. The original high school participants rounded up twenty-five volunteers for it, and our one sophomore boy and his friend Carolyn continued in their participation.

Our experiment was successful not only in this one school, but also in influencing other schools to set up similar programs. It was reported in written form at the meetings of the

Group Psychotherapy Association in January 1964 and in the January 1964 issue of the *N.E.A. Journal*. It has been a factor in pointing the direction of some programs in community attacks on poverty, where the use of college youth to help high school students was in part based on our experiment.

Summary

I was fortunate in having been invited to consult at Clements, since I had a chance to work with a principal who was open to new ideas and willing to try them. The racial and economic background of the school was such that we learned a great deal about the aspirations of middle-class Negro parents. I was not surprised to find that they exert the same pressure for academic achievement on their children as do the white middle-class parents with whom I have previously worked. In this case the pressures are exacerbated because the status of the Negro is currently improving. These parents see education as the "open sesame" to a place in the sun for their children, and they push all the harder. On the basis of contacts with a small sample of poorer Negro parents, it seems to me that they share the same aspirations and push even harder. The result is that, in addition to the ordinary problems of growing up and those superimposed by membership in a minority group, the children at Clements also showed problems that arose in response to these pressures. I think our method of on-the-spot consultation—that is, making weekly visits and accepting things as they are— was successful in alleviating some pressures which handicapped the climate for learning in this elementary school. Several factors contributed to this success. One of these was direct intervention. Perhaps the way I functioned at Clements might be looked at dubiously by some social workers and psychotherapists who are committed to a non-directive approach in helping other people. And yet I am quite sure that I came to be accepted and used by the principal and the teachers just because I took over a class from time to time when the need arose, or held a conference with a parent, or spent time with an individual child who was in need at a particular moment. One teacher expressed this to me on the last day of school. She said, "We are going to miss you. You aren't just doing a job or gathering data for research, you really care about us and the children." Perhaps it is partly because my background was in teaching that this eclectic, sometimes direct, sometimes non-directive, approach was the best for me to use. It would seem that different backgrounds offer different styles and approaches to consultation and that there may be more than one road that leads to Rome.

[A different consultant with a different background approached consultation in a different way. In this connection, it is useful to add a few striking excerpts from two other elementary schools where we consulted. The first school, Hoover, was a school in a lower-middle-class neighborhood with an enrollment of over 500 children in seventeen classes with a staff of twenty. The principal, Mrs. Adams, was an active participant in the schools' in-service training programs and eagerly requested consultation as soon as she was told of our plans to consult in an elementary school.

[The excerpts from Hoover are chosen to point up certain problems or occurrences during consultation that did not show themselves so clearly at Clements, while those at Lincoln show the kind of problems consultants face in a school with a multitude of special cases. The two schools were both worked at in the first year of our project.

[Mr. Howard Kitchener, a psychiatric social worker whose interest in schools began even before his participation in the original Child Research Branch of N.I.M.H. under Dr. Fritz Redl, consulted in both. His skill in this kind of work may help to indicate what traits are needed to make a good consultant of the kind we have been talking about. Since he, Mrs. Bloomberg, and I all came from different backgrounds, it is clear that these traits have something in common but that the common ground need not be similar professional experience.]

Hoover Elementary

(Howard Kitchener, Consultant and Reporter)

Airing of Teacher's Anxiety about Consultation

While eating with a group of teachers in the lunch room, I was discussing the "show and tell" activity I had observed the previous week while visiting one of the kindergarten rooms. Several of the teachers joined in and made jokes about an article in the latest *N.E.A. Bulletin,* in which a parent expressed concern about what the children were telling in school. Mrs. G. apparently felt I was paying too much attention to one segment of the group, and she rather abruptly asked me if I knew that Mrs. F. (on her left) was their Head Teacher. I assured her that I had met Mrs. F. the previous week and mentioned that I knew she taught first grade as well as being Head Teacher. Mrs. F. seemed pleased. I started to inquire about the duties of Head Teacher when Mrs. G. went on to call my attention to another teacher, who she said "was formerly acting principal; she had been here the longest." I turned then to her and several of the teachers began joking about their length of service. I told them I was really interested in the subject and thought twenty years as a teacher was something to respect. One of them reminisced a bit, recalling what it was like years ago when the area was rural. As the conversation rolled on, it appeared that Mrs. F. was second in seniority, the rest were all "newcomers" of two or three years, and Mrs. G. was a focus of strength, supporting the old as well as the new organization.

Friendly, informal conversation continued for about twenty minutes, with discussion of the recent presidential election, changes in the neighborhood, longevity of service of various teachers, and other subjects.

Suddenly there was a dramatic shift in the tone of the meeting. The teacher of a low-I.Q. class, sitting in an isolated spot down the table, interrupted the flow of conversation to ask in a loud voice: "Mr. Kitchener, I've been wondering, just what it is you're going to do here?" The general chatter stopped and all the teachers looked expectantly at me for an answer. It was as if all the lively, polite talking had been screening this question for each of them.

The teachers asked if they would have to keep anecdotal notes on various children. I told them that it was not our job to prove anything to anyone and that we were free to find the methods of communication most useful to us. I added that I thought we might find anecdotal notes useful in some situations, but that our purpose was to make life less, not more, burdensome for them. There were sighs of relief.

Discussion then developed about the extent of teacher involvement in some classroom problems, and finally Mrs. G. raised the question directly, "Aren't you trying to treat the teachers?" I answered that this was not our purpose. Our focus was really on the child as the problem-producing factor and, if we succeeded in relieving some of the stress, it should enable the teacher to work more effectively at her own job.

There was a noticeable reduction of anxiety in the group as this point was clarified, and later, when the meeting broke up, Mrs. G. said, "What we were most concerned about has been answered to our satisfaction." It was clear to me that she was referring to the issue of "treating" the teachers.

After the teachers' fears and questions about the consultant's presence had been allayed, requests for consultation and observation increased at a remarkable rate.

Reaching a Principal Whose Standards
Were as High as Her Defenses

On many occasions I observed that when a child was having a talk with the principal, Mrs. Adams, and started to express negative feelings, she shut the child off with such phrases as "Oh no, you don't feel that way at all; you just have nice feelings about that boy" (a fellow who had just called the boy a name or hit him). One day when she asked a small boy why he had misbehaved, the child answered that sometimes he "just felt all black and hate inside." Mrs. Adams denied that the child could have such a feeling and told him he must be mistaken because he was really a very nice boy. The point is that psychotherapists, and many teachers, work for hours to get a child to acknowledge negative feelings as a natural part of himself in order for him to accept himself and behave more healthily. Mrs. Adams could understand in general that children are not all bad and that they need to feel self-acceptance, but her denial of their negative feelings prevented her from helping a given child at a given instance to make constructive use of his awareness of them.

After I had been at Hoover several months I began to realize how frequently Mrs. Adams was missing our regularly scheduled conferences. She was often out to lunch with a colleague or busy with chores about the building. One day I suggested that we meet at a nearby restaurant for lunch. Mrs. Adams was delighted with the idea, and our talk turned out to be one of the most productive discussions we had.

While waiting for lunch Mrs. Adams made some comment about the difficulty of talking in her office, where there are frequent interruptions or where she is often involved in other duties. I mentioned that the nature of her job made unusual demands on her and that it was sometimes hard to know where to focus attention. Then she began to talk about a recent hassle between two teachers over the transfer of a child. The child was moved from a younger teacher's room to a brighter group under an older teacher's charge. The older teacher expressed criticism of the child to the younger teacher, stating that the child could never measure up to the performance of the brighter group. Later the younger teacher asked to see the principal and was quite upset at what she felt was implied criticism. Mrs. Adams handled this nicely by telling her that they all knew this older teacher had too exacting standards for many children, that she shouldn't be concerned about implied criticism because the principal was the one to do "evaluating," and that she was well satisfied with the younger teacher's performance. Mrs. Adams went on to tell me that this younger teacher is a "worrier" who drives herself with great expectation, but the fact is that she does not have the kind of children who will show dramatic results.

Then she started to discuss a teacher with whom she felt she had not been able to communicate successfully. She seemed to be criticizing herself in much the same way as she had reported that the younger teacher criticized herself. I carefully asked her how she could so effectively help the younger teacher see that success wasn't dependent on reaching all the children, but then couldn't allow herself the same latitude with her teachers. Mrs. Adams saw my point briefly but then the characteristic denial took over. She said, "Oh, I don't feel inadequate in any way; I have a good relationship with all the teachers. We have our little conflicts now and then. But who doesn't?" I told her I thought we all felt inadequate in one way or another. I cited as an example that when there seemed to be blocks in my communication with her I felt responsible and despaired of resolving the difficulty.

A little later Mrs. Adams was much more relaxed and talked about her long struggle with one of the older teachers in the school, a woman who had been there before she came. This teacher was overly strict and tried to run the school. The department wanted to transfer her, but Mrs. Adams had asked to have a chance to try to work out their difficulties. Recently, when a supervisor visited the school, he was "astounded at the transformation" in this teacher. Mrs. Adams had carefully assigned to her functions which would enhance the status of this older teacher, and this treatment showed quick results.

Here we see some of the sympathy and awareness the principal brought to bear, despite her tendency to deny the problems around her. She was aware of the personality conflicts between some members of her staff and was willing to make some allowances for what couldn't be changed immediately. She knew it would have been a devastating blow to the older teacher to be transferred, so Mrs. Adams had given her managerial status. The teacher then began to relax her earlier rigid attitudes about managing children. The supervisor, impressed with the teacher's performance, was also impressed with the principal's manner of bringing it about.

A Teacher Asks for Help

After our luncheon conversation, there was a noticeable change in the way Mrs. Adams began to use my services. A few weeks later she said she wanted to discuss some difficulties she was having with one of her special teachers. She told me she regretted that she was unable to spend more time with these teachers. She understood that they had different and sometimes more difficult problems to deal with than the regular classroom teachers did. The supervisor who evaluated Miss Z. (who had a mixed class of low-I.Q. and emotionally disturbed children) wanted to give her a lower rating than the principal thought she deserved. Earlier I had observed some of the children in the class and was able to support Mrs. Adams' contention that the teacher possessed reasonable capacity, but there was no question that she needed additional help in understanding the difficulties of the children. Miss Z. seemed to be caught between a need to express her distress to the principal in the hope of getting some help and the fear of exposing her shortcomings. She was sure exposure would only substantiate the supervisor's evaluation. Mrs. Adams asked me if I would concentrate on this teacher and hold conferences on a regular basis in an effort to help her.

This manner of referral was entirely different from that in force at the beginning of the program: Mrs. Adams had insisted on scheduling conferences only for teachers referred by herself. At that time there was no indication that the teachers understood or wanted such conferences with me, and referral by the principal would have been resented, so that any effort on my part would probably have been negated. Now, since Miss Z. had already asked me to observe her class and discuss her problems, it was easy for me to note that the severity and number of problems in her room required regular conferences in order to keep up with them. Mrs. Adams arranged, to have a "room mother" cover the class so that Miss Z. would be free for such conferences, and said she would occasionally cover the class herself if necessary.

How a Consultant Can Help a Teacher in Trouble

I had noticed earlier that the teacher and the children in Miss Z.'s classroom were unbearably tense. Miss Z. spent much time trying to outyell the children, and she seemed too demanding and hostile toward them. Yet one had the impression that she wasn't this way most of the time. In one earlier conference she had talked about the problem of yelling at the children and had asked me to suggest other ways of getting their attention which wouldn't be so wearing—and incidentally would not make her feel so bad.

In each of the conferences with Miss Z. she had two or three particular laments, usually about the most aggressive, demanding, or hostile children. Later the laments shifted to her feelings of futility about ever getting anywhere with some of her low-I.Q. or disturbed pupils (for example, the nonreaders). Still later, she was distressed by the frequent turnover of children in her class: She felt burdened by having to constantly regroup the class and handle the new pupils individually. It might be useful to illustrate these laments, as they show some of the basic concerns of such a teacher and possible solutions for some of her problems.

One of her first concerns was Jack, a big thirteen-year-old slow learner who seemed headed toward delinquency. He was often defiant and provocative with her, although she was not at all afraid of him physically. After listing his misdeeds, Miss Z. began to speculate about how this boy might feel about being in her class, which was sometimes referred to by the children as the "dumb class." She said that when he was transferred from a sixth-grade class he showed considerable embarrassment about being seen with this group, which contained several younger children. He would frequently line up with his old group in entering the building. She admitted that she had reached such a point of irritation with anything he did that she could no longer be objective about evaluating his behavior. I started her talking about another big boy in her room with whom she got along very well, and then she began to see that if this boy were doing some of the same things that Jack did she would not react so strongly. She agreed that she might try to use this second boy as a guide to controlling her overreactions to Jack, and she later reported that this seemed to work for her.

Later her concern was focused on a particularly difficult big girl who tended to try to control the class and was defiant and boisterous. After two or three meetings in which we discussed this child, Miss Z. raised the question of the necessity for her remaining in the special class. The girl had progressed to low performance for her regular grade level except in one subject. Within a few weeks we arranged to have her transferred back to her regular group, while she continued with Miss Z. for the one subject in which she needed individualized help.

It is noteworthy that week after week Miss Z. could raise meaningful issues to discuss with me and usually some plan could be worked out for the specific difficulties. However, she would periodically revert to a general complaint about the exasperations she experienced in trying to resolve permanently some of the problems in her special classroom. I began to raise with her what seemed to be the more basic issue she had to resolve: Since many of her chronic laments were inherent in the nature of teaching such special classes (more turnover and less measurable progress), perhaps she had to think about whether this was the kind of teaching she wanted to continue to do.

Miss Z. gained some support from my comments about the similarity of her problems to those I had heard from special teachers in other schools. She could then begin to sort out specific problems about grouping, promotions, and so forth, with which Mrs. Adams could be of further assistance, since they raised some issues that only the principal could decide.

For example, Miss Z. found that when she had eighteen or twenty children she could eventually divide them into five or six groups of various levels of performance. However, whenever a new child was assigned to her class she often had to work with him individually for several weeks before placing him in one of the groups. If two or three children were assigned to her room within a short period of time, she found she could not keep up the work with the individuals and the several groups, too.

She faced a similar problem with promotions of children back to their regular classes. She disagreed with the policy that forced her to replace her more advanced children before they made what she felt to be sufficient progress. When she could raise these questions with me, Miss Z. found she could formulate her views more clearly and thus make more productive use of conferences with her principal in which such issues could be resolved. For example, Mrs. Adams could better control the rate at which new children were assigned to the class and old children removed when she understood the grouping problem more explicitly.

Aside from the help on specific issues which this teacher raised, the teacher appreciated the consultant's attention to her class. Such special classes in a regular school are often the forsaken classes. The teacher was supported by the fact that the consultant and principal had demonstrated that her situation warranted special attention. Thus her role was regarded seriously and her status enhanced. Mrs. Adams was somewhat relieved because the teacher could begin to raise specific issues with which the principal could more easily help her.

Excerpts from Lincoln, an Elementary School for Special Problems

(Howard Kitchener, Consultant and Reporter)

Lincoln Elementary School had a far greater proportion of disturbed children than any other elementary school in the system. In fact, it was known as a dumping ground for children with a variety of atypical characteristics: over-age, low I.Q., emotionally disturbed, and so forth. For this reason, the principal selected for this school was unusually skillful in handling children who are hard to manage. At the time of consultation the school's population consisted of 350 students and a staff of 25, an unusually high teacher-pupil ratio for this overpopulated system. Mr. Graham, the principal, always a forward-looking man, asked for consultation as soon as he heard of our program. The specialness of his school and his welcoming attitude made us eager to consult there. The following excerpts show the quality of the principal, the effect he had on the staff, and the quick, good use made of the consultant.

First Visit

I arrived about 11:30 in the morning for a con- ference with the principal, Mr. Graham, and we spent ten or fifteen minutes in getting acquainted and discussing ways to use the services I could offer. I tried to show that I was very much interested in his school and implied that if he found he could talk freely with me he would then feel safe to in- vite his teachers to do the same. I felt we could establish a good working relationship because this man was very able as a principal. He was an introspective, sensible, firm person who used his unusual intuition to operate effectively in a very difficult and complex school.

Mr. Graham wanted to know more about the background of our service and I mentioned the long-term project with severely disturbed boys at the National Institute of Mental Health. I told him that all we had learned in that specific venture would not be worth the money put into it unless we could also find out which parts of it could be translated into usable measures for people like himself who were dealing with the children who needed such help.

He told me something of his experience with consultations and demonstration staff conferences, which were held through a special services program of the school system. He cited the "staffing" of a child, listing all the school personnel involved. He questioned whether such a procedure would be feasible in his setup because he had so many children who needed to be "staffed" and because many of the staff's recom- mendations just couldn't be carried out among so many groups of children to plan for and manage. We agreed that the "staffing" method of conference might not be the most useful method of training in some schools because very little can be done to change the program or reassign children. I commented that, even in situations where few overt changes could be effected, understanding the pressures made it easier to continue to live with the conditions. Mr. Graham added some examples from his school. He mentioned the problem of managing particularly difficult children from deplorable home situations which cannot be changed.

Mr. Graham suggested that I take a few weeks to become familiar with the total setting and then begin to focus on specific areas which needed attention. He seemed unusually comfortable about beginning with a fairly unstructured program for me. He discussed the possibility of a group meeting with his faculty and decided this might be more productive after I had spent a few weeks around the school. He suggested that we begin by taking a tour of the building so that I might meet all the teachers individually in their classrooms.

During this initial tour of Lincoln, it was apparent that the teachers and the children were accustomed to have the principal drop in on them for unobtrusive observation. In most classrooms, if a class discussion were in progress, they simply continued until there was a convenient point for the teacher to interrupt: She might pause to explain the context of the discussion or offer Mr. Graham an opportunity to make a comment or to participate as he wished. Other teachers simply proceeded without any interruption when there was no indication from Mr. Graham that he needed their attention. In classrooms where desk work was in progress, the teachers came over to meet me and to chat briefly. In each room it was apparent that Mr. Graham was leaving it up to the teacher to decide whether this were an opportune moment for interruption. The quality of this respect for the autonomy of the teacher was striking and seemed to characterize his relationship with his staff. Some classes were quiet and some noisy; some were involved in highly organized activity while in other rooms diffuse individual activities were in progress. It was noteworthy that whatever the activity, noise level, or organizational style, none of the teachers seemed defensive or needed to explain why they were working in the particular way they had chosen. The atmosphere of easy communication and implied trust between Mr. Graham and his teachers became even more noticeable later during the lunch period.

As the noon-hour bell rang we stopped in at the teachers'

room. I realized that this was a shrewd move on Mr. Graham's part. The informality provided a chance to chat with the various teachers as they came in for a beverage or to eat lunch. The first few who came in were quite uneasy, as they thought they were interrupting a conference between their principal and me. They accepted Mr. Graham's invitation to join us, and we then had two or three there at all times through the next hour. There was lively talk as the teachers tried to figure out who I was. When they were told that I would be around to help with some of the problems with the children, they enthusiastically related recent experiences in their classrooms—some disturbing and others humorous or pleasurable. They were sharing their reactions in a way I suppose they ordinarily did with Mr. Graham, but now some of the conversation was addressed to me. In the course of this interaction I received from Mr. Graham what I thought a high compliment. One of the teachers, Mrs. K., related an anecdote about a large, rough girl in her class. She wanted to go on to tell about something she had done with the girl the day before, but before doing so she turned to Mr. Graham and asked, "Is it all right to tell him?" (The implication was that what she had to say might be irregular for outsiders' scrutiny.) He answered, "Sure, you can tell *him* anything, he's going to be one of us." The illustration had to do with her rather brusque handling of a big girl who was trying to intimidate her.

This kind of observation tells us a lot about the particular setting and the atmosphere within which consultative work may be done. Mr. Graham was aware of the consultant's needs for casual teacher contacts which can facilitate easy communication, and he had no fear about allowing it. In fact, he set it up smoothly. The teachers, in turn, were comfortable about reporting anecdotal material and, even though aware of the possible wrongness of some of their rougher handling, they were not so defensive that they had to explain it away. Rather, they were able to describe it meaningfully. They also revealed a most important ingredient that characterized their relationship: trust in their principal's judgment as to what was or was not communicable to outsiders. This, in turn, reflected their expectation that he would protect them when they needed it and that he had good judgment of what they could afford to reveal. It also indicated the range between what he approved publicly and what he would question, but still allowed them to tell him personally without their needing to fear his misuse or reprisal. Generally, it showed their comfort in asking for help about questionable incidents.

When the teachers had gone back to their afternoon classes, Mr. Graham expressed his concern about the fact that he had more difficulty with his shop teachers than with the regular classroom teachers. As he continued, I was curious why the shop teachers felt "second class" in a school where prestige seemed to be based not so much on academic achievement as on success in managing and programming for these unusually difficult youngsters. When I observed that the shop teachers might be in a more difficult spot with these particular children because they had to deal with hammers and saws, where the academic teachers had pencils and erasers, Mr. Graham immediately grasped my point and wondered aloud if he had been successful in letting his vocational teachers know that he understood their difficulties were greater in some ways. This led to a more general questioning about his methods of dealing with his staff. He said he tended to emphasize an individual approach to each teacher's particular difficulties and strengths. While conceding that this method had much merit and operated quite successfully, he now realized that he needed more group discussions with the opportunity to point out to all the staff the additional pressures that the shop teachers were under. He concluded that such attention might help the vocational teachers gain more respect. It occurred to me then that the problem might be that these teachers didn't have a group of youngsters of their own. In each class in woodworking, sewing, cooking, etc., that we visited that moring, Mr. Graham had remarked,

"Let's see, this is part of Miss So-and-So's group, isn't it?" While the children were pleased that their principal identified them correctly, the teacher who was with them at the time was not associated with them and seemed to receive less recognition in his encounter with Mr. Graham. For me, the openness of Mr. Graham's concern was as relevant as the content of the concern itself, and I felt that this resourceful man would find his own ways to modify the problem now that it had been clarified.

Back in the principal's office, we agreed in general on the approach to be taken for the next few weeks. Instead of "lecturing" at a faculty meeting immediately, I would "float around and play it by ear." I would take my lunch to the teachers' room the next week and start chatting about some of the children, then get myself invited by the teachers into some of the classrooms for observation. Since most of the staff had met me on the tour, Mr. Graham would tell them in the next faculty meeting that I would be around regularly one afternoon a week and available for discussions.

Second Visit

When I arrived the whole school was in assembly for Election Day. I joined Mr. Graham, who was standing near the door, and we watched the program for about fifteen minutes. We then went up to his office for a short talk. He told me about a problem concerning the big girl who had been discussed in the teachers' room during my last visit. She was becoming more defiant and aggressive; she had hit another girl and seemed to be intimidating her teacher, Mrs. K. I realized that while Mr. Graham was aware of the emerging difficulties between this girl and her teacher, he was not at all alarmed and apparently did not feel it was time for him to take any action. His attitude and strategy for handling such situations became clearer to me as the problem unfolded during my visits.

I observed that it must be time for the teachers to be gathering in the lunch room and Mr. Graham said he would go up with me. There were two teachers already there, and after Mr. Graham introduced me to the one whom I had not met before, he left. It seemed clear to me that he was giving his staff and me a chance to talk freely together without him. I started a conversation with the teacher I had just met, who seemed somewhat depressed and unenthusiastic. She lamented that she just couldn't seem to accomplish anything with her low-I.Q. group—the "scrapings" from other fifth grades. Our conversation was interrupted by the entrance of several other teachers, including Mrs. K., who seemed to focus the attention of any group on herself. Last week she had dominated the conversation with an account of her problems with the aggressive girl, and this time she plunged into election issues. She was teased a bit about her "campaigning" and then a couple of the men teachers began ribbing her, in a friendly way, about her "big" girl. The way they did this revealed their awareness that she was becoming physically afraid of this student.

By this time I had become aware that a great deal of barbed humor flowed among the members of this staff. It did not seem to be essentially hostile, but, rather, was used to probe and to help the person being barraged to express what the rest of the group knew was being repressed. It was an unusual mechanism which seemed, in large measure, to account for the level of relaxed give-and-take that went on.

With engaging humor Mrs. K. launched into an account of her latest trouble with the girl. She said, "This morning she took the window pole, supposedly to open the window, but I just didn't know what she might do with it." One of the men tauntingly asked, "What did you think she might do?" (implying that she intended to hit the teacher). She answered directly, now without humor, "Well, it's true. I am beginning to get afraid of her. In fact, I've been thinking that since she seems to like men so well, she might do better with one of you." (Here she turned with warm, seductive humor to me and quipped, "Don't misunderstand me, Mr. Kitchener, so do I."

Then a general discussion evolved about the pros and cons of assignment of difficult children with reference to the sex of the teacher. One of the older women suggested that if a girl had a bad relationship with her mother, she should have a woman teacher to counter the negative influence of the mother. Two of the men expressed a similar view to support assigning many boys to men teachers, especially when fathers or male substitutes for identification are absent from homes. Both groups of teachers went on to question whether girls, too, didn't need a positive relationship with men teachers to compensate for the absence of fathers in the families of many of these children. When the members of the group had raised several cogent aspects of this issue, I tried to clarify the various arguments. I agreed that often the child's relationship with the teacher compensates for what the child is missing at home. However, if it becomes too close a "substitute" it may become too complicated and painful to both teacher and child, especially if the child transfers too much of his conflict about his relationship to his parents into the classroom experience with the teacher. For example, some girls, such as the one cited here, have a negative or destructive relationship with their mothers, and a more wholesome relationship with a woman teacher might counterbalance the bad home relationship. However, they may, in some cases, transfer these negative feelings to the teacher so completely that it is no longer possible for them to differentiate the "good" teacher from the "bad" mother. Despite the teacher's efforts to relate to her, the girl may unconsciously use every opportunity to negate these attempts and, by so doing, maintain her distorted image of all adult female relationships, rather than suffer the anxiety of changing her perceptions and adopting a new way of relating to adults of her own sex.

If such a girl cannot give the teacher a reasonable opportunity to demonstrate that she is, after all, quite different from the girl's mother, then perhaps the girl and the teacher (and the rest of the class) should be spared the struggle which would be fought out in the classroom. Sometimes when such girls can be provided with a male teacher they are more able to accept a relationship with a peripheral woman teacher, for instance in art or music, and begin to use this less intense relationship constructively.

I went on to illustrate how these same considerations might apply in deciding to assign a difficult boy to a woman teacher until he was more ready to do part of his work with a man.

The conversation then turned back to the particular from the general. Mr. A., who teaches the "life adjustment class," started a discussion with another teacher about a boy who had been temporarily transferred to his class from hers. It was clear that Mr. A. wanted to keep him and his former teacher wanted him back. Both prefaced their remarks with "I've been meaning to discuss this with Mr. Graham," as if this were the natural channel of communication and that Mr. Graham could be counted upon to support each of them. Mr. Graham told me later that he usually leaves it up to the teachers to work out questions of reassignment of students, although he assumes responsibility for the final decision. This explained what Mrs. K. was trying to initiate in bringing up the question of whether her girl would do better with a male teacher.

As the group was breaking up, Mr. A. suggested that I observe his class that afternoon. When I saw what was going on in his room I was fascinated. There was an over-all sense of control with all of the youngsters, and yet tremendous latitude within which each seemed to operate. He conducted a nice language class (nouns and verbs) while five or six other students went on about their individual pursuits. When I went back to say good-bye to Mr. Graham, I told him how impressed I was with Mr. A.'s class and he seemed very pleased.

Third Visit

I had a brief conference with Mr. Graham when I arrived. He told me that the school psychologist, Mr. V., had been there that morning and would return during the noon hour in order to meet me. He implied that there might be some questions as to just what each of us was supposed to be doing. I agreed we might find some overlapping of functions and suggested that it would be useful to clarify our roles so that each could operate most productively. I asked what areas Mr. V. had been working in, and Mr. Graham described his function primarily in terms of testing the children for grade placements.

He then brought me up to date on the developments between Mrs. K. and her problem girl, Patty. The situation had become more intense and, since Mrs. K. had asked directly that something be done, he had started the routine procedure for psychological study referral. He mentioned that he'd been away from school for a day earlier in the week and that, before going, he'd told Mrs. K. that if she had trouble with Patty to take her to Mr. A.'s special class and he, himself, would deal with the matter when he returned. I was impressed with the coverage and protection he offered this distressed teacher when he could not be there himself. He added that Mrs. K. had come to him about Patty again this morning, and when he heard "I was talking to my husband about it," he knew the pressure was mounting to the point where he would have to intervene.

At noon, Mr. V., the psychologist, joined a group of us in the lunch room and he and I started to talk about our respective jobs in the school. Suddenly Mrs. K. broke into the conversation to ask whether the special services department could tell her how far she should be able to go in managing a given difficult child, "because maybe the child is beyond what can be coped with in public school, anyway." A lively exchange developed here, with several other teachers joining in. They, too, wanted more definite answers about what kinds of children they should be able to work with, and where they could get the additional techniques they felt they needed. Then I inserted a question about the divergence of points of view being expressed. I noticed that Mrs. K. wanted some outsider to be able to tell her the limits of possibilities for her classroom. I pointed out that she was really selling her own experience and observations short. Just because she was stymied by about 5 per cent of the more difficult children, why did she feel that she *had* to be successful with every child —or why did she feel that she needed an outsider to tell her they were impossible to deal with? After she agreed that such a proposition was untenable, I reminded her of the 95 per cent with whom she is able to work successfully. Mrs. K. then acknowledged the contradiction in her feeling a failure just because she was unable to succeed with every child. In the course of the discussion, I used the opportunity to mention that even with the 5 per cent there was evidence of some success—for instance, I was aware of the basic affection she expressed toward Patty. Later, Mrs. K. told Mr. Graham that she had been thinking over some of the ideas discussed in the lunch room: She realized that she didn't have to let Patty's provocative behavior become so upsetting and, "anyhow, the girl isn't really so bad, after all." When Mr. Graham told me that Mrs. K. had also urged him to encourage more of his teachers to make use of these lunchtime discussions, he indicated that he understood that a teacher, under particular pressure, needs additional recognition that she is struggling with a very difficult situation. I pointed out that he had really set the climate for Mrs. K. to express herself openly and thus make use of my recognition of some of her troubles.

Reaching for the Stars— And Those Who Can't

One day when I was eating lunch with the teachers, two of them started comparing notes on the composition of their respective groups. One commented that she had the "scrapings" from three other fifth grades, while Mrs. X. had a "regular" fifth grade. When I asked how the "regulars" were selected for a school like Lincoln, the implication of the answer was that they were the undesirables and the misfits. Mrs. X. remarked that some of these children were not academic or behavior problems but that their parents were particularly difficult, which might have been the reason they were screened to attend Lincoln. I asked questions to elicit comparison of what was considered a more flexible program at Lincoln with that of the other elementary schools. While accepting the staff lament that Lincoln often got more than its share of the difficult children because of its flexibility, I suggested that it also got "regular" ones who would do better with this kind of program. Several of the teachers agreed with me and gave examples of children who did much better here than they would in another school.

Mrs. X. spoke of some of her former pupils, who were extremely deprived and yet had more zest for learning than some of their more fortunate classmates, and gradually built up to her greatest success in all her years of teaching. She described a boy whom "the school had salvaged from a rat's nest—a bright boy with an I.Q. of over 140." She went on about the glories of this boy's attainments: "He became a jet pilot, married into one of the best families, and now he's right up there reaching for the stars." This was a very moving moment in the lunch room discussion. There were eight or nine teachers in the room, and it seemed to me that they all identified with Mrs. X.'s satisfaction in her achievement and longed for a similar opportunity to experience and measure success in their own work.

I commented on the natural satisfaction there would be for a teacher who could look to such absolute measures of success but wondered how to measure success when you have a child with an I.Q. of 70 or so and ultimately are able to help him function at his capacity. They all pounced on this question, and there was a half-hour's lively discussion about sources of replenishment for the teachers of children who are never going to "touch the stars." Some spoke of pupils they've had who have come to be able to hold a steady menial job in the community; others cited examples of former students who keep coming back to Lincoln for visits now that they are married and working. One teacher suggested that some of her former pupils are now better parents (than their parents were), as evidenced by the fact that they now come regularly to P.T.A. meetings.

One could readily feel the sense of worth the teachers experienced in this discussion. They all seemed reluctant to leave, although they were five or ten minutes late back to their afternoon classes. When I stopped in to tell the secretary I was leaving, she remarked, "It must have been a good discussion today—some of them stopped in here on the way to classes, and you could tell they'd had a good meeting."

3

Consultation in the Junior High School

Campbell Junior High School

(Ruth G. Newman, Consultant and Reporter)

There is a semi-residential area composed mostly of deteriorating row houses and other slum buildings, but which contains also a small, new, fashionable section. In addition to urban variety, the area has its share of rats and dirt and far less than the city's normal share of trees and parks. In its center stands Campbell Junior High, built in 1920, a red-brick structure surrounded by asphalt playgrounds and metal fences.

During the year I was a consultant at Campbell, the student population numbered 780, 85 per cent of whom were Negro. There were thirty-six teachers, about half of whom were Negro. The administrative staff—principal, assistant-principal, counselor, and secretary—was white.

The Neighborhood and Its Population

This was not the worst of the city's neighborhoods and did not bear the stigma of the area surrounding Urban High (Chapter 4) but the school was plagued with vandalism and visits from the police were not infrequent. It was close enough to poor men's bars, centers of prostitution, and the jail for the pupils to be city-wise and for some teachers to prefer to teach elsewhere. It was equally close to one of the greatest libraries in the world, although it is unlikely that students felt sufficiently at home in libraries to use this facility. Since the residents of the fashionable section were either childless or private-school-minded, Campbell's parent population ranged from clerks in stores, government workers with low salary ratings, garage mechanics, restaurant employees, day laborers, and domestics to the intermittently or permanently unemployed. The neighborhood had experienced a recent population expansion, consisting largely of new families of Negroes from the South.

As a matter of fact, the years following the project described have not dealt with the neighborhood kindly. More and more it has become a center for transient populations; less and less have repairs or improvements been made. The trend seems to be downward.

As we came to learn, the children from rural or segregated communities were not familiar with white teachers, middle-class expectations, or the language, pronunciation, and idioms of Campbell and its neighborhood. Many of them had little or no experience with large-city concepts, vocabulary, and patterns of behavior. Their parents complained bitterly that they were taken advantage of and held in low esteem, that their children were often set upon by the city-wise, higher-status kids of the "old families." Many parents feared their children would take on evil city ways and loose morals, and consequently held their children almost literally in bondage with unreasonable curfew hours and rigid restrictions. The children often complained that they were not even allowed to stop on the street for a Good Humor on the way home from school or to go to a friend's house to borrow a book or play a game, but had to go directly home each day on pain of being beaten or restricted further. Many of these children had low test results because of the lack of opportunity for intellectual and verbal stimulation. Many more performed poorly in academic subjects because they felt lost and uprooted and were too inarticulate and intimidated to question what they did not understand.

The teachers at Campbell often found their task bewildering. It was difficult to make these youngsters feel comfortable when one could barely get them to speak up at all. Answers were usually "Yes, ma'ams" or "No, sirs," leaving the teacher with no sense of whether or not she had reached the child. Concepts plain to the teachers and simple for the city children drifted above and beyond the heads of these others, until a test showed how little they had got from explanations that hitherto had been clear enough for all the pupils to understand. This aroused in the teachers feelings of impatience and despair, a conviction that these students were hopelessly stupid, or a fear that they were very poor teachers.

Selection of the School

Campbell was one of the first experiments in our project. It and two elementary schools in the same system were given psycho-education consultation during the first year of the project, whereas our work at Urban High, the nursery school, and other institutions was undertaken in the second and third years.

We first met the principals of the schools we soon became involved with at a meeting called by the Superintendent of Special Services in the Public School System. She had made a list of twelve schools whose principals were all eager to try the kind of assistance we had to offer. She discussed these people and their schools with us in several conferences, and then she suggested the three she thought most suitable; both from the standpoint of our project and from that of her department's needs. She was familiar with our National Institute of Mental Health experience, our current research plans, and particularly those aspects of it that were of special interest to her. She was engaged in a pilot project at that time for training her department to consult with principals and to help them use more rewarding consultative practices with staff, children, and parents. The similarity of aspects of her project with aspects of our own was striking, and we agreed to help each other where the projects had common ground.

In the beginning, the three principals representing the first three schools were not sure exactly what they were buying—nor we precisely what we had to sell. The Superintendent of Special Services had outlined the process, insofar as she knew it, and they knew they wanted help. At our meeting with them, the Superintendent, and some members of her department, we and the principals brought up all the questions we could think of. On our side, we made it clear that we were not part of the school system, would have no influence, for better or worse, on the status of staff members in the schools we were visiting, and that we were in no sense raters or judges. We emphasized that we did not think we had all the answers and described our desire to explore and to be of use, within our competence, in those areas where they asked for our help. After outlining our project and defining our assistance as limited to the problems of emotional disturbance in the classroom, we asked each principal how he thought we could be useful in his school and which aspects of our project particularly interested him.

The principal of Campbell, Mr. Ponsell, first mentioned his social adjustment classes as a focus for consultative aid, but then said perhaps it would be better to begin with individual problem children throughout the school. He mentioned that he had difficulties with some of his administrative staff and said he would also like the psycho-education consultant to work closely with the special class teachers.

The Principal

Mr. Ponsell was a middle-aged, good-looking man who had been in the city school system many years and had been the principal of Campbell for a good part of this time. He was proud of his reputation as a solid, forward-looking, and ambitious principal. He was bright, dedicated, opinionated, liked friendly informality when *he* chose it, and was fond of keeping the reins of authority in his hands. He was well versed in the necessary art of tightrope walking between the school system's regulations and the needs of his own staff and pupils. He did not bother to fight battles he knew or believed could not be won, but tried instead to circumvent them. For instance, when one person in the central school administration attempted to hamstring a program of his, he did not fight; he simply approached another person who could either give him permission to go ahead or could talk the first fellow into giving it. When he had to live with an untenable situation, such as a teacher incompetent to deal with students or with the rest of the staff, he built up enough of a case against her teaching at Campbell that it was unthinkable for her to be assigned there the following year. In other words, though not the most insightful of souls, he knew well how to negotiate the system.

Mr. Ponsell was particularly interested in curricula and methods for teaching youngsters who were retarded academically. (This retardation was said to be due to low I.Q., but in many cases it was complicated by or confused with emotional and/or cultural problems.) He believed strongly that retarded children could and should learn if given appropriate material and teaching methods. This attitude, so different from the more or less prevalent concept of the custodial function of low-I.Q. classes—"give them busy-work and keep them off the streets"—strongly and positively affected the atmosphere of the whole school. While Campbell was by no means a school for the mentally or academically retarded, being a "regular" school within the public school system, it contained a disproportionately large number of Basic classes. (Basic track included children who were considered educable but who had severely low I.Q.'s. The concept of tracks and their meaning is explained in Chapter 4.) Within the student body, I.Q.'s ranged from the low 60's to 130; of the 26 classes, 9 were designated as low-I.Q. classes. Mr. Ponsell wanted his Basic-class teachers to try new materials and methods that were being developed for teaching children with severe academic problems. When this program worked, new problems occurred. When many of these youngsters skyrocketed in I.Q. from the 60's to the 80's—or occasionally to the 90's or 100's—there was often as much distress among the teachers as there was joy. For in many cases it was clear that it was the more individualized pacing of material, closer attention to the child's needs, and small subgrouping that had made this growth possible. But as soon as the child's work began to show improvement he would be moved from the Basic track to a higher one, at a time when he might not have sufficiently solidified his gains to be able to cope successfully in a less personalized atmosphere. Moreover, since Campbell, unlike other junior high schools, had specialized in curriculum and methods for Basic track students, it was felt that this track afforded much better teaching and learning than the third, or General, track. If anyone needed proof that more care in teaching and more support to teachers would pay off in gains for the children, or that what could be done for the Basics might well be undertaken for those less severely handicapped academically, Campbell Junior High School had such proof. After consultation occurred, retracking on a grand scale took place. The question of what to do with the newly elevated children to help them catch up or stay up has been a severe instance of the concern at Campbell with these graduates of Basic.

Mr. Ponsell was equally concerned with the management of students who had severe emotional problems. In addition to the nine special classes for the slow or non-learners there were, in the year I acted as psycho-education consultant to the school, two "social adjustment" classes. These were composed of boys who presented the wildest behavior problems, regardless of mental ability (the I.Q. range was from 58 to 110). Mr. Ponsell's ideas of handling some of these maladjusted youngsters were often not executed for therapeutic reasons so much as they were for punishing or controlling behavior deemed unacceptable. He instituted a system of hiring young male teachers with physical-education majors upon their graduation from a local college, having them take over the most troublesome classes, and encouraging them to take special courses. These young men were energetic, vital, not over-thoughtful; their relationship with some of the troubled youngsters was often salutary. It was Mr. Ponsell's conviction that it was the strong male outlook which made the boys behave, and so, without theorizing about the qualifications of special education teachers, he simply decided that such men would be good for these boys. It was the same kind of empirical decision so many people in the clinical field have made concerning the aptitude of nursery-school teachers for working with the disturbed. The choice of nursery-school teachers has been defended on the basis that they have deeper training in child development, more acceptance of primitive behavior, more arts and crafts and project skills at their command, and are used to relating on the warm individual basis so needed by disturbed children. In this instance, the substitution of strongly physical males for frequently nonexistent fathers or ineffective fathers was intended to do the trick. Sometimes it did. It may well be that Mr. Ponsell's selection of a male physical-education major for the troubled boy of junior high school age was a good clinical choice. His system worked better than many others. Sometimes he would find a man truly gifted in working with these boys; often he found well-intentioned ones who could cope with the situation. Special training, along with good-heartedness and the male image, would have added to the understanding and effectiveness of the teachers. I spent much time in consultation with these teachers, both in groups and individually. It is true that these men had an easier time with their colleagues than do teachers of special and basic classes in many schools. The atmosphere at Campbell did not relegate such classes to the dump heap, and consequently the special teachers did not feel that they, themselves, were considered pariahs by their colleagues. Also, since there was more general (though superficial) knowledgeability in this school about the fact that certain children need special classes, the other teachers were not jealous of the smaller sizes of these classes, being aware that ten "socially maladjusted" could harass a teacher far more than thirty "regulars." Mr. Ponsell's attitude toward special classes of all kinds set the tone for the school. Many principals are not so eager for large numbers of maladjusted children or understanding of the difficulty the teacher has in handling these youngsters, not to mention trying to teach them. Mr. Ponsell often expressed the complaint that demands on his time and energies were so great. He was often out of the school at meetings or tied up in his office with an overload of administrative details. Often he was not able to see his staff members as much as would have been useful, not able to keep the lines of communication between staff members as open as he would have liked, and not able to have consistent contact with pupils except those few who kept reappearing in his office.

The Teachers

I first saw all the teachers together at the faculty meeting I attended on my fourth visit to the school. They seemed a fairly young and lively group, most of whom appeared to get along in an easy and friendly fashion. Later I became aware that there was a division between the races in the cafeteria, the whites sitting together at one half of the faculty table and the Negroes at the other. My impression was that this behavior was at least partly unconscious, and I'm not sure how significant it was. Mr. Ponsell's attitude toward his Negro staff members was always courteous and respectful but lacked personal warmth and contained a suggestion of distance and patronage. There was, nonetheless, a feeling expressed by a large majority of the faculty that Mr. Ponsell would treat them fairly according to his own rather rigid lights.

Though the children in the school were from lower-middle-class and lower-class families, the attitude of the administrative and teaching staff was distinctly middle and upper middle class in terms of behavior and goals. This is fairly typical of most public schools; the pitfall is that often the youngsters simply mouth what they soon learn to know is expected of them. If their experience of reality is such that what is handed down to them doesn't seem to fit their lives, the school's precepts become, in fact, more academic than educative. There are, of course, youngsters who do succeed in imbibing these values and others who, without thinking, go along with them, but for many the divergence between what they know from their own lives and what the school presents as valid is such that they begin to distrust the process of education as false, or hypocritical, or just not for them. At Campbell, although there was an understanding attitude toward deviations in accomplishment, there was not much leeway for deviation in values and goals. When, as so often happened, the youngsters experienced the difference between what was being taught them in school and the values of their parents, they felt that their heritage was being slighted or held in contempt. The parents often felt this way, too, and often shunned efforts made by the school to talk over the problems of their children. The teachers were often given a double dose of suspicion from the children and from the parents and were not sure what they did to deserve either the fiery rebuke or the sullen withdrawal. Often it was this unspoken undercurrent that made the teachers' lives so difficult in their teacher-parent conference or in some crisis with a student. It reminded me of Jerome Weidman's short story of a Christmas party held in a Jewish immigrant slum by a well-meaning teacher who, out of her small salary, had bought Christmas candy for her class. The children greeted this kindly gift with suspicion, with hostility, and some with fear—knowing the sugary sweets would cause unbearable pain in the cavities of their uncared-for teeth. The story, as I recall, ended with the breach between the cultures wider than before. It is this kind of breach that consultation seeks to mend.

Campbell, in addition to its individual problems, reflected all the difficulties common to junior high school teaching. Of all academic levels, this is probably the most difficult, as it marks the beginning of fragmentation for child and teacher alike. An elementary school teacher deals with the same children all day long. Though this may be deadly on given days, she has the satisfaction of being able to know well each child in her class if she wants to do so. She can see him when things are easy for him and when they are hard. She knows what will make him mad, sad, or joyous; she knows the tasks that will be too simple or boring, and those that will be a challenge or too difficult and frustrating. She comes nearer even than his mother to knowing the whole child, for she can see him alone and with his classmates, in a personal crisis or lost in the group. Not only does she have close contact with the individual, but she can tailor-make her lesson plan for the whole class, from day to day, and experience each child as part of a group. The junior high school teacher sees no child whole: she sees the group—an ever-changing group from hour to hour. In addition she has hints of the clique, and only some facets of each individual who passes through her class, period after period, all day long. She is trained to concentrate on subject matter, and when a student is outstanding as a success or as a failure in her class she often doesn't know if that is how he responds with other teachers in other subjects or whether it is her subject or her personality that is affecting him. She has had only peripheral training in child development, and she is confronted with a series of youngsters who vary emotionally from near-babies to near-adults and physically from little boys and girls to bearded or curvaceous teen-agers. She is supposed to keep order in her classroom at a time when everything we know of child development tells us that youngsters in this age bracket need to move, to talk, to daydream, to defy—to be grandiose one minute and help-lessly dependent the next. She sees each one for only one period a day and, like the teachers in the classes before and after hers, she is intent largely on making that period go without too much disruption. Unlike the high school teacher, she cannot, even at the worst, urge a pupil to drop her course, because at this age school is mandatory and most of the courses are required ones. She often has little support from a too-busy principal. She has less support from a supervisor who often comes only to rate her on how she maintains discipline (meaning quiet) in her classroom and whether she is following the prescribed syllabus, regardless of whether that fits her particular class at the moment. Because she is aware of her limited contact with her students, she is particularly uncomfortable when dealing with the disturbed child. Often she cannot confer with the counselor until the behavior has gone beyond her control—and, once she does confer, it is doubtful the counselor will relay back to her the results of a parent conference, of diagnostic testing, or of referral for treatment. It is true that the principal of Campbell attempted to alleviate these trials of teaching and management. On the surface, he welcomed help when he could get it, though often he was too busy to get the help he needed or to relay it to a bewildered teacher. Nor was he open-minded enough to accept areas of help which he, himself, didn't initiate or wasn't led to believe he had initiated.

Consultation

Upon my arrival at the school for the first day of psycho-education consultation, I found that the principal had been waiting for me in his office and was very eager to get started. Referring to our initial meeting the week before, he said he had concluded that I would be most useful to him, his staff, and the school if he could tell me about a few particularly troublesome pupils, and if I could help all the staff to a better understanding. Just then Mrs. Listmeyer, the counselor, came in. As she started to tell the story of a girl who was a severe behavior problem, we were joined by Mrs. Chase, the assistant principal, and Mrs. Drew, the nurse. So my consultative role was established in the first phase of a pattern which was gradually discovered to be, with a few variations, the classic one regardless of the school or principal involved. For the first few months my time and services were requested by the administrative staff, and some of the teachers, almost entirely for observing and discussing individual children. While the emphasis on individual children continued throughout the year, other kinds of problems were gradually brought to me. At Campbell I was never asked to hold a conference with a parent, but I was soon asked to help the principal or counselor or some of the teachers to prepare for such conferences and to discuss these with them afterward. After I had been there about three months the principal and counselor consulted with me about two of their "problem teachers." And finally the teachers and other staff members began to talk in informal groups about personal matters which they felt were affecting their professional lives or to propound their own theories of education, management of children, and school administration, or simply to express some of their own doubts and worries about the day-to-day jobs. One danger the consultant must guard against is a school's use of him to get rid of bothersome children. Campbell had a reputation for this, and I was on my guard not to become entrapped, but to be as objective as possible.

I shall use excerpts from my weekly reports to illustrate the range of problems presented in the course of a year's consultation. However, the very first one, the case of Susy, the girl referred to on my first day at the school, was one which I followed so consistently and intensively that I shall summarize it here from my notes.

A Case

In my first conference with the four members of the administrative staff of this school I learned that Susy was a thirteen-year-old white girl who had been transferred from another junior high school the previous year because her aggressive, impudent, and rebellious behavior was considered intolerable there. The Special Services department of the school system decided to try her at Campbell, feeling that the staff in this school could handle such behavior better. For the rest of that school year she had done well in the new setting, and there had been no major difficulties either with her school work or her classroom behavior. In the new school year, however, things had taken a turn for the worse: On the two preceding mornings she had been caught "making out" with a twenty-one-year-old boy on the school grounds. She had been kept out of classes and sent to talk with the counselor and then with the nurse. I had been aware upon first meeting her that this nurse, Mrs. Drew, had a remarkably natural, pleasant, and understanding manner. After I had been around the school for a while I realized what a great asset she was, particularly with the more difficult children. She told us she had given Susy some jobs to do around her office and had then driven her home: Susy lived in a reasonably adequate house in one of the worst neighborhoods in the city. After various aspects of the case were talked over, it was decided that the counselor would gather together all the information she could about the girl. On my next visit I would observe Susy in her various classes and would then meet with everyone directly involved to review and go into the problem.

On my subsequent visit I looked up Susy's I.Q., which was at minimum an 85, and wondered why she had been put into a class with the low-60 I.Q.'s. It occurred to me that this program didn't fit her, that perhaps she was bored, and that she could do better work. No one seemed to know why she had been placed there. The teachers all agreed that when she did come to school (which was not too regularly) she could make up in a day the work it had taken the others a week to do. We looked up the record from her previous school which proved her capable of doing "regular" work. The answer finally came from the counselor. She said that since Susy had been transferred to Campbell as a behavior problem, it had been felt that the teachers of the low-I.Q. classes, having been carefully selected for their skills, could handle her better than those of the regular classes. We had another meeting with all interested parties. Clearly, the counselor was very well aware of one part of the story; the assistant principal, who had a quite good relationship with this girl, was aware of another part; the principal of a third; and the nurse of still a fourth. None of them had the whole story, and the three teachers involved had virtually no knowledge of it at all. This is typical of fragmented communication in the secondary schools, and communication is precisely one of the bridges that consultation can build.

On my third visit I arrived to find that Susy had run away and had been reported to the Missing Persons' Bureau by her mother. It was Mrs. Drew who found out where she was and tried, unsuccessfully, to talk her into returning to school. Susy had protested that she was sick, and Mrs. Drew, a remarkably well-intentioned and interested nurse, said, "Oh, come now, we know you're not sick." At this point Susy did a characteristic thing, which all of the teachers had described in their contact with her. The minute she felt criticized, or when people did not take her at her word, she completely withdrew. It was as if a veil came down over her. Mrs. Drew said she talked with Susy for a long time but that Susy, after that first comment, became very polite, vacant, distant, and flatly refused to go back to school. Mrs. Drew returned feeling helpless and discouraged.

In the group consultation that followed, I tried, without being critical, to suggest to the nurse, or to ask the nurse to suggest to me, what she thought might have been going on. The nurse described her helplessness when the veil came down. The other teachers joined in and said that they had had the same experience. All felt helpless with Susy except for one teacher who seemed to be able to get through. She said she felt this girl had been handled too indirectly. She herself was very direct and honest with Susy: She said how she felt and what she meant and Susy usually kept in the picture for longer periods. At least she didn't feel helpless when Susy became uncommunicative; she felt she could just leave Susy alone at that point. I reflected that this girl had a way of making nearly all adults feel helpless, that this was exactly how the mother felt and probably how Susy herself felt— pretty helpless to do anything. The only approach we had found so far that seemed to work was directness. Since there had been much talk of her many complaints of ill-health, I asked the nurse why she had said, "Oh, but you're not sick," and she replied that she felt Susy was malingering. I agreed on that possibility, but I said that indeed Susy might feel sick in a non-physical way. I added that sometimes it is useful to go along with a statement even of feigned illness: The malingering of a person like Susy meant something and we needed to find out what. Since the girl had said, "I have cramps," I suggested one of many possible replies, i.e., "Well, I know how uncomfortable that is. Why don't you come with me and have a cup of tea to warm your stomach?" Mrs. Drew got the point— that acceptance of the hurt might have kept her in contact with Susy longer than denial of her statement, and might have given the nurse more information.

As a group we tried to discuss this girl's dynamics. One of the things achieved was to get a summary of the whole story. There were moral issues involved in this girl's story—a deserting father in and out of jail, the mother's long-term illegal alliance with another man, jealousy between mother and daughter over attention from this man—all things the teachers either were really shocked about or had to pretend to be. I increasingly felt that Mrs. Listmeyer, the counselor, deceived herself into thinking she was shocked because she ought to be, but was basically an earthy soul. Consultation helped her to allow her basic, human good sense to overcome sterotyped middle-class rigidity of judgment. Mrs. Chase, the assistant principal, really was shocked, however. I soon learned that Susy's best contacts were with Mrs. Chase, a definite, expressive, and often rigid woman, and with the teacher who happened to be the most rigid of the group in the classroom. So I pointed out that this was a child who had had a very loose background, that the mother claimed she was quite incompetent to handle the child, and that when threats of bodily harm were ineffective the mother became helpless. Therefore, this girl appreciated the distinct limits set out in the firm way that the assistant principal and the teacher were able to do. At the same time we got a strong group re-action to the moral issues which, eventually, were looked at more humanely.

Sometimes a personal attitude or specific experience of a teacher affects an area of his relations with students or with a particular student. Susy had expressed a genuine fondness for one of her male teachers, Mr. Frome, and so I asked him if there were times when he could talk to her in a casual, friendly way. His reply was that, when they were alone to-gether, Susy acted seductively and that this was frightening to him. I questioned this a bit (there was something about this statement that didn't jibe with my impression of pale, forlorn, not very seductive Susy), and he then told me of a quite traumatic incident in his own teaching past. He had been alone in a room with a girl student who had suddenly screamed "Rape, rape!" It was only by luck that there were other people nearby who had seen that this was not true. Mr. Frome was determined that he was never going to expose himself to that kind of thing again. Clearly, this was an unfortunate example of transference of past panic to a present situation. If this teacher had been able to accept Susy's presence, he could have been more useful to her. The principal suggested that perhaps the teacher might talk to her in the office next to the secretary's with the door open, and I came up with the idea that the principal, being a man, might be able to get into the act too. (Susy hated her mother, her sister, and women in general; she needed a man because she had been rejected by her father all her life.) Mr. Ponsell answered that he would like to do so and then genuinely ex-pressed his regret that he had so little contact with the stu-dents because he was so involved in administrative details.

When Susy returned to school after running away, she had, of her own accord, gone to apologize to the principal. Natural-ly, all concerned were happy and encouraged. But it seemed to me that they did not realize, on the one hand, how much they were really doing for this girl and, on the other, how un-realistic it was to assume that the problem had been "solved"

or that they could expect steady improvement. The first set-
back came a week later. Susy had come to school and had complained of a sore throat. Mrs. Drew found no symptoms of any
consequence and suggested that she gargle and go up to her
classroom. Susy refused and walked out of the infirmary. The
nurse, distraught and disappointed, reported to me that Susy
had left school. This was not true; she had simply not gone
with her class to music but had gone to Mr. Frome's room,
where she was quietly working. When her class reconvened
there, I joined them. Susy was talking quietly but happily to
the girl next to her. Having looked at her watch several
times, she suddenly asked the teacher for a pass to go to the
nurse, saying her throat hurt. Soon after she left I followed
her down to the infirmary.

It was a big room with little privacy for anyone. The waiting children sat in chairs, there was a curtain hiding four cots,
and in front sat the nurse. Her procedures and conversation
were heard and seen by everyone. Susy not only waited patiently but, when Mrs. Drew said it was her turn, she said,
"No, Patty came first." Since Patty had come in with me a
good bit later, it was clear that Susy was stalling and I wondered why. When it was her turn she complained that her
throat had become worse. Mrs. Drew, apparently remembering our talk about accepting these symptoms at face value,
sympathized with Susy and offered her medicine, rest, and
a gargle—none of which was accepted. Susy said she didn't
want to go to Home Economics class but wanted to go back
to Mr. Frome's room. Mrs. Drew gave up urging alternatives
and agreed that she might do so. It seems, at this point, Susy
simply went out the front door, leaving the principal a note
saying that she was ill. Though this was not a proper excuse,
she did not just walk out but tried to do it legitimately by
way of the note. What she had clearly wanted from Mrs.
Drew was permission to leave school. I remembered how
many times she had looked at her watch while I was observing her and how, in the middle of a cheerful and lively conversation with her desk mate, she had seen the time and asked

to be excused. She obviously had a date of some kind, but wanted her absence to be legitimate. The nurse, the counselor, and the assistant principal felt discouraged. I said that I did not, that her effort, however devious, to leave school legitimately indicated an attempt on her part to stay within some authority limits. Knowing this, perhaps the staff could help her help herself to stay longer some other time.

In this case I was wrong or too late, or both. Things went from bad to worse. Susy appeared at school only one day in the next two weeks. Her mother professed complete helplessness to deal with her. She said she hated to see her daughter sent to the training school but it was clear she could not cope with the problem; welfare and the attendance officer had control now, and she would be sent to the receiving home. All three staff members felt disheartened and discouraged, especially since they felt the school had done a good job with Susy, and Susy had done well with them. I handled this by first talking with the staff about what could be done, such as placement in a residental treatment home or possibly a foster home. We thought up techniques for dealing with the mother and with Susy when we would talk to them about these last alternatives to the training school. We discussed the unlikely possibility that the trauma of being at the receiving home might make Susy more amenable to suggestions. Then we talked over what the school had done and where the school had been limited. I tried to show them by my questions that, on the whole, they had done a job and that the major stumbling block had been Susy's home. All agreed that *had there been a social worker on the case* from the moment of her transfer, who would have seen the mother regularly, gathered pertinent information, and related it to the school, things might now be different. (The need for a school social worker to make home visits, unify the records, and perform liaison among the teachers became apparent again and again. There are now a few social workers in the system, but at the time there was only one in the entire city school system.)

Susy managed to resolve the situation exactly as she wanted to by marrying, at the age of fourteen and with the consent of her desperate mother, a sixteen-year-old bakery assistant. The young couple moved to a nearby state where, as a married woman, Susy would not have to continue in school because of her age, as would have been the case had she remained in the city.

Problems with Individual Children

Although I was more involved with Susy than with any other child in the school, I always had a list of children to observe, discuss, and follow through with if possible. I found in discussing children with whom the staff wanted help that most of the teachers had observed their behavior well and accurately. They had often made insightful guesses as to what caused behavior, but hadn't been able to put their observations together or to have confidence in their hunches without outside support. Sometimes, however, as in this first excerpt, stereotypes—racial or otherwise—clouded the thinking of the adult, so that the child's problem was seen as something quite different from what it was.

Excerpt 1. Fantasies and Impulse

"Mrs. Listmeyer, the counselor, brought up to me in some detail the case of a boy she was very worried about, whom she wanted me to have on my agenda. James was a good-looking Negro boy who had never got into trouble in school before the last couple of weeks and who had been especially helpful as a monitor outside Mrs. Listmeyer's office. He had talked at length one day, just prior to the onset of difficulties in school, about his 'evil mind.' Mrs. Listmeyer took this to mean sexy and questioned him generally. James defined 'evil mind' as not sexy, but murderous. He described in some detail a temper tantrum he had had in fourth grade which had shaken him deeply. Under very slight provocation, he had broken a bottle and attacked another little boy with it. He said he feared his temper and he feared his inability to forget a grudge. As if he had asked the authorities to help contain him, the day after this talk he got into severe difficulty, using verbal and physical threats toward an extremely beautiful white girl in his class. The girl claimed she had done nothing but throw a scrap of paper on the floor. James had got in a rage, chased her down the hall to the locker room, and threatened her with physical attack if she didn't stop teasing him. He reverted to the same behavior the next day when sitting in class with her. His sister reported to the counselor that he had a fierce temper and was suspicious of everyone and everything. I suggested, having observed both characters in the classroom, that James might, at his age and state of development, be having sexual fantasies about this beautiful and seductively dressed girl. Like many growing boys, he might well be defending himself against these fantasies by fights and fury. Mrs. Listmeyer concurred. I suggested that at least his seat be changed so he didin't have to sit and look at the girl. This subject caused Mrs. Listmeyer to bring up questions and tales about Negro lechery and sexual potency.

"She brought forth, in a musing way, the statements that all Negroes were more sexually able and more sexually directed than whites, that sex and music were what Negroes did best and most. I commented that this was a commonplace myth often used to maintain race prejudice and a stereotype that not only had no basis in fact but did little to help one group understand behavior patterns of another. Indeed, there were some Negro sexual athletes as there were white ones, but whether there were more, I didn't know. As far as I knew, Negroes had the same sexual difficulties and successes as the rest of the population. I added that in the Depression it had been found that the unemployed or intermittently employed —white, Negro, and Oriental alike—had more time to devote to acting out sexual fantasies, and that it might better be put that since poverty and irregular employment are often the lot of the Negro, energies devoted by the middle class to work are often directed by them to sexual activities when no work is at hand. I also said that more economically privileged types had more varied outlets for entertainment and for expressing anxiety, frustration, need for power, and a desire to escape. The poor everywhere, of all races, were always accused, often rightly, of higher sexual, drinking, and drug rates, but there was no evidence I knew of that Negroes had the market cornered, as it were, nor did they have greater needs or larger sexual organs. 'Really?' she said, in wonder. 'If that's true we whites needn't be so afraid.' In a most untypical fashion and with her urging, I began in a lecturing way. I said, 'Not so afraid or so envious. If we could see that employment and economic conditions are more equalized, we would not need to be so concerned about many aspects of Negro life that now concern us. Sex is one aspect and it is often used as a defense against despair, as an act of aggression and an affirmation of identity by all of us. If we leave little room for other outlets, then obviously the economically or work-deprived individual may turn to sexual acting out if he is able.' 'Really,' she kept saying, 'people ought to know about this. You ought to tell all the white faculty this.' She seemed stunned and truly amazed. I decided to increase my advantage of suddenly becoming 'the expert' and the 'eye-opener' on sexual mores and mentioned that many white girls and women, especially Southern ones, used Negroes in their fantasies to express sexuality both out of desire and out of fear. These were only fantasies and, as pleasant as they might be, or as scary, they were harmful to an understanding of an ethnic group and helped to build a wall of fear. The Negroes react to the stereotype by building a counter-wall of resistance which is typical of people who give up trying to interpret themselves to others. Finally, some may understandably say, 'If this is all you think of me, then that's what I'll be.' In the sexual department this myth has too high a status as a symbol of ability and power not to be exploited by both Negroes and whites! Mrs. Listmeyer kept urging me to say more and more and to speak to all the faculty on this. She assured me she had learned so much that it would change her entire thought processes. While I did not believe that, I think I made a dent. Maybe I am being naïve—dents are not made easily and not by lectures."

Here I should like to make a point about the sometimes illusory or perhaps transitory results of consultation. At the time, I felt that this conversation had got through to Mrs. Listmeyer and enabled her to look at some of her biases in a constructive way. Several years later, in the course of our project with the school psychologists in this school system, we were discussing in seminar a principal and her problems with the race question. This woman believed herself to be a champion of integration and, by intellectual intent, might be thought to be so. But the parents in her school sensed an undercurrent of unconscious prejudice against the Negro families, which showed itself in odd moments. An incident was reported in which she, along with other administrators, requested that the Negro children shampoo their hair with a disinfectant, although she did not concern herself about the heads of the white children. When a Negro boy displayed a knife (although he did not use it in any way), the principal assumed aggressive intentions, but confessed that with a white boy she would have been more upset because "you don't expect white children to carry knives." Thus, prejudice of which she was unaware kept cropping up. Commenting on this kind of person, one of the psychologists in the group said, "That's just like Mrs. Listmeyer, the counselor at Campbell. She is another one who is known to be anti-Negro although she, too, would deny any prejudice." I said, "Still? Even now?" They all chorused, "Oh, yes." So my conversion of Mrs. Listmeyer was a mere romantic wish.

Excerpt 2. An Impossible Responsibility

"When I came in through the outer office, a number of bedraggled and dejected boys were sitting in the hall. Adults were milling about in great confusion. An ambulance had been called to take one boy to the hospital and Mrs. Drew, the nurse, was all over the place trying to reach the hurt boy's mother, to get the authorities, and to tend the boy, all at the same time. Mr. Ponsell had just finished talking to the major culprit, who was led out to the bench in the outer office. When I went into the inner office, Mr. Ponsell exploded about the trials of the school, about the number of fights that had been going on lately, and he described this particular one. It seems the large boy I had seen on the bench had been expelled from a residential school for disturbed children. He had subsequently been released from a training school and then assigned to Campbell. He had been kept under some control in one of the special adjustment classes, but that morning, while the special teacher was absent, he had cut loose in the halls, got into a fight with a small boy, and kneed him until his penis was crushed and bleeding. Considering that this fight had come on top of two other serious fights, one involving girls, Mr. Ponsell, Mrs. Chase, Mrs. Listmeyer, and Mrs. Drew were justifiably upset. I played the role of the sympathetic listener. There was nothing much I could contribute since the grownups were too upset by these events to want to go into them at the time. I only said something about the possibility that this fellow might be one of the 'impossible' ones. I pointed out that, in the light of his history at two residential centers, he may have been discharged too quickly or put into a home setting with too little watchful support. He might well be one of those children who shouldn't be kept in a school of any kind and needed to be hospitalized. Later I asked if it were possible to provide someone who could offer a one-to-one relationship with such a boy who could be available when the boy was edgy or when the class teacher was absent. If not, this kind of a boy could probably not be maintained in an open setting."

This was a situation, I felt, where the adults were desperately asking themselves *how* to handle this boy and it had not occurred to them to ask if they should be expected to deal with him at all. It was clear when all the facts were looked at that either this child should not have been released from residential care or, if he had been considered ready, insufficient support had been given him in his home and school environment to enable him to maintain himself outside of hospital life. The lack of information and communication between the hospital and the school increases the rate of recidivism, damages the child, and frustrates the school. I felt that had regular, on-the-spot consultation already been an established procedure, this kind of trauma to child and school might have been avoided. The consultant would have contacted the social worker at the releasing institution and gotten recommendations for handling this boy. He, or she, would then have helped the school staff carry them out and would have provided support for both the child and the school during the initial period of adjustment. If it became apparent that the child could not be contained in a regular school setting, the consultant would have investigated possible alternative ways of caring for such a child and relieving the school of a problem it could not and should not have to handle.*

Problems with Individual Teachers

When the principal first asked me to help him with Mrs. Green, he explained that she was a young Negro teacher who had been very successful with a regular home economics class the preceding year (her first at teaching) but that this year she was not doing well with a low-I.Q. class. He felt that her strictness, humorlessness, and inflexibility were bad for her students, and he wanted me to see what could be done to get her to lighten her touch, be more kindly, and adapt herself with humor to the level of her class. While we were discussing this, the counselor asked if I would also help with another teacher, Mrs. Hunt, a temporary teacher, new to the school. It was said that she had a terrible temper, hated everyone (particularly men), and consistently made a mess of every situation inside or outside the classroom. Mrs. Listmeyer had tried to befriend her and could handle her personally without becoming angry, but she agreed with the principal that Mrs. Hunt was impossible as a teacher.

---

* See Ruth G. Newman, "The Way Back: Extramural Schooling as a Transitional Phase of Residential Therapy," *The American Journal of Orthopsychiatry*, XXX, No. 3 (July 1960), 588-598.

I was aware at the time that these two requests were quite dissimilar in purpose. I was being asked to help Mrs. Green become a better teacher through an improved understanding and a better attitude toward her pupils. In the case of Mrs. Hunt I was being asked (and this was openly stated) to provide support for the principal when he advised his superintendent that this woman was unfit to teach. The latter situation made me feel uncomfortable because I was not sure that this was the proper role of a consultant. But I decided I would at least observe Mrs. Hunt in the classroom to see if she were as ruinous a teacher as these two people considered her to be.

Excerpt 3. An Army Sergeant in the School Room

"I went to see Mrs. Hunt, a poor soul who shouldn't be teaching. She has a thing about men. She has been in the armed services, is quite disorganized in her planning, and conceives of teaching as army discipline. I saw the end of one class and the major part of the second. On noticing my presence she got quite anxious. She was not prepared for my visit since Mr. Ponsell had neglected to tell her I was coming (which is against our consultative rules). Her response to anxiety was to tighten up like an army sergeant and give the children all sorts of idiotic, meaningless, disciplinary tasks. During the second class she lined up all the students (evidently the third time in two weeks), reassigned seats, and appointed a monitor who was supposed to dole out minus points on the most complicated point system I ever heard of. It was marvelous mathematics practice for this fellow, but the subject she was supposedly teaching was English. Then, though she had come over and explained to me she had a monitor so that they would hate him, not her, she would stop and point to a minor infraction of the class rules and scold the monitor for not seeing it. She would then count a given number of points against both offenders, monitor and culprit. The poor monitor was craning his neck all over the place to be sure to catch the terrible mistake before Mrs. Hunt pointed it out to him. There followed a lecture on her point system, her class honor roll, and her class failure roll (actually!), and then she passed out new books. The students, reasonably enough, wanted to look over the books, which is supposed to be what a teacher wants them to do. They were leafing through pages. She stopped this as if they had been shooting BB guns—not in an unfriendly way—just 'Stop reading, don't look until I say open.' Then she had them read the first page, publisher and all, and then the preface. They never had a chance to see the contents of the book itself. The books were then collected while the monitor scored up new misdemeanors. This was English. Poor soul, I think she was scared to death of me and was afraid she couldn't teach content anyway, and so she wanted to show me what she thought she could do that I would respect—maintain *discipline*. It was all terrible and pathetic.

"She had a system I have seen used before by teachers with 'excellent' reputations as disciplinarians. It involved a kind of continual musical chairs on the basis of bad behavior. Seat one, to the extreme left of the first row, was premium. Anyone who committed a misdemeanor had to move to the extreme right, last row. There was not only a constant interruption of classes by people moving bag and baggage from front and middle to back and from left to right, but kids, knowing a source of fun when they see it, delighted in getting those to the left of them in trouble so that they would have to move right rear while everyone else moved toward left front. This not only distracted and halted teaching and learning but encouraged sadistic or just plain mischievous trouble-making. A great system."

Excerpts 4 and 5. Just Plain Scared

"I arrived five minutes late for my appointment with Mrs. Green, a very good-looking, young Negro teacher. We just had time to get acquainted before the children came in. She told me about her feeling that these children had no motivation and were unwilling to learn. She said she didn't mind teaching a slow class if they cared. We talked about slow learners and the process of motivating, in an informal way. I asked her if she had tried the project method at all. She said no. She said there were individual children she wanted to talk to me about. At this point her class came in, and we ended by making an appointment for lunch the next week. I observed her class. She seems to be quite teachable or supervisable. She tends to be too rigid and perfectionistic in an unimportant way with these kids, but I didn't feel her rapport was really bad, and she does have a sense of humor which came out every time she was comfortable."

The following excerpt is taken from a report written about a month later.

"I went up to my appointment with Mrs. Green. I like her and now she likes me well enough to open up quite frankly. We talked about the materials she used, and she complained about the materials that the school gave her as being inappropriate and inadequate for the Basic-track kids. . . . We then got to talking about how she had felt catapulted into teaching the Basic track from teaching home economics to a group of 'bright' kids. She said she didn't mind teaching the Basic track, as a matter of fact she liked it, but she *did* mind having so little notice and no help in learning how one teaches basic subjects to low-I.Q. kids. She said she didn't know the materials to use, the methods, techniques, or anything—and how uncomfortable and stiff she had felt. She told of how she nightly called her friends from the school where she had taught two years before. These teachers had taught beginning reading to Basic kids. She hounded them for advice, materials, clues, and interpretations. She said she wouldn't dream of asking her supervisor since this would endanger her rating and her permanent status—to reveal your lack of skill or knowledge to a supervisor was considered suicide. She had picked up what she could and had used it and now she felt a good bit more comfortable. She talked about how bad she felt not to be able to feel free to ask for real help from people who ought to give it. She asked me to help her where I could and, of course, I said that was what I was there for. It is clear that with growing confidence—which still has much, much room for improvement—the stiffness and lack of the light touch and overstrictness which Mr. Ponsell complained about decreases. She actually has, I feel from observing, a nice relationship with the children and a nice manner. She is just plain scared, not temperamentally scared, but scared of being found out to be ignorant and of being caught short and exposed. She is also angry at being put in a position where she feels inadequate, where before she had felt and had been successful. The times this kind of shift happens in schools, whether out of need to fill a salary or from bad guesswork, is staggering and damaging to everyone."

Mr. Ponsell and I worked on this problem of teacher placement in our subsequent conferences. Mrs. Green's plight, being given a class that needed special teaching methods without herself being given any additional training or guidance, is one in which a great many teachers find themselves. This is particularly true of the teachers of "social adjustment" classes where the problems of management are even greater than those of teaching. While there are some school systems which use specially trained teachers for pupils with extreme behavior problems, this, unfortunately, is not the general custom. Nor are there a sufficient number of well-trained special education teachers. Sometimes a teacher is chosen for such a class because the principal realizes that he or she is naturally gifted in the handling of difficult children. Sometimes a teacher is given such a class because he or she is a beginning teacher and thus low man on the totem pole of assignments. The practice at Campbell, of hiring young, athletic men usually trained as physical-education teachers, had some advantages. The boys, so used to females, had an opportunity to relate to a male teacher who might serve as a male model. This could be especially useful for those who had either no men in their families or who had weak or irresponsible ones. The choice of such teachers also made physical control an easier matter. The disadvantage in this procedure was that these men had little or no training in the underlying psychological meaning of the behavior of the youngsters and were therefore often handicapped in matters of clinical management or appropriate curriculum planning. Many of them were quite aware of this lack and begged for help. The following four excerpts cover about two months of consultation, and Excerpt 10 is taken from a report written about a month later.

Teachers' Hunger for the Meanings of Observed Behavior

Excerpts 6–9

"I went directly to the special adjustment class taught by a young manly type, not very articulate, but obviously very competent, Mr. Ennis. He told me how eager he was to use some of the long morning blocks of time on group personality tests and asked if I could confer with him on the various tests. He was curious about the dynamics of the kids and felt the records gave him next to nothing. He and I made a date for this coming Thursday at 2:30 when he will be free.

"When Thursday came around I met with Mr. Ennis and outlined the various tests he wished to hear about. I explained the meanings of each and the purpose. He was entranced with the House-Tree-Person test and one other drawing test. He said he would get drawings from the kids and asked if I could go over the productions with him. I explained the two tests in detail, and he said he would show me the pictures next week."

The following week:

"At this point Ennis appeared with a sheaf of House-Tree-Person drawings and some others and said, 'Analyze them.' I explained what could and could not be done and how I could say things, like a fortuneteller, but it would be much more valuable if we had the kids' records to look over. These, with the pictures, might throw some light on the knowledge he already had about the kids. I added that this was a legitimate use of projective tests: They were not made to test how much the tester could guess, but to help him learn as much as possible about the kids tested in order to help them. So next week I am to get the very faulty records they have."

Two weeks later:

"Mr. Ennis and I had a long conference going over the House-Tree-Person tests and the reports that I had done for him on the members of his class. He was impressed with how well the write-ups jibed with his own observations, and we talked in detail about ways to observe kids and how one can tell what attitudes beneath surface behavior may be revealed in the classroom. He's an attractive, enthusiastic young man with an instinct for teaching though not a great deal of knowledge about techniques and methods."

Excerpt 10. More of the Same

"I went to Mr. Jones's room at his request: he had been sold, somewhat oversold, on the psychic fortune-telling job I was supposed to have done for his class neighbor Ennis in interpreting the House-Tree-Person test and another drawing test, and also on how well I had been able to sum up the personalities of the kids. He asked if I would do the same for his group of not socially or emotionally maladjusted, just plain, backward Basic children—I.Q.'s supposedly 56 to 72. I agreed, but later on, in talking with him, managed to ask him what value he wished to get from the tests and how he hoped to use them. He's a nice, young physical-education type, handsome and pleasant but a little insensitive—well, a lot insensitive though he likes the kids and obviously cares about them. He had collected the drawings for me and insisted upon talking about each kid right there in the classroom. I said this made me uncomfortable and that I would be happy to go over the test, write up a paragraph as I had done with Ennis, and go over the stuff with him when I came next week and when we could arrange his conference at a time when the kids were not in his room. He asked for observation of his class another day since nothing was going on there now but study hall." This problem of doing consultation with teachers when children are about must be dealt with promptly and carefully.

Requests for observation of a class as a whole and for help with the teaching and management problems of a group came after the teachers had asked me to observe and discuss individual children. I had to become a familiar and trusted figure before they felt comfortable enough to shift the emphasis of consultation to their professional competence with a whole class. Later still, some of them were eager to talk more deeply about general professional theories, aspirations, or concerns. Occasionally someone would launch into purely personal and private confidences, and I found it a delicate task to refocus the conversation on its professional aspects without damaging the relationship of trust that had grown over the months of consultation.

The principal, who with a few exceptions had some sort of conference with me every time I visited the school, quite often spoke very freely of his professional concerns both within the school and in the wider outside educational world. The following excerpts about the principal come from notes I made over the course of most of the school year. The excerpts of teachers' conversations are from reports written in the middle of the second semester.

The Principal Talks about Himself

Excerpts 11–13

"Mr. Ponsell became quite expansive about his philosophy and the need to keep emotionally uninvolved and be objective. We talked back and forth. I tried to include in his thinking an awareness that feelings could help as well as hinder. I did this by indicating to him some of the good interactions I had seen him have with teachers and a few kids. I cited these as examples of what one did when one didn't deny one's own feelings but, at the same time, didn't allow irrational feelings to determine one's acts toward staff or children.

"He then talked about his entire schedule; how he had

changed it over twenty years, the mistakes he had made and had been able to change and those he felt he was still making.

"After this Mr. Ponsell and I went to his office and I confronted him with my concern that at our original meeting, when planning for consultation, he had said he had one severe problem, namely the disagreement about methods of discipline with someone on his administrative staff. He had felt Mrs. Chase was much too authoritarian, too strict at the wrong times, and often made life more difficult for teacher, child, and parent. He agreed he had told me of his concern but said he had worked with this woman for twenty years—fifteen in a position of boss to underling—and that he and she had never agreed. She was soon to retire. He liked and respected Mrs. Chase outside of disliking her professional approach. He said he had not done anything about it directly this year because he felt it was basically useless to teach an old dog new tricks but that he had hoped to find ways, through me, of circumventing her. He felt that if I could help the teachers so that they would not find it necessary to send the kids to her, this would be one way. Mr. Ponsell tried (not too successfully) to make himself or the counselor more available to the kids that did get sent down and he had busied Mrs. Chase with other jobs so that she would not so often get into difficulties with the kids. He felt this maneuver had been successful and went on to tell me of Mrs. Chase's assets and loyalties, even though she overstepped the bounds of good judgment and his guidelines. I felt quite good about this conversation because I had been worried that this one first plea of his had never been dealt with, and I began to understand that, without directly approaching it, he had used my presence to help him circumvent it."

Some Teachers Talk about Themselves

Excerpts 14–16

"Mr. Kent, who is a very pleasant, knowledgeable, eager, and intelligent young man but quite a talker—one might even say a non-stop talker—stayed on with me after

Mrs. Green left for her room. I had observed his class a few weeks before and thought he did very well with what the other teachers called the trouble-makers and the weirdies. He was full of humor, casual, helped make the work as interesting as possible for them, and had some intelligent notions behind his teaching. He used kinesthetic methods, non-boring repetition, and good books. He was tough when he had to be but treated the kids with a genuinely friendly interest. Children he found no trouble were always in trouble with the teachers they went to for other classes. On this occasion he wanted to talk—his theories and philosophy of education, feeling about the kids, feeling about their needs, all were put into a non-stop hour-and-a-half outpouring. After this, which was pleasant but tiring, my visit ended with another non-stop talk by Mr. Ponsell on his favorite subject, the basic learner and the need for corporeal handling.

"I had a long conference with Mr. Jones about the millions of House-Tree-Person tests I had done for him on his kids. This not only lasted two hours but involved his telling me his dreams, his own concerns, and his love interests. I tried to get back to the kids' tests as fast as possible without either being rude or seeming evasive. I did manage to focus on the job, and we finally finished up nearly all of his kids before it was time for me to observe a boy in the woodworking class.

"In the cafeteria Mr. Ponsell asked some of the teachers to join him and me and to talk about the kind of things they would like to hear from me at a faculty meeting. They all began to talk about teacher anxiety—the confusions of what to do, what to take seriously and what not to, when one feels inadequate and when one can do something about it, and when one simply feels inadequate and can't. It was a good talk . . . we got to the meat of some of these problems and there was a good bit of quite undefensive honesty about the experience of dismay for the teachers."

These excerpts should give the reader a glimpse of the variety of problems facing the consultant in a junior high school.

Since we were novices at that time, there were many methods of getting together that I overlooked and many I handled awkwardly. Later, for instance, I would have done much more consultation with small, homogeneous teacher groups to minimize the fragmented, isolated feelings of staff and students in the junior high.

At Campbell it was possible to talk informally with many of the teachers in the cafeteria at lunchtime and to get some feeling of relationship with small groups. At Urban (Chapter 4) the teaching and administrative staff was so much larger and the organization and scheduling so much more complicated that it was possible to establish only a number of individual relationships with some of the staff members. The bulk of teacher consultation was done in small groups.

Despite its smaller size, however, the junior high presents some specific problems in consultation. For one thing, the junior high finds itself in charge of a greater variety and range of pupils than does the senior high. There are, for instance, a large number of youngsters who can barely, if at all, achieve graduation from the ninth grade and are simply serving time until they are sixteen. There are the college-bound gifted students and the college-bound pedestrian pupils. There are the non-academic-minded youngsters who need a different kind of curriculum. There are the great majority of kids who are drifters and don't yet know what they want or what they are capable of. They are waiting until some life goal hits them, and if one is not allowed to have doubts about life goals at this age, we are living in a sad society. Adolescence blooms in its variegated form all over the junior high. Underdeveloped little youngsters who look like fifth-graders sit by the side of giants replete with bosoms or beards. There are the ones who already date and the ones who have entered into the phase of rebellion against adults—"I won't" behavior, dress fashions, or out-and-out rudeness. There are those who have become adolescent isolates along with the pre-puberty friendly kids. Moreover, changes occur from day to day so that what one says of John or Sue in February may be meaningless in May. Considering the tremendous turmoil and challenge this age group presents, it is not difficult to see that staff problems run high, and one defense against problems one doesn't understand or feels helpless to deal with is denial.

Many junior high school teachers feel they are not good enough or experienced enough to make senior high school, which is considered a higher-status job. They have not been trained even as much as elementary-school teachers in the dynamics of growth and behavior. They are often at a loss to deal with the multitude of problems present and take refuge in concentrating on subject matter. Behavior problems are sent to detention hall or the assistant principal's office and seldom followed up by the teacher who sends, or the disciplinarian who receives. Rarely does one teacher get to know how a troubled or troublesome child behaves in his other courses, unless the child gets into so much trouble that he becomes a school scandal, or unless a consultant can institute staff meetings on a given case or a series of problems. Many a junior-high-school teacher feels that to stay on in junior high is a sign of low status, low success, and low recognition. Most of those who can, move up to the senior high, thus creating rapid staff turnover. This further fragments a junior-high student's learning experience by reducing the opportunities for stable teacher relationships. The difficulties and potentials of this age group require the best planning, understanding, and teaching. Many of those teachers who stay on feel like failures and act accordingly. Though there are many excellent teachers in the junior high, there are not enough and the low regard in which they are held discourages their staying there.

Consultation to the junior high, therefore, tends to concentrate on building up professional self-awareness and self-esteem among staff, acknowledging the multiplicity of the tasks, and indicating the opportunity that exists to reach a variety of kids on a variety of levels. It has to try to make clear the meaning of individual differences in growth and how a given piece of behavior may fit into developmental patterns. It must demonstrate or imply that the patterns a teacher likes or dislikes in a child may, at this age, be set for good or may vanish according to the response of the adult. Particularly important for the consultant in the junior high is the task, similar to that in the senior high, of setting up lines of communication among staff and among outside specialists: the psychological services of the school and the community, the clinics, the hospitals, and the vocational and recreational groups. Moreover, the school needs consultative help in receiving information, and using it, from the elementary schools, and in relaying appropriate, well-thought-out information to the senior high or vocational school.

To my mind, junior high is the most complex division of the twelve grades: it is composed of the most challenging age group and is often the least equipped in terms of staff and physical facilities. Its goals and purposes badly need rethinking and replanning. The whole concept of junior-high-school education is open to question. Since the consultant must work with the schools as he finds them, he must try to help, as best he can, to define the concepts and the goals. Together with the staff he can search out a plan by which children of this age can best be served—in what kind of setting, with what kind of curriculum and methods, with what kind of attitudes and ancillary services.

4

Consultation in the High School

Urban High

(Ruth G. Newman, Consultant and Reporter)

The high school is often the stepchild of the school system when it comes to mental health programs and other extracurricular help. A valid insistence on the importance of special services at the elementary level drains funds and staff for similar programs away from the secondary schools. Moreover, those undertaking action-research projects often are frightened by the feeling that anything done in secondary schools will be negligible in terms of the needs. Thus, high-school students get the least individualized, and often the least informed, help at the very age when emotional instability is to be expected, when crises concerning identity and choice abound, and when decision-making is of the essence.

We decided we would try consultation in a high school despite the many difficulties it presents. The school for which I was consultant—Urban High—is a large, sprawling structure with higher ceilings and more air and light than are customary in newer schools. It is situated on top of a hill with a remarkable view of the downtown area of the city. However, the building is in poor repair, lacks modern equipment, and suffers periodic attacks of vandalism. The student body is 99.58 per cent Negro, the de facto segregation caused by real estate values and the happenstances of urban development. There is a small group of students whose parents, most of whom are attached to a nearby university, are well educated and on a relatively high economic level. There is a larger group whose parents own or rent homes, often shared with other families, and who have skilled or partially skilled jobs. The great majority of students come from poor economic backgrounds with parents, or parent-surrogates, who are sporadically, seasonally, or sometimes permanently unemployed. There are many broken homes; most are one-parent homes.

The Principal

Dr. Beatrice Tilden, a gifted and well-educated woman, was the principal of Urban High during the period of our consultation program there. She and her husband grew up in this city and were prominent members of the Negro community, having gained recognition as skillful leaders in their respective fields and in the Negro movement throughout the country. Before coming to Urban, she had worked with adolescent boys too disturbed and disruptive to attend regular schools. She felt strongly that one of her basic responsibilities was to meet the challenge of suiting education to community needs, particularly those in Negro urban areas.

Many of the staff members were holdovers from the previous, conservative regime who feared or resented her programs and her methods. There were those who approved of the new approach but were unable to keep up with her pace. They felt, often justifiably, that she was too occupied with projects within the school and in the community to give sufficient attention to the necessary details of school administration. And there were loyal and able followers who were willing to function under a great deal of stress because they were dedicated either to her ideas or to her personality. Despite the discouraging number of problems and complications caused by intra-staff factions, there was, when I entered the school as a consultant, a sense of excitement and hope and something to fight for.

Consultation on a Specific Program

On my first day at school, when Dr. Tilden and I met to decide on a plan of action, we found the task of making a choice among so many areas of need a rather overwhelming one. We finally agreed that I should start by helping with the work-study program which was just being launched. This was in the hands of a teacher, Mr. B., and a new, adept counselor, Jenny Jones. Although Mr. B. had his teaching certificate, he had not taught for years but had been in charge of custodial and janitorial duties at Urban High. The plan was for him to train about twenty selected boys in the various individual tasks which comprise maintenance work. As soon as possible they would be assigned to assist the maintenance men or custodians in other schools in the area and for this work they would be paid a small wage. They were to work four hours and then return to Urban for the rest of the day for courses in Basic English and arithmetic. In addition, they would be supervised in learning skills in carpentry, electricity, and plumbing which would stand them in good stead in possible future jobs. This project, conceived by Dr. Tilden, has spread to other schools in the system and is considered very helpful by most of the students, including those not directly involved.

The account of setting up this program, as well as the accounts of other kinds of consultation, is taken from the reports I wrote for our consultation project at that time. In some places I have summarized; in others I used the notes verbatim.

Excerpt 1. Launching the Work-Study Program

Mr. B., Jenny Jones, Dr. Tilden, and I met to select about twenty boys from a group whose records of truancy, behavior difficulties in the school, low academic achievement, and lack of motivation pointed to the probability of their dropping out. We discussed the criteria for selection and agreed that applications must come from the boys themselves, with the consent of their parents, and that preference would be given to those in such financial straits that even the small amount of money to be earned would be of great help. We also decided that the boys should be given this program for a full school year and not just for one semester as originally planned. Dr. Tilden made the point that all those being considered had done so poorly in academic subjects that they needed a more intensive program than the remedial one now being offered. This would mean developing a curriculum that would cover the kind of arithmetic they could use and the kind of reading and English essential to holding a job, not the usual academic courses.

Excerpt 2. Miss Jones and the Work-Study Boys

I spent time with Jenny, who gave me a rundown on all her selections for the potential dropout, work-study group after the program had run for three months. She reported in glowing terms the meeting that had been held with the group and what the kids had said about it—what it meant to them, how it affected their desire to stay in school and learn, and also what faults the kids had seen in the program. For example, one kid had validly objected to being exploited on the job. She talked about a few of these boys as special cases. She was worried about them and wanted to refer them to private sources for therapy. We went over these cases and found a way of approaching each parent on her list so that they might find the suggestions acceptable and practicable. We also got a list of clinic facilities.

Excerpt 3. Mr. B.'s Troubles with Some of the Boys

While Mr. B. is deeply dedicated to this program, he is over-conscientious. If any of the boys don't live up to his expectations, he becomes angry and so disheartened he

wants to eliminate them from the program. Jenny has pro-
tected several of the boys. A case in point is Peter. His mother
was living with a transient paramour; for this reason, in typical fashion, the welfare department had stopped giving her
relief. Now, no paramour, no money, no heat, and for weeks
now the boy has been sleeping in an unheated apartment with
all his clothes on because it was too cold to undress. He has
been supporting the family by working on a job from eight to
twelve at night. He has been late for school and for the work-
study job, which gives him a little extra cash—enough to get
the heat put back on when his check comes. Mr. B. wanted to
remove him from the job because he was late for work and
because he fell asleep in class. Peter did not confide in Mr.
B., so that, not knowing the circumstances, he was hurt by
Peter's attitude. Jenny wanted me to speak to Mr. B., and I did.
Sensing that he thought I had come to criticize, I purposely
didn't get to the point until we had chatted for a while about
the program and the screening for new boys. Then I asked if
we might meet, he and I, for half an hour weekly to discuss
those kids he feels disturbed about or who seem not to be getting as much out of the program as he would like. The rebellious ones don't tell him what's happening in their homes,
especially because he's something of a moralist. They do tell
Jenny. I suggested that he and I get the folders and all the
material on Peter and another boy, the two boys he said were
the most troublesome, and then meet and talk again next
week.

Excerpt 4. Mr. B. and Psycho-Education
Consultation

I met with Mr. B. Again a couple of boys were
being discarded for not living up to his standards. He has
great pride in the jobs he gets for the kids and bends over
backward to please employers. If the boys don't act like ver-
itable Boy Scouts, they're in trouble. He cares so much that
when they don't show up on their jobs he visits their homes.
For some kids this kind of caring works marvels; from others

he gets legitimate resentment for interfering and fresh talk or some show of resistance. He and I talked and we got somewhere, though he was skeptical about what he considered my loose standards. He confessed that he had lost one boy by becoming too involved and then resenting the fact that the kid didn't appreciate his efforts. As we talked he began to see how his visits to the home were interpreted by the boy. He went there so often and spent so much time talking to the stepfather that the boy felt Mr. B. had become lined up with the hated stepfather and had further alienated his mother from him. Mr. B., drawing on his own memories, came to understand that this boy, like many adolescents, needed to keep home and school separate to protect his emerging identity. This is in contrast to the elementary school; a teacher's visit to a young child's home serves the purpose of showing the child that teacher and parent are united in their efforts to help him.

The Use of Consultation Spreads

My initial contact with Jenny Jones was through the work-study program. Soon she was consulting with me about individual boys in this program, other students with whom she was involved, and other projects she was developing or wanted to initiate.

Another staff contact that I made through the work-study group led to the development of an important program that became an integral part of the school's services to students. Mrs. H. was a business teacher who had worked with Mr. B. in starting the work-study program. She was assigned as both a home-room teacher and a business teacher to one of the most difficult classes of boys in the Basic track. In addition, because Dr. Tilden had no dependable, trustworthy secretarial help, Mrs. H. did all the important office work for months until a suitable secretary could be found. In the meantime, her group had gone to pieces, and she was being criticized by the rest of the staff for helping Dr. Tilden and not teaching her class.

She was torn between jobs, but since she was truly afraid of the boys in her class she was willing to be pulled away to work in the office. Despite her difficulties and conflicts she had creative ideas, and some of her proposals, conceived in desperation, developed into very useful programs. It was she who suggested that some of the women from a community service organization, who had volunteered to help out in the school, be trained to give remedial tutoring to her class and to other students who desperately needed extra help.

While many volunteer groups were doing a variety of jobs in the public schools, the group of women at Urban was the only one, at that time, interested in working in a senior high school. Most volunteers feel more comfortable with younger children, while adolescents tend to arouse in adults fears about discipline and management. Dr. Tilden wanted me to help her provide tasks for these ladies that would be genuinely useful to Urban and at the same time would not alienate the students or make work for the staff. It took time to appraise the group and decide how to make maximum use of individual talents and abilities. Three areas of activity finally emerged. Some of these ladies gathered statistics about attendance records, truancies, and potential dropouts. Some were used to interview parents by telephone to determine reasons for absences, tardiness, and truancy. Others expressed interest in tutoring the children although, at the beginning, only one of them was trained in remedial techniques. This was the group with whom I worked most closely and regularly, continuing as their consultant even after our project at the school was finished. From the outset I expressed my strong conviction that less than twice-a-week tutoring, especially for the very slow children, was often worse than nothing. Increasingly, more tutors came twice and sometimes three times a week. Once the group was established I met with them once a week and helped them by means of group consultation on various aspects of their work, ranging from the teaching of skills through the exploration of relationships. I believe that without regular, continuing consultation with and supervision of the volunteer tutors, this much-needed program would not have become firmly established as an extra service to the students at Urban.

Volunteers' Needs for Training and Regular Consultation

Excerpt 5. *The Statistical and Interviewing Volunteers Get Started*

Before my first meeting with them, the women had collected a great deal of necessary data on absentees. While a few of them were fascinated with the information that could be gleaned about the kids just from objective facts, most of them were impatient to get on with the telephone interviewing, having collected the statistics only because they had been told to do so. Dr. Tilden handled this well, pointing out the value of facts as indicators for future investigation and programming, and then turned the meeting over to me.

One woman wanted a formula at once for exactly what to say on the phone to parents; she thought she could start right away that morning. I replied that since this was an important and delicate job we should be careful to work out appropriate ways to get information. We discussed this for a while, then they suggested role-playing as a means of learning to interview by phone. I thought this a fine idea. I spoke of the importance of using non-ambiguous, understandable, but non-condescending language. We talked at length about confidentiality. A procedure was set up for getting records from the counselor and consulting with teachers when necessary. I explained how to use school records and discussed group tests. The impatient one again wanted to get started; she wanted to get ten files and records and begin phoning next Wednesday. Others helped me hold her back by saying "Ten!" I suggested that they would be doing well to get three each to start—these we would discuss in detail next week.

Excerpt 6.   Trouble Setting Up the
Reading Groups

I had hardly entered the school when Mrs. H. pulled at me to hurry and get to the volunteers and get the reading groups assigned. I was perfectly willing to do this, but I wanted to know my schedule for the day first and also wanted to know exactly which volunteers were interested in the reading program. There were other things I needed to know about the members of the school staff who were to be involved with the tutoring group, but Mrs. H. was too frantic to listen to my questions and rushed me into the room with the volunteers. I started to assign youngsters so that each child would get two hours of remedial work with the same tutor, instead of just one hour a week. I felt, and said often, that one hour a week for these kids in bad reading trouble was not only not better than nothing, but often worse than nothing. When these children who have asked for help think they have got it and then get too small a dose to do them any good, it simply reinforces their feelings that they cannot be helped and they become more discouraged. Then Mrs. H. asked about her "little angels"—the boys she was supposed to be teaching in business class who had become anything but little angels. She had devised this whole tutorial structure for Dr. Tilden and me partly to satisfy her conscience about her frequent unavailability to these boys because of all the office work she did for Dr. Tilden. Since the boys should have been included in the program, I asked why they weren't. She said she didn't know why, but they weren't. When lists were brought out and all the names of the participating students put down, it turned out that all of Mrs. H.'s boys *were* on the list, and some of them were already being seen by two of the volunteers. I said I couldn't talk about this any more until everyone from the school gave me enough information on the kids for us all to appraise them properly. I insisted on a long, intensive session next week to see how everyone wanted to go about this task and who would do what for how long with which kids. I only partly succeeded in containing my annoyance; my irritation with the sloppy, confusing communication must have come through. Those people from the school most particularly interested in the project appeared to be making it impossible for the program to get started out of anxiety or unconscious mixed motives.

Excerpt 7.   The Reading Groups Get Under Way

I held the big meeting, which I had insisted on, with all the reading people. Heaven be praised. It will be held weekly from twelve to one, and I made it urgent enough so that I wasn't sorry when one person felt guilty about not being able to come next week. We got a lot of group suggestions and group questions. Some people brought up specific problems they were having, and we went into each one a bit. I suggested that Mrs. Q. bring in a case in full next week and that we use that as a good jumping-off place to begin a diagnostic handling or programming for each kid—which in time we will get to. This went much better than I had hoped, with Jenny coming in and filling in information about the kids or about the health service when we needed it. L. works with one kid who obviously needs speech therapy; there is a question about his hearing, so we'll get the school doctor to give him a test. There is another child with double vision and Miss N., the nurse, can get hold of this. This is a rather nice way to involve the school health personnel in consultation.

Consultation and the School Nurse

My final comment in the preceding excerpt reflects the concern I had felt, even before coming to Urban, over the fact that in this school system the people directly concerned with the children's health are often quite isolated from the rest of the staff. School nurses and school doctors are employees of the city Health Department, and this would seem to be one factor in the marked lack of interdisciplinary planning and communication.

Excerpt 8.   Some Problems of Physical and Mental Health

Again I went to see Miss N., the school nurse. She is a bright, energetic, well-meaning young woman. She works hard and she gets frustrated because the school program so little includes her. She draws up schedules for dental, eye, ear, and physical exams, trying to interfere as little as possible with the academic life of the kids or teachers, but because of lack of time and machinery for communication, the administration and the teachers don't cooperate, and she is left with her own schedule and programs dangling. Today she was particularly frustrated; she had wanted me to meet the school doctor, who had already come and gone. It seems that the secretarial staff had failed to put Miss N.'s notice of physical examinations in the bulletin and then had failed to include it on the list for the public address system, so that instead of thirty kids only five had come to be examined. This is a school where health problems are tremendous, and she was horrified that this opportunity to do her job (and for the doctor to do his) had slipped by. When I commented that I was sure Dr. Tilden would be as concerned about this as she was and suggested that maybe the thing to do was to take her notices directly to the principal, she was dubious and resentful, feeling that Dr. Tilden was involved with so many things that this procedure wouldn't be any more efficient. She complained, too, that in crises people send her problems she doesn't know what to do with and has no authority to deal with. For instance, today there was one acutely schizophrenic boy who was having hallucinations and was sent to Miss N. by a teacher for "medically peculiar behavior." The boy had decided that World War II was on again, started by an African king, and that the dogs were winning the war. He had got into fights with kids and came as a medical problem, with a cut eye. This she could deal with. (The handling of this incident by the teacher was unhappily typical of people who do not understand the quality of mental illness. In order to show

Miss N. and me that he was no sucker for malingering, the teacher told us that at first he thought he was being kidded, the boy's stories were so wild. So he pulled the boy aside, threatened to hit him, to club him, to beat him up. "But you know," he said, "the boy really believed all this because he kept on saying these things.") Other boys then came and told Miss N. that this boy had had a similar episode in junior high and lately had begun to act peculiar and say strange things about voices and visions, and today all hell broke loose. By the terms of her job description, Miss N. could do nothing. There were others in the school who could call a hospital, but they either could not be found or were unwilling to do anything until the parents were notified first. No one was permitted to help until the parents had been contacted, and this proved impossible. We tried to set up emergency measures at a nearby hospital and still protect the school personnel for this and future cases.

The Consultant and Teachers' Meetings

Excerpt 9.   Planning a Teachers' Institute

We had a lunch conference today about a Teachers' Institute to take place next Wednesday. Last year, at a similar Institute, Dr. Tilden had had a panel discussion in order to air her revolutionary plans for Urban. She had made it clear that it was no longer a business school and had introduced her many-sided program, including the Honors track. (The very idea of starting the latter at Urban had brought laughter, scorn, or doubt from her staff. Now they are beginning to believe in it and some of the staff feel proud of it.) This year she wanted something exciting, stimulating, morale-building, involving, and preferably not talky. We all thought. Finally I suggested that since she had inspired me with the variety of programs she presented, I thought she might get a tape of W.'s Honors class (a free discussion like one I had just sat in on), one of the work-study class (like the discussion Mr. B. and Jenny had got from the boys about what they were doing and how they felt about it and what it meant to them), tapes of a business class or a print-shop class, and one of a good straight academic class. Then she could choose the most dramatic three and present them to the group. W. then suggested an open-end evaluative sheet for the teachers to fill out on their reactions to the tapes. I was elected discussion starter and provoker. I suggested small workshop groups, each led by a strong teacher, and time for me to summarize at the end.

Excerpt 10. How the Teachers' Institute Went

The session started with a very intelligent math teacher giving a good paper on the whys and wherefores and purposes of the Institute and what was to be hoped from it. I took over and tried to smooth down what I knew to be ruffled feathers. The feathers were ruffled not only by some hostility to Dr. Tilden and her programs but also by the fact that another white specialist was in their midst, and a friend of Dr. Tilden to boot. The business-class tape was first, and the teacher began by explaining away everything and defending herself before she was attacked. The next tape included two math classes, a slow one and a more advanced one, on the same theorem and corollary in geometry. One was taught in a group method, the other by child-initiated questions and visual demonstrations. In both cases the teacher built in a mental set for attention, then related past learning to present problems and possible future solution. Next came a tape of R.'s print-shop class for a group of Basic boys. His tone was very friendly and informal although he addressed each boy as Mr. So-and-so. The method used was the Socratic question-and-answer technique, very skillfully handled as a means to solve the practical problem of printing the school newspaper. When he explained that he used "Mr." to give these Basic boys respect and dignity, the other teachers burst out in approving applause. They were also genuinely admiring when he explained his other techniques. It was nice to see. He is a new teacher and might have been put down by this cliquey faculty, but was not. Then came W.'s tape, an excellent one of a free discussion class—a quite remarkable feat in which the kids discussed a book in terms of their own problems, white supremacy, and unfair treatment. After the tape was finished, one teacher questioned the freedom of the discussion and wondered whether the teacher should have intervened and directed more. The fact of the matter was that, through an emergency, W. had been out of the classroom part of the time, so it was a nice example of how a class of kids, once stimulated and involved, can carry on by themselves, manage themselves, and continue the free discussion. Criticism of this method was brought up on the basis that only a few people get to talk and therefore monopolize the group. I pointed out that this was life and that if the habit of such discussions gets going, a teacher can use subject matter or an occasional directing word to set up a climate in which most of the people, or more people, get educated to participate. We talked about how the listener also gets something and about the undesirability of forcing the painfully shy and withdrawn ones to speak up. The talking back and forth between staff and me felt good, and the meeting ended with a great deal of discussion. The excitement among many of the teachers was enough to mark this as the first of a series of such discussions instead of as a failure.

Excerpt 11.   Regular Meeting—Grading, Tracks, Black-White Attitudes

Dr. Tilden came into her office, where we were to meet with W. to set up the teachers' meeting that afternoon. The monthly meeting is the one time Dr. Tilden has a captive audience of her whole staff, the hostile ones and the friendly ones. There is so much on the agenda that the great plans we make for provocative, stimulating discussions on important issues just get a surface covering because time has always run out. This meeting was to be on grading. After the school day was over, the faculty meeting began with forty-five minutes devoted to many announcements. Dr. Tilden said a few words about why she wanted the subject of grades to be discussed and threw the meeting over to me. Much of the morning had been spent in arranging for Jenny's presentation first of actual statistics on grades to be given, so that it wouldn't always look as if I were briefed by Dr. Tilden to say just what she wanted said. I was supposed to ask some provocative questions after the presentation. However, contrary to our plan, time made it necessary to begin with me. The sea of hostile faces, many of which when met individually are friendly and even inquiring, was somewhat appalling. I said practically nothing that I had planned to say in the speech which was supposed to provoke discussion because my time had run out. Probably the best thing that happened was that Dr. Tilden and I had to leave, because then Jenny *had* to take over the meeting. She told me the next day that everyone talked—violently, argumentatively, and profitably. They were glad to adopt my suggestion that instead of changing to yet another subject at the next faculty meeting, they pursue this one. I gather there was actual applause when Jenny mentioned that perhaps Honors should be treated, as it is in many other schools, not as a total course but only for some courses in which a youngster has special aptitudes. Thus, those particularly interested in and able in English or math or history should take Honors in only one or two subjects instead of a total Honors course. I have here enclosed Jenny's statistical breakdown of grades given, showing the number of failures and near failures at Urban. Next time she will break it down into subject-matter gradings instead of sectional gradings.

Office of the Counselor—Urban High School

Tenth-Grade Scholastic Profile Summary

Passing all subjects	35%
Failing one subject	27%
Failing two subjects	18%
Failing three subjects	10%
Failing four subjects	7%
Failing five subjects	3%

Distribution of Grades

	No. of A's	5%
	No. of B's	14%
	No. of C's	29%
	No. of D's	22%
	No. of F's	27%

Track Distribution

Honors	Passing	21
	Failing	8
Regular	Passing	13
	Failing	19
General	Passing	94
	Failing	243
Basic	Passing	33
	Failing	107

The reason the subject of grading was such a vital one was that in addition to its intrinsic educational dynamite there were economic and discriminatory factors mixed in. Neither students nor teachers had recovered from the feeling that Urban was a school populated by students of low achievement and potential. Consequently, morale was low. Low morale was reflected in the meager expectations of both teachers and pupils. Since changing this is part of Dr. Tilden's crusade, it is particularly important to get across clearly how each one of the teachers who grades in a despairing, defeated, and often unconsciously hostile manner contributes to the low morale of the whole school, the low status of the school, the lack of Honor-group stimulation, and the increased number of drop-outs. The subject came up after the first eight-week reports had come out. Jenny Jones and W. had gotten excited because the Honors group, who by definition are A and B students, had been given F's, D's, and C's. Students in the regular academic track, who need college approval, had been flunked and downgraded in large proportions. Many from both groups were thinking of dropping out—"What's the use, we can't make it in the intellectual world from this school where our efforts are rewarded with this kind of grading."

Although there are instruction books for grading in reference to the track system, there is still much confusion about grading in the minds of the teachers. To try to explain: The

Honors track was set up for the very fast students who volunteered for an enriched, more difficult, more exciting program. Only comparatively high-I.Q. and academic-minded kids are included, and it is voluntary on their part. If this track is marked on its own curve, it is often quite unfair to give Honors students C's and D's. If they had stayed in the regular academic curriculum, they would still be receiving B's or even A's in the less difficult, intense, and sophisticated courses. Therefore, it is a general, but evidently not widely understood, rule of the city that one does not grade the Honors track on an Honors curve, but grades the students as if they were part of the Regular track curve. This makes sense, but many teachers forget or do not understand it. Others, for such reasons as unconscious jealousy of the very bright, and sometimes because of hostility toward Dr. Tilden's attempt to uplift the school, manage not to take this into consideration. Some teachers give these Honors kids, especially the ones beginning in the ninth grade, horrible marks. This so discourages them that their work falls; some drop back to the Regular track or, worse, they drop out as soon as they reach sixteen.

The Regular track grading problems are less acute and confusing and far more usual. Some of the teachers have the disease of wanting to be loved by every student and give indiscriminately high grades (the dearth of such happy jewels in Urban is marked). The far more usual and prevalent disease in this school is that of thinking of oneself as a good teacher only if one is considered a tough grader who fails and downgrades. This is especially true in the first grading period in nearly every high school. A teacher seems to dread being looked upon as a soft grader by the students, forgetting sometimes that the wonderful fresh spurt of energy many kids have in the fall gets squelched by a discouraging first low grade when they have put out their best effort. Confusion exists in the Regular track when, despite the low marking of Honors students who are supposed to get A's and B's, the teachers reason that if Regular track kids were really A and B students they would be in the Honors track—therefore they often feel that Regular track kids should not get more than a C. Thus the Regular track also tends to be downgraded.

We now come to the General track. Again there are the usual problems of grading on a complete curve, but students suffer from the knowledge that if they were A and B caliber they would be in the Regular track and there would probably not get more than a B at best, since they presumably are not academic-minded. The philosophy of the track system, in addition to grouping according to interest, is to have a full range of ability within each track, except the Basic track. Thus there are supposed to be as many A's and F's in the General track as you would find in any normal curve distribution. Everybody gets excited over this, Dr. Tilden included, because if they give A's in General track, which is vocational, business, and job-centered, then what do you do with the Honor Roll? Does an Honor Roll at a school mean an abstract standard of academic excellence or fine performance in relation to one's ability? Last year the valedictorian of the school was a boy from the General track who was chosen by grades. I can't see what's wrong with that, but many people get into a tizzy over it. They recall all their 140-I.Q. Honors track kids who didn't get as many A's, but who, being academically adequate students, might better represent the goals of the school.

We now come to the lowliest of the low—the unacademic, hard-to-teach slow learners, the Basics.* These are kids whose I.Q.'s are either quite low or whose learning motivation and emotional structure make it impossible for them to learn academically, especially reading and arithmetic. Many of them are on an elementary-school reading level, and low elementary at that. They are supposed to get remedial teaching and have limited educational goals based on concrete, practical needs. However, the planning and curriculum offered this track is still replete with busy-work and involves custodial care. However, the high school has the advantage of many ex-

* The track system has been revamped and the "Basics" are now called "Special Academics." In the new system, children of under 70 I.Q. make up the Special Academics. All others, regardless of how academically retarded, are supposed to be in higher tracks.

cellent vocational opportunities, such as the print shop and the work-study program, which is new and experimental. Many of the volunteers are being used to help these kids improve their reading in a one-to-one tutoring relationship. The theory of marking, rarely followed here because of the contempt often felt and shown for these kids, is that if they do their best and if they are improving at their own level, that's A or at least B work. However, many teachers think that if the kids are in the Basic track they are automatically D and F pupils and ought to be marked so. Moreover, many people feel that kids who get A shouldn't be kept in Basic. In addition, they feel that since so many kids are placed in the Basic track because of "false negatives" in testing or cultural disadvantage (such as having just moved from a rural deprived area) they must be moved out of Basic as soon as possible. For people who feel this way, a grade of A would indicate that they function too well to have been put in Basic track in the first place.

Dr. Tilden feels strongly that the danger in the track system is that the categories tend to get frozen, and that once a kid has been labeled Basic or General he will have a hard time being moved into the higher tracks. She has been fighting against this, and feels that when a kid gets A in Basic, he ought to have a chance to get into General. I see the point, and part of me goes along with it. The other part of me feels that if a kid works hard and well at his own level, he should be rewarded with high grades (since we insist on using grades in our society). If he feels he can never get above a C in Basic, what's the use of trying? Also, the classes are smaller in the Basic track and the work is tailor-made. Therefore, if a kid operates well when he is given greater attention, it does not necessarily mean that the great variety of the General track will fill his needs. If he is promoted to it he may slump down in motivation and in achievement to the bottom of the heap, from where he had for the first time in his life elevated himself. There is more to it than just this. Everyone is afraid that a Basic kid who applies for a job is in competition with a Regular track or a General track kid. If the Basic boy shows B's and the Regular boy shows D's and C's, the Basic boy might get the job even though he may not be so competent as the General or Regular boy. I'm not at all sure competence on a job relates to I.Q.; it depends on the job, doesn't it? Nor am I sure that the I.Q. is the soundest measure when it is derived from a group test.

The whole issue becomes confused because the second fundamental rule of grading, which no one seems to understand, is that every kid's record that goes to agencies of any kind is marked in large letters—Basic, General, Regular, or Honors —and everyone can judge accordingly. People such as Jenny Jones and W. felt that that mightn't be enough. W. mentioned a weighting system used in another state whereby an Honors A meant, let's say, ten points, a Regular A nine points, and so forth. Jenny, whose direct, unstatistical approach appeals to me, thought we might give out grades such as A (B)–Basic, A (R)–Regular, A (G)–General, etc.

Grading is also a tender subject at Urban because some teachers are using grading to fight what they least like or feel least comfortable about in Dr. Tilden's program. They feel they should leave things alone. The attitude behind this laissez-faire desperation is that these kids are going to have a tough time making it in the white intellectual world. "Why not either train them in General and Basic material or make it as tough for them as we know it was for us so they'll know how rough things are when they get out?" they say. This is hard on budding but discourageable ambitions. As in many, many schools, some teachers grade for good behavior and tend to downgrade the questioner, the misbehaver, the rebel, who may very well be in the Honors track—the very kid who is most inquiring and is not just a good automaton. I have found that some Negro teachers, knowing society to be white-middle-class-dominated, feel that if they are training students to get along in the white middle-class world, the children learn that it is unlikely that they will be rich and that few will reach high status, so they must train them to behave in a docile, passive fashion. Therefore they reward and reinforce what will work in present-day society, not necessarily what they wish for or what could strengthen their ethnic group. It is a dismal point of view, but they think it is realistic, since it often grows out of their own bitter experience. I am beginning to note Dr. Tilden's stifled irritation with this attitude among her more despairing Negro staff members. She feels that they are helping the enemies of the Negro. Being a fighter, she finds it difficult to work with these people patiently. One can hardly blame her; yet her irritation is often not the most effective tool. In some ways, strangely enough, I am not sure it isn't easier for me to get the message across to the group since I am white and child-centered and not so racially involved.

Consultation to Students—A Group

Staff members often asked me to see individual students for a variety of reasons. Although I saw my role as one of indirect help to the children through working with the teachers and other staff members, I did talk with any youngsters who were referred to me. However, I did not see them more than once unless I felt the staff members could benefit by gaining, through several joint conferences, a better understanding of the disturbances these pupils presented and the working out of more appropriate placement or management. There were also a few youngsters whom I tried to see regularly in order to help with teacher programming and attitudes until something could be done to get help for them. I shall present the cases of two of these students. But first I shall give an account of some boys whom I was asked to see as a group.

Excerpt 12.   Meeting with a Group of Boys

In a crisis, Dr. Tilden asked me if I would see a group of boys who were causing a lot of trouble. They were Mrs. H.'s "little angels," a ninth-grade Basic group who were supposed to have an hour's business class with her regularly.

However, she was often busy in the office during that hour, and they had taken to vandalizing rooms in the school while she was otherwise occupied. Since I didn't have time to think before I was whisked to the spot and introduced to the boys, my unease at being used directly as a fixer-upper was never articulated. I sat on the desk, informally, and got the boys talking in no time at all. They talked all at once and had many complaints. They said that Mrs. H. had contempt for them because she thought all but her "two favorites" were dumb. (I doubted this statement, but during a later conversation with Mrs. H. she admitted that, with two exceptions, she is not over-fond of the boys in this group.) In any case, they interpreted her absence as lack of interest and thought her hostile and ungiving when she was present. The kids got so excited talking about why they thought they had resorted to vandalism, about their resentment at not having enough work to do, about their boredom, that they didn't want to stop and asked for more time to talk. I arranged to see them later in the day, in English class, where we began to discuss their difficulties in English and reading. Mrs. H. had left the room when I was talking with them earlier in the day, but Miss K., the English teacher, did not. I was getting things under way, asking a couple of the boys what jobs they had held, in order to bring about some formulation of what they felt was needed from school to make a success of life after school. During the friendly discussion Miss K. interrupted to scold one boy for not listening. He had been reading a book, not disturbing me or the others. I couldn't keep the flow going, so I politely said to Miss K., "That's all right, he'll listen when he wants to." She said, "No, this is the trouble with this group, they can't listen. They don't pay attention, their attention span is short, they can't follow directions." Whereupon came a tale of woe about today's English class. I tried to get back to the boys, but by that time they had sunk into sullen apathy, some looking at me from under half-closed eyes to see what I'd do. Then the bell rang. I told the boys I would talk with them next Wednesday. I hope I can get them back. Certainly I will need

to talk tactfully with Miss K. to help her see how she reinforces the low self-image of these boys by her carping. I then
talked with Mr. F., who often pinch-hits for Mrs. H. with
these boys, leaving his own classes to do so. He is a dedicated,
intelligent teacher and very good with this group. I said that
I thought everybody *talked* too much to these kids, used too
many words, and that they had acquired a deafness. They
should *do* more. Teachers should try to get them into the act
in some of the ways he was doing already, only more so. We
talked about the way they presented themselves, their sense of
being stupid, their mumbling, the lack of respect handed out
to them by adults and their consequent lack of respect for
themselves transformed into lack of respect for anything.

Excerpt 13.   The Boys Again

I went, as promised, to my group of Basic van-
dals. I had been concerned that the English teacher had lost
them for me, but this was not the case. They talked all at once
and very badly. They mumble, slur words, so that if they say
anything wrong it can be taken back. Various regional drawls
combined with shyness, fear, and the desire to play it safe and
be ambiguous make communication difficult. If I were an
English teacher I would concentrate heavily on speech. I
would have lots of free discussions, a few short role-playing
dialogues, very brief scenes from modern plays in decent English. I would insist on their speaking so that I could understand them, though I wouldn't insist on good grammar. This
time I soft-pedaled the gripe session about Mrs. H. because
I felt it could get to be a seductive thing of lining up adults
against each other. They told me how badly they read and
how they didn't understand. We made a list of those who
wanted extra help in reading and those who wanted tutoring
in the reading program. Some time after this I had a conference with Mrs. H. She says herself that she is a good teacher
for the very bright but not good for Basics; I am sure it is so.
It seems a shame to me that we waste good teachers by not
developing and using screening techniques to assign a teacher

to the kind of child with whom she does best. There are many teachers who, if status were not an issue, and if we could get them not to consider themselves "dumb" because they are teaching "dumb" kids, would do much better with the slow or recalcitrant learners. They find it a challenge. They like developing new materials and using imagination on creative projects. They like the personal contact necessary to help these kids along, and they are often the ones who under-stim-ulate and under-expect with the quicker kids. Teachers like Mrs. H., who are excellent with the quicker youngsters or who have genuine sparking power with the academically adept, are often given classes which bore and frustrate them and in turn bore and frustrate the children.

Excerpt 14.   Misplaced Students

In relation to the academic placement of the boys in my vandal group, I had a conference with Mrs. H. and several other teachers, and we decided to survey the rec-ords of the whole ninth grade. We discovered, by looking at test scores, that many students had been placed in inappropri-ate sections and had stayed there throughout the year until now (March). Lots of other things emerged from looking over the list of the ninth-grade kids and their ratings in class, their grade averages, their I.Q.'s, their academic achievement, reading, and arithmetic level. For instance, what was a kid with 122 I.Q. and a ninth-grade reading level doing in one of the two lowest Basic classes, supposedly for those of no more than 70 I.Q. whose reading levels were below fifth grade or certainly below sixth grade? From what little I could glean, it seems that since he has been placed in this section he's given up and does nothing. Not too surprisingly he turns out to be one of Mrs. H.'s two favorites and resents the slowness of the other kids. On the other end of the scale, why are there some kids in the General track with high reading levels and with higher I.Q.'s than some in the Honors track? Why is a kid with an I.Q. of 95 and a reading level of barely eighth grade in the Honors track, where the I.Q.'s are 120 and above and the work hard, fast, and intense? It came out in my later conference with W. that this kid is doing badly in English. Another teacher tells me he is doing badly in everything but he is a very nice kid, wants to stay in Honors, and tries desperately hard. So no one in this place, where it is felt that so few kids are motivated, wants to risk putting him into Regular track where he belongs and where he'd probably do well. The idea of status is so important that he feels it better to get D and F in Honors than C and B in Regular. Cross-tracking, which might solve the problem, is so difficult to schedule that the administration is afraid to try it. Later I had a long conference with Dr. Tilden and several others, including the remedial-reading teacher and Mrs. H., about including 50 of the 168 pupils in the ninth grade who are below sixth-grade reading level in an experimental program with emphasis on reading, vocational placement, self-presentation, and skills. Dr. Tilden agreed on 25 pupils, as less disruptive to the over-all schedule. We got to work on this plan and on the wrongly placed Honors kids and decided to give Honors in some but not all subjects; also to get that 122 I.Q. out of the Basic track! [This was written two years before everyone in Basic track was retested to prevent such misplacement.]

Consultation to Students—Two Individual Cases

I selected these two students, whom I saw often, as examples of issues commonly arising in an inner-city high school. Also, the cases of Amy and Fred demonstrate several kinds of interaction that occur as a result of individual student consultation followed by conferences with teachers, and point up the absolute need for extra help and support from the school for children in crisis periods.

Amy: (a) The assistant principal in charge of girls, hostile to psycho-education consultation in the past, became more accepting of my services through my seeing Amy. (b) A physical-education teacher, whom Dr. Tilden considered unreachable, was reached and felt she had learned something through my talking with her about Amy's problems. She herself told me so in the evaluation and became most cooperative in her inter-staff attitudes thereafter. (c) It was made clear that homosexuality is such a frightening thing for high school staff that the handling of this problem becomes particularly delicate if the teacher's own fears and feelings are not to be inappropriately transferred to the students. (d) The question arose of how to give a student enough support to keep her from dropping out.

Fred: (a) People often have a false concept that the severely deprived child who is also deeply emotionally upset is unmotivated and incompetent to deal with school work. This is often proved to be simply not true if some help comes in time to support him. (b) It was demonstrated that the gifted child with troubles needs extra curriculum planning and placement with appropriate teachers. (c) The need to take care of pent-up hate so that it will not erupt in school to the detriment of student, class, and teacher was made clear. (d) The problem of the teacher who befriended this boy showed the need for deeper understanding and acceptance of such a role by the school.

Excerpt 15.　Amy (Aged 17)

The assistant principal had asked me to see Amy, a homosexual, troubled girl. I had seen her once in what I considered an unproductive interview, and I had thought she would never come back again unless forced. To my surprise, she asked to see me again. I saw her for half an hour. She told me that she had behaved better in school this week and that she was trying to hang on but she didn't think she'd make it. I had no idea we had got together well enough for her to trust me with these feelings. She said that on the whole her relations with her grandmother were better. I noticed that she would begin sentences about "this girls' group I go with" with a smirk, and her tongue would pop out like a little snake. I had noticed this the last time we had seen each other and noted that every time she was censoring a remark about her sex-

ual activities or thoughts, or others' sexual thoughts about
her, out came the tongue. This time I mentioned this to her
and said, "If there is something you are trying to say, feel free
to say it. I am not here to judge you." She hesitated, and I
said, "It has to do with sex, doesn't it?" "Yes," she said, and
then out poured a miserable story. There were periods of
blocking on her part, purposeful and concealing, but, with
virtually no urging, out came more. She is actively involved
in a girls' homosexual group. We talked about the compan-
ionship of the group and how it helped with her deep loneliness—both the affection and the camaraderie of it. We talked
of how she had not had much affection or fun in her life. She
spoke of her father's psychotic episodes. Her mother had described them to Amy after she had left him. Now Amy had experienced them with him when she visited him at the mental
hospital, where he had been for years. She talked briefly about
a sexual experience with a boy a couple of years back which
she hadn't liked because it had been forced on her. She spoke
then about how the mother's paramour had many times forced
intercourse on her and her sister, which explained the hitherto puzzling fact that the court had ordered her to live with a
most unsympathetic grandmother rather than with her own
mother.

In the next interview, she went back to talking of not being
able to finish school because she had to go to Detroit. She said
this in a sad and frightened manner. I asked her why she "had
to." Who was forcing her? After a few halting beginnings she
said that two years ago, when she was just sixteen, she had
gone to Detroit and she had got married. I really didn't know
whether it was to a male or female. So I said, "You married
a guy up there?" She said, "No, a girl. And now my husband
insists I come up." Then came the story of this twenty-seven-
year-old girl who had been coming down to see her monthly,
sending clothes and money, and who expected her in Detroit
right now. Amy is obviously scared of this woman. I explained
the law, even about boy-girl under-eighteen marriages, and
said she wasn't committed and if she didn't want to go, no

one could make her. She said she didn't know anymore. She used to be scared of the woman but now she looked forward with some fascination to her visits. The woman, who had a house of gals, "a harem," had promised her a great deal of fun in Detroit. Our time was up and she had to get to class. I don't have enough facts to do anything constructive. Except for Dr. Tilden, I wouldn't tell anyone here of the kid's communication because they all get so excited about homosexuality that they'd drop her quickly. I invited her to come in if she wanted to, and only if she wanted to, next week. She said "yes" with alacrity and then "please." I left feeling worried and depressed, and wondered what I could do, what agencies, legal and otherwise, I could contact without revealing the girl's confidence.

Excerpt 16.   Amy and Fred (Aged 16)

I went down the hall and found that my friend Amy is not in school today. Amy's home-room teacher, who was supposed to be uncooperative and whom I found very cooperative, though frightened of the homosexual aspect of the case when I first talked with her about Amy, rushed up to tell me that Amy and her sister had left their grandma's house and gone to their mother's. How? The sister, not Amy, had had a blow-up with the grandmother, who then kicked them out. This may be fine, it may be terrible, nobody knows. The mother had not yet been reached. I was only worried that because of geography Amy would not come back to school, having established last week that she does have enough credits to graduate. All she has to do is be there, and I knew the mother lived out of the neighborhood. It seems that somehow or other Amy had been getting to school except for this day. I do hope it keeps up and that I will see her next week. The teacher felt she had been able to handle herself much better since I have been seeing her. My last interview with Amy was not so encouraging. It was clear to me that, indeed, she was committed to an overt homosexual way of life. This is O.K.

with me, but I had hoped I might be able to help her handle herself in such a way that she doesn't throw it around and does not get pressed into activities beyond her ability to cope with, such as the Detroit "harem." I hoped that she would be able to curtail her sullen and hostile temper toward the school people long enough to graduate and be able to see some usefulness for herself in dealing with her anger in more appropriate, less ruinous ways. Her desire to graduate was reinforced by her desire to join the WAVES or WACS. I figured that if she made it into these organizations she would at least get free psychiatric help. If not, she'd have her high-school diploma to help her get a job.

Now Fred. Jenny told me that he had come to her office one day asking for a hammer and nails because he said he was so popping mad and so ready to split that he needed to get his anger out by pounding nails. He feared he might explode in school if he didn't. He had just come to school in January or February. Why was he mad? His aunt kept him in the house after seven, no going out, no television, no records, no smoking, no nothing. His hostile and punitive aunt had destroyed the records he had bought with his own money, his house was full of noise and fights, he was not fed if he wasn't there by seven. Fred was going stir-crazy and needed to talk. Fred's mother is a very sick woman who had tried to keep her son but had been unable to. The father, a severe alcoholic, lives in Chicago and is utterly good for nothing. At times when the mother tried to work, a grandmother kept the kid, but got tired of doing so and has disappeared from sight. He was sent to an aunt, who died, and then the mother came and took the boy and lived with him in another state. At this point he had tuberculosis and was hospitalized for a while. He went back to live with the mother for a pleasant period, until the mother had what was clearly a severe schizophrenic breakdown and has been, and is now, in a state hospital, where it seems that she is likely to remain. So the kid seemed to be on his own. He was put in institutions and foster homes and then was taken by his father's brother, to live with him. The boy did all right in school at that time. He is clearly an exceptionally bright, articulate, motivated kid, but he is also evidently one of the acting-out, neurotic children given to uncontrollable rages. He was expelled from the Chicago schools for getting into violent rages. At this time he lived with his alcoholic father and the father's girl friend, who made overt passes at him. He kept out of the house as much as possible. He got a job as a junior counselor in sports at a church, did well there, was liked by the settlement house people, and may have been taken under their wing. He has great skill at getting people to become interested and involved with him. Though he roamed the streets and was in and out of gangs, often beaten up by various rival gangs, he managed never to get thoroughly lined up with delinquents. One of his acquired skills was that he managed never to be around when the police caught people. This in itself showed a measure of brains, judgment, and self-preservation. He tells this with pride as a demonstration of the fact that by his brains he learned to spot cues and to keep out of trouble when trouble was about. His father didn't have money, or refused to give him any, and also refused to feed him. He got to eat one meal a day, which he managed to eat at friends' houses, through careful and opportunistic planning. He would visit a different friend daily and stick around and be invited for dinner, just once a week. He was careful not to accept invitations more often, so that he could spread his meals out. He also told me techniques he had developed for getting money from people without stealing it. All this gave him confidence in being able to take care of himself by the use of his wits, so long as he didn't let his temper go. In the daytime, being out of school, he spent time around the University, read a lot in the library, and cultivated literary and philosophical friends whom he encountered on park benches and library steps. He has actually read Freud and some Greek philosophy. (If he hasn't, he nevertheless knows the names, chapter headings, and what the books are about, which is more than many a high-school student from middle-class background can say.) He stayed out of his father's miserable house, where he was afraid of losing his temper, till two and three each morning. Finally, his father and his girl friend were involved in a street brawl and both were arrested for disorderly conduct. Because of his fear of his own tendency to violence, Fred got money from an uncle to come down here and live with his aunt. He says, "Look, I was kicked out of school once. I've got a good head. I like books. I want to write. I want to go to college. I'm eighteen and in tenth grade [he said eleventh and then amended it]. If I have to stay in school till I'm twenty-five, I'm going to get a high-school education. It's dull and boring. Some subjects are much too easy for me, new ones like French and Spanish are not too easy, and some are hard but I can do them." The school, recognizing his intelligence, put him in one of the two Honors divisions, but unfortunately he doesn't have an imaginative English teacher like W. He is doing well in school but is terrified of losing his temper. He says he can't live under his aunt's restrictions. He knows he has to be polite and get along with his aunt. She wants to get rid of him because he brings in no money, and she's going to move to a smaller place and threatens to throw him out. He knows he'll have no place to live, and he doesn't know anyone in this city as he did in Chicago. He knows his temper and tolerance for frustration are at the breaking point. He fears his fantasies at night when he is made to go to bed to please his aunt, much too early for sleeping and without reading materials or permission to keep the lights on. Besides, he recognizes his own signs of breaking loose. When he was teased by a group of male homosexuals in a bar, he became frantic. He says about homosexual activities: "They can do what they want. It is just not for me. How can I love someone who has the same thing I have? I got mad at the taunting by the fags and someone's laughing at my refusal to accept the pass made at me. I started a tremendous fight. I was pulled off this guy and became even more terrified that I'd mess up, because I didn't think I could stop my rage once it started." He tried a job at a restaurant and was horrified to find that he lost it by losing his temper there, too, and he has tried to work on self-control. He feels if he had a few more releases, in walks about town, in later, freer hours, through books and records, in some privacy, he could get himself together. We talked over the possibility of his taking on a job so that he could get out of the house more or, as he said he'd like to, pay board and keep a room somewhere in the Urban school neighborhood. I said I'd find out from Jenny about facilities, and that he could use me as an outlet for the need to talk for half an hour weekly. Jenny is cooperative in her talks with me about this boy. I feel we can help Fred, and by doing so, help Jenny with techniques which could be useful to other kids in tough circumstances.

Excerpt 17.   Fred

Fred was delighted to have changed to W.'s class (which I had arranged) and finds it very exciting. Mrs. M., the English teacher from whom he was transferred, was angry about the change. This was understandable because Fred was by far the best in her class. She used him as an assistant teacher, which was good for his ego but not for his learning, and she didn't want her one A student to get away. Next time I must not make such an obvious and terrible gaffe. I must remember to talk with the teacher from whom I am asking somebody to be transferred so that she will understand. But at least Fred has W., which is what he needs for stimulating and interesting English classes. He has also taken to tennis and has launched himself with a girl friend, but he has many qualms because he can't tell his aunt, for fear of criticism, that he's taking out a girl. He is hanging on to his home and to his temper, but it may not last. I think he needs to be helped with his problems, some of which are real and some of which have a strong paranoid flavor. I offered to see him here next week if he calls, even though it is Easter. I am eager to get Jenny to work on getting him a good social worker or psychologist to take over when school is out, so that he will get help. I don't want to leave him hanging. He had written a powerful poem on loneliness which he handed to me as he left.

Excerpt 18.   Fred Again

This summer the Northern Colleges Tutorial plan will be available at Urban. Volunteer students from Ivy League colleges, who are home for vacation, will participate. Each volunteer will work with a boy or girl to fill in cultural gaps, explain, motivate, and stimulate on a course of study the student chooses. It is not remedial but for extra trimmings. Fred signed up for two courses—one in biology, which he likes and does well in, and one in algebra, which he doesn't understand but thinks he would with individual tutoring and explanation. Talk about motivation! People complain that the slum kids are unmotivated. Not the ones I've seen! They are more Abe Lincoln-minded than middle-class kids. They have great odds to overcome and surprising courage so long as they get adult support and understanding. Fred is surely a case in point.

Dr. Tilden had told me about the adult support offered him by Mr. X., the math teacher. Fred's aunt had made a fuss concerning Mr. X.'s interest in the boy. It was clear to me that Fred was not going to bring it up in our conference. Mr. X. had been a counselor of Fred's in Chicago at an institution for neglected kids, and was the only person Fred knew down here from old times. Mr. X. had befriended Fred, helping him when he was miserable or lonely. He had shown him where things were in the city, taken him to the library, shown him where the stores were, taken him on an outing or two. Mr. X. is married and likes kids in a good way. He found Fred worthwhile and interesting as I do. Fred was grateful and, from time to time, has paid off some obligations by offering to wash Mr. X.'s car. The aunt accused Mr. X. of having homosexual interests in Fred because he didn't bring Fred home until nine one Saturday night. In fact, he had dropped Fred at the girl friend's house and Fred knew he'd be locked out for having a date. He had thought to lie and say he had been with Mr. X., thinking that would be legitimate. The aunt called the school. The two assistant principals are both ready to believe the worst and had hauled Mr. X. into the office. Mr. X. adequately defended himself but had decided not to do any more kindnesses for Fred, such as planning picnics and library excursions. I led Fred to talk about home; he told me about some nasty fights with the aunt, but not about this one. I waited, and then with a bit of very gentle prodding he came through and told me about his rage over this mess about Mr. X., his humiliation, the flood of violence he felt well up in him toward his uncle and his aunt which he could barely control when they accused him and Mr. X. He was defensive in insisting on his manliness: Tears came into his eyes when he repeated that Mr. X. had never done anything but be kind and that they had had fun together. I handled this first easily and honestly, by getting mad and outraged along with him, giving him support and getting rid of some of my own rage at the aunt, and privately at the stupidity of those school people who would take the word of this woman over that of a good, conscientious, and respected teacher. Fred then told me how badly he felt that he had brought shame to the one friend he had by his aunt's gossip. Now he, too, was afraid to talk with Mr. X., lest he cause him more trouble. I encouraged him to hold his temper a couple more weeks and by then we'd work on getting him a job and a place to live away from the aunt.

Consultation with a Teacher

Excerpt 19.   A Teacher's Dilemma

I had heard Dr. Tilden say what a fine teacher Mr. X. was, that he put in extra time and work to help many of the kids with math or with other problems, that he did this gracefully without any fuss, and that she was very pleased to have him at the school. I thought I should tell him how much I appreciated all he had done for Fred and that I felt Fred could never have regained equilibrium without the support and friendliness Mr. X. had offered. When I made an appointment with him he seemed scared and sure that my purpose was to accuse or pry. I made it clear that I knew from Dr. Tilden what a fine teacher he was and that I knew from Fred how much he had done to get him straightened out and feeling like a human being. I said that my continued work with Fred would never have had the good effects it seems to have had without his kindness and interest in the boy. At that, Mr. X. breathed a sigh of relief and told me the story of his own fears and moral conflicts. "Do I let gossip waylay me and keep me from doing what I feel is right and know is O.K.? Do I go ahead seeing Fred and another boy after school anyway, or do I guard my own reputation and maybe just teach kids, not befriend them?" We went into this at length, and I supported him strongly in his interest in the kids. I did say that, since Fred was going to be living with the aunt for only two more weeks, he might protect himself and the boy by waiting for outings until after the boy had moved but that he should most certainly not stop a projected library trip, lifts home, and giving advice and help on jobs—the point was to stay away from the aunt.

I felt this was an important session since it is just this kind of situation which, if not caught and talked over when the conflicts are being experienced, often makes a teacher—especially a young one—bitter, disillusioned, and discouraged. At this point it would be easy for a teacher who has much to offer to turn into a person who decides to stay out of emotional or moral involvement and never again allow himself to be vulnerable. Such people need support for their good feelings and good intentions and help in using judgment and foresight in trying to prevent unnecessary complications.

After the Project Ended

Dr. Tilden had found our one year of psycho-education consultation useful to her and the many programs she held dear. She wanted to make this kind of consultation an integral part of her school, and she was enabled to make a

start toward this by a federal grant for a complete action attack on the Urban school area. She asked me to keep up some
of the work I had started until she could incorporate more of
this consultative function within the school. I volunteered to
keep on working with two groups—the reading group of volunteers and interested teachers and a combined group of Urban High teachers and young Peace Corps members. The
latter had returned from overseas duties as teachers in underdeveloped countries and were incorporated into Urban under
an intense, supervised, in-service training program, for which
they would be given graduate credit from a university involved in the project.

In the course of my second year's visits to Urban, I found
that I was again asked to help deal with a number of problems, particularly those of individual, disturbed students. In
order to do this I used part of the time that was supposed to be
spent in writing our report to form and work with groups of
staff and students. After the grant expired I made arrangements to continue some of the groups under the auspices of
a city university where I was working on one of its special
projects.

Peace Corps Returnees

Dr. Tilden and some of her staff members work-
ed out an intriguing plan whereby twelve Peace Corps returnees would learn while teaching at Urban. The purpose of this
project was to use the fresh approach of young service-dedi-
cated people who had had the experience of working with
the inhabitants of underdeveloped countries abroad and who
had returned wanting to use their skills in their own country.
It was hoped they would add something stimulating and new
to the curriculum and methods used at Urban. They taught
a variety of classes from all tracks under the close supervision
of three master teachers and were given specially tailored
seminar courses for which they were granted graduate credits
toward an M.A. One seminar was devoted to the subject they
taught, and concentrated on developing new material and

methods. Another seminar, given by a sociologist familiar with the Urban background, focused on social issues of class, race, economics, and attitudes. I led the third seminar, which was addressed to the psychological aspects of growth and development, particularly those of adolescents. In addition, experts in behavioral sciences from all over the country came to lecture, to demonstrate, and to see. The goal was to help the returnees to observe and perceive the students they taught as individuals in a given setting, beset by a multitude of pressures, and having various needs, assets, and liabilities.

There were problems, such as friction with the regular staff, some of which could have been avoided by more careful planning. The newspapers jumped in too hard and too fast, and the published interviews with some Peace Corps members caused resentment (against the project and against Dr. Tilden) in the school population, because the reporters emphasized the lacks and the poverty surrounding the school. Many of the students felt that this jeopardized their chances of jobs and scholarships and objected to the implied reflection on their parents and their homes. The project itself was sometimes misused by some members of the school administration as well as by some representatives of the President's Committee as a political football. Nonetheless, the Peace Corps program survived its trials and indeed yielded good things to the school and the community—good enough so that after an evaluation committee from outside the area had observed it, it was expanded in numbers and scope for the year to come. It was interesting to note how these Peace Corps people could accept primitiveness in foreign places but found Urban primitiveness horrifying. This called for talk and help.

The Volunteer Group

The women of the volunteer reading groups had asked me to continue to help them in the selection of cases and to supervise them throughout the year. It was rewarding to see the greater confidence and efficiency with which the alumnae members of the first-year group operated. New members were assimilated and helped by the group itself to understand that often their function was to inspire hope in the student and increase his ability to relate to an adult rather than to work for higher grades or giant strides in reading. Although spectacular achievement sometimes occurred and was gratifying, it was not to be expected.

The major difficulties of the volunteers centered on their isolation from the rest of the school and lack of communication with or cooperation from some of the faculty members, although a new remedial-reading teacher had been put on the staff at Urban and attended all the meetings of the volunteers. The school counselors varied in their skills and attitudes, to say nothing of their hospitality to new projects which made demands on their time. Consequently, students whose counselors were hostile or apathetic often got far less from the program than those whose counselors were willing, or even eager, to cooperate with schedule-planning, home contacts, and interviews with students, volunteers, and subject-teachers. In any program such as this it would help for a volunteer representative to be invited to faculty meetings and to have regular consultation with grade counselors.

Eleventh-Grade Group

In addition to these two adult groups, I worked with two student groups, always in combination with one or more counselors or teachers so that they could be trained to take over these or other groups. One group was initiated at the urgent insistence of Jenny Jones. She had asked me time and again to see a number of bright eleventh-graders who were in dire trouble. Some were about to drop out, others were failing though they had the ability not to fail, others were in disastrous emotional or situational messes. Jenny and I got them together, as a group, and worked with them weekly. I asked that Mr. S., a new counselor, join us so that we would have a male involved and so that he too could experience this group method of counseling. In times of major crisis, one or the other of us saw individual members in addition to the regular group sessions. When it seemed desirable, class sections were rescheduled and parent interviews held. Although we certainly did not "cure" the group members, none dropped out. They either maintained or raised their grades, and some who were in great economic need were helped to find jobs.

The Summit Group

I now come to one of the most interesting groups of kids I have ever worked with. It all began because of a widespread school crisis initiated by my old friend Fred. In the fall of the year, after our consultation project, as such, had ended at Urban, at a time when Dr. Tilden was in the hospital, Jenny Jones called me to come to the school on urgent but unexplained business. I also had a call from the assistant principal, in charge during Dr. Tilden's absence, asking if I would help out in a very bad situation. I will take the explanation of this to-me-unexplained crisis from the notes I made at the time.

Excerpt 20.   The Rebel

As I entered the outer office I heard fire alarms ringing and saw some students walking out. Inside sat Fred, head down on the table, dejected. I went over, genuinely glad to see him for the first time since June, shook his hand, and asked him how things were. He answered that he was in the process of being kicked out of school. "What for?" I asked. "For this," he said, handing me a four-page mimeographed paper. I sat down and read it. It was a lurid but not completely inaccurate account written by Fred of some of the bad conditions at Urban. Though smacking of yellow journalism, much of it had a basis in fact. It was calculated to make the most of any racial discrimination that existed, or could be interpreted as existing, in the school system and angrily pointed out the better conditions for learning at high schools in wealthier and whiter neighborhoods. The fire bells and the walkout were a demonstration by some of the students against

Fred's impending dismissal. Fred had not, in fact, been expelled, although an irate assistant principal was threatening him with it. It seemed that he had fallen, like so many politicians before and after him, not on the issue of the paper and its contents—although it was reasonably clear that that was what was behind the excitement—but on a technicality. In a rage, he had refused to give his home address since he no longer lived with his aunt, and the school had a right to expel him if they had no proof that he lived in the district. By that time he had calmed down sufficiently so that I could say, "Oh, for heaven's sake, Fred, give them your address, then let's deal with issues here at school where maybe something can be done about some of the things you brought up, and let's see how to do it. If you get kicked out nothing will be gained." He blurted out his address, which was in the Urban district. The assistant principal, though still angry, decided to let the matter go. I started to talk to Fred about the good things in the paper and also about his use of exaggeration, distortion, and forgery in making his case.

I used the word "forgery" in my notes because, while the articles in the paper were signed by several other students besides Fred, these others were objecting to the use of their names, since the articles they had submitted bore little relation to those printed. I asked if I could see all the students involved—some were members of the student government—and said I wanted to see if we could tackle some of the problems mentioned in the paper. Thus, what I called to myself "The Rebel Group" got started. There were four boys and six girls, and all of the tracks, from Honors to Basic, were represented. At first Jenny Jones and I were the only interested, participating adults; later several teachers became actively involved. The group met every week for the rest of the school year and then continued on a monthly basis, with replacements made as members graduated. (It is still going on.) Within three weeks they were called "The Summit Group." I do not recall who gave it the name—it was not I—but the name stuck. They considered themselves a policy-planning group and did, indeed, affect the school and its policies.

We began by sorting out the problems Fred had brought up—which ones we, as a group within the school, could do anything about and which required more community social action. In time, members of the Summit Group became quite active in writing letters to the newspapers and making appearances on radio and television on subjects relevant to the city's problems or youth viewpoints.

I shall summarize, briefly, some of the concerns and activities of this group. The most immediate problem at Urban was the student body's fear of "outsiders" who broke into the building—often with knives, sometimes with guns—and made serious trouble. Groups of these outsiders, many of whom were dropouts from this and other nearby schools or unemployed graduates, hung around outside the building intimidating, blackmailing, and beating up Urban students on their way to and from school. The Summit Group made suggestions about what the students themselves could do and asked for faculty help in guarding doors. They also asked Dr. Tilden and me to approach the police for better, and more understanding, coverage of the block at certain times, and this was the beginning of some work with the police on their attitudes toward and relations with teen-agers.

Within the school, the first issue that emerged was the fact that the school newspaper served no function of communication. The journalism teacher insisted on an expensive, high-standard product which could enter into competition with papers of other schools for prestige and awards. The students found this frustrating because measuring up to her standards meant printing only one or two papers a year. I suggested a weekly newsletter which could be cheaply mimeographed and distributed and would be quite distinct from the "ideal" school newspaper. Many of the teachers became interested and cooperative. English teachers, typing teachers, the faculty sponsor of student government, all helped and some worked hard on the actual physical production—proofreading, typing, mimeographing, collating, stapling. The newsletter came out for two cents a copy and became a regular feature of the school life. It served as a place for editorial comment on problems, for communication of school and personal events, for reports on programs, and for discussion of issues. When Dr. Tilden took a leave of absence she used the newsletter to address the students, telling them where and why she was going. The Summit Group was rightfully excited and proud.

Another in-school problem that was tackled was the almost unbearable noise and confusion of the cafeteria. The Summit Group planned movies and social activities, record and combo playing at certain times during the lunch break. Cooperative teachers helped them to tempt masses of students out of the cafeteria and into fun activities away from the overcrowded lunchrooms and neighboring halls.

Of course there were issues that did not lend themselves to direct practical solutions, but these were, at least, aired and discussed. Child labor laws (originally made for their protection) prevented many youngsters from getting needed jobs after school. According to the law, no one under eighteen can work after ten o'clock at night. Restaurants and all-night garages don't want to hire anyone who has to quit at ten, since this would necessitate a second shift. The Summit Group reported that many kids who wanted to continue in school dropped out because they had to work full time and could do so only in the daytime hours. Some stuck to night school, some soon gave up. It was through the Summit Group also that I learned of the difficulty some bright students had, not in achieving college loans or scholarships, but simply in raising enough money to *apply*. Lacking the ten- or twenty-dollar fees, many gave up the idea or chose inferior colleges simply because of the lower application cost. (The volunteers from the Council of Jewish Women generously started a fund to take care of this when it emerged as a problem, but it is clearly not a problem unique to Urban High.)

As the year progressed the students trusted me with their fears and resentments, knowing I was not there to judge them and was genuinely interested in their feelings and ideas. Many faculty members cooperated in helping them with Summit Group projects. Beginning with the newsletter, and continuing on through the next year, the faculty sponsor of student government attended all their meetings. He liked them and they him, and it was not long before he helped them to articulate their problems even more clearly than they had before.

In December of that year I was asked by an educational organization to get a tape of student opinions on the difficulties in the high school which contribute to discouragement and to the decision to drop out. I asked the Summit Group if they would like to help me. Seven of them agreed enthusiastically when it was established that neither their names nor the name of the school would be given. This would leave them free to be honest and still not get themselves or their faculty in trouble. I warned them that my name was often associated with Urban. I pointed out that if the tape were picked up by the press (and it was), the connection with Urban might be made. They still agreed to come to my office to make a recording. On the appointed day five of them appeared after school; the other two were sick. Here I include a summary of their criticisms, their positive statements, and their constructive suggestions.

Students' Thoughts about Why Fellow Students Drop Out

1. There is not enough selection of elective courses, and students are bored with those available.

2. Necessity to work often causes drop in grades and discouragement.

3. Inability to cross tracks prevents academic students from taking business courses which in turn means that they lack money-making skills at graduation. (It seems that academic students must take five academic majors, leaving them no time for courses such as typing. In addition, typing classes

are already overcrowded, so there is no room for the few who might manage to carry the extra-heavy schedule.)

4. There are not enough counselors. This means that the counselors have no time for the kind of individual relationships and mental health counseling that the kids feel they need. Most teachers are too busy or too harried to offer individual encouragement to students.

5. Teachers put pressure on bright students to prepare for college regardless of students' own inclinations.

6. The classes are large and overcrowded. There is need for more business classes. Some subjects, such as language and math, should be taught in much smaller classes.

7. Students over eighteen are not eligible for school tickets on buses. For some, the extra cost of fifty cents a day is prohibitive. This is most likely to affect Basic or Regular students.

8. There is pressure on good students to excel in *all* subjects, as well as in extracurricular activities. These factors, in addition to outside jobs and home chores, do not allow for proper rest.

9. There are not enough textbooks; in some courses there are too few, in others there are none. Those that are available are often outdated and are often issued weeks or even months late.

10. Students are asked to buy supplementary books that they cannot afford.

11. There is inadequate equipment and a lack of facilities, especially for science courses.

12. Reading problems are usually a big factor in dropping out. The subject matter of readers used in remediation is insulting to high school students. There should be emphasis on reading in the low grades and individual remediation should be offered in the upper schools. Mobile libraries at all school levels should be expanded.

13. To stay in school it is necessary to have pride in oneself and in one's work. Teachers don't help a student build up such pride. Instead they often give false praise which the stu-

dent knows is not deserved, or they withhold praise from the student who needs it.

Suggestions Made by Students

1. The work-study program is very good. It should be available to more students in the school and extended to other schools.

2. Remedial reading help from the volunteers is very good, and the program should be enlarged.

3. There should be more counselors; they should be better trained; their work load should be reduced.

4. There should be two kinds of counselors: (1) mental health counselors and (2) grade placement and section placement and vocational counselors.

5. There should be better testing to determine aptitude before track placement is made. There should be consistent review of students' records and achievements for more flexible placement and checkup on requirements for graduation.

6. More high schools should be built and staffed.

7. There should be special counseling services for possible dropouts who are in precarious positions. They need to talk; they also need special attention.

8. There should be better-trained teachers interested specifically in Basic students, so that there would be less busy-work and more learning.

9. There should be adjustment in scheduling and school hours to make it possible for students to have jobs and continue their schooling at the same time.

10. Volunteers should be used to lighten the counseling and clerical load at rush periods, such as the beginning of the school years, mid-semester, and report-card times.

11. All students should participate in some extracurricular activities. Then they would have more pride in their school and more sense of belonging to it. Expansion and re-examination of areas of particular interest to students should be made to revamp the extracurricular program.

12. There should be more personal contact between teach-

er and student wherein a teacher will listen to a student and find out what help is needed.

13. There should be recognition of the outside interests and problems of high school students.

14. There should be more recognition of true economic need and more imaginative ways to meet this need within the school program.

Summary

As we had anticipated, the high school presented tremendous problems of fragmentation and lack of communication. This is deeply reflected in staff and students. There is a sense of impersonality which increases loneliness and despair and which decreases the possibility of understanding a student's needs or a staff member's anxiety. Discouragement, resignation, and apathy are all too prevalent among staff and students alike. We felt that psycho-education provided a means of improving communication so that fragmentation might be lessened and so that students and staff would have more hope of achieving appropriate goals.

We realized that this kind of consultation in a high school requires more than one visit a week. Even if not much more time can be given by the consultant, it would be better to schedule two four-hour visits each week to insure a closer follow-up of issues, programs, and individuals. It also became clear that whereas it is possible to work successfully with individual staff members in the elementary school, and it is sometimes necessary and possible to do so in the senior high school, great economy of time, with gains to everyone, can be effected by holding small, selected staff or pupil group meetings. In many ways group meetings are the optimal way to achieve communication and to bring about change in what is essentially a bureaucratic structure. Many different kinds of groups can be formed according to the needs, the sophistication, and the requests of the people involved.

At Urban we found many of the usual school problems complicated by the black-white issue. In some cases the self-image of the Negro made teachers feel a burden of over-responsibility for the achievement of the pupils; the burden can extend to the children, often with unfavorable results. At the other extreme, self-hate made some teachers feel that these young people would never amount to anything and that therefore the aspirations for teaching them should be on the lowest level. There was among the staff the usual fear and jealousy found among adults when confronted with adolescents whose life and power are just opening up. This was complicated by a concomitant jealousy of the greater opportunities that were emerging for the Negroes coming to adulthood. The task of revamping a curriculum to better suit the needs of this group was often approached with antagonism or anxiety. This was especially true among the staff who had been taught old study plans and old curriculum designs and who often, though dissatisfied with what they had, were understandably afraid to try new methods for which they felt ill-prepared or inadequate. This problem emphasized the need for constant in-service training and for a great deal of inter-staff communication. The psycho-education consultation program served as an indicator of what needed to be done and where and how the problems could be approached.

5

Bayside Treatment Center

As our society grows increasingly aware of the need of children too emotionally disorganized or too disrupted to remain in ordinary classes, more day-care and residential centers come into being and more are planned. Some cities and states have already included such centers either in their school systems or hospital systems. But up to now many, if not most, of these centers have been supported by private funds or local community funds.

We consulted in one such center in the environs of Washington, D.C., for two years during which time budget problems characteristic of such ventures caused a series of unsettling reorganizations and mergers. Some time after that two-year period, the center merged with a completely separate institution, not mentioned in the following selections, and gained more stability. But the turmoil and chaos at Bayside, although extreme, was not unlike the experience of many struggling treatment centers. This chapter indicates how consultation can help, how it differs from consultation within ordinary schools, and what special skills are necessary for a consultant to bring to such a setting.

Work in a treatment center demands extraordinary involvement. A characteristic result of consulting in a treatment
center is that one inevitably gets to know staff members intimately. Their individual styles of interacting with the children, with their colleagues, and with the professional staff of
other disciplines are so important to the primary task of working with the children that close scrutiny into each of these
areas is essential. Furthermore, the staff at a treatment center is
open to intensified anxiety from a number of sources. Teaching children with emotional and learning disturbances is
difficult—regression is frequent, improvement slow in coming
and hard to judge. Such children have a low frustration level,
and their anxiety is contagious. Where staff direction and supervision are not adequate, the resulting instability can become contagious as well. The quality of the relationships between staff members and children shares paramount importance with those between individual staff members, between staff groups, and between supervisors and supervised.
Therefore, these relationships must be scrutinized far more
intensively than is required in a normal setting. Change is
particularly threatening in such an interpersonally sensitive
environment, whether at a high level or low. Interaction and
the response to changes among children and staff are closely
tied together. This is true of any treatment center and implies
the necessity of solid directorship and close interdisciplinary
staff communication, support, and supervision, in which
psycho-education can be of significant help.

The less stable the directorship and the less clearly defined
the treatment goals, the more necessary, more frequent, more
difficult, more involving the tasks of the consultant become.
But, although active intervention may be necessary, the consultant must be constantly on guard against intervening in
the policy and philosophy of the center to the point where his
role as objective consultant becomes less neutral and more
contaminated.

Stable directorship in a treatment center depends on the
background of the directors. The job requires understanding

in the combined fields of psychiatry, psychology, social work, group work, education, public relations, and business administration. Without a good part of these attributes—in the director himself, or properly delegated to a strong supporting staff—or without consultative help, the survival of the institution is in jeopardy.

To do a useful job, even in a stable treatment center, requires that the consultant spend a great deal of time with the directors and assistant directors. This is not in itself different from the time required to gain the cooperation of the principal of a school. The difference here is qualitative. The consultant who works in a treatment center must have a multi-disciplinary background and understanding because emphasis in consultation varies. When working with directors whose expertise is psychiatric, the consultant must do far more in the way of intervening through educational means. This is in contrast to the type of work with school principals, who require more emphasis on mental health aspects and the dynamics of child and staff behavior.

In small, privately run or community supported centers, budget concerns create makeshift efforts where planning is required. Budget limitations often mean hiring inadequate staff members, where even the best trained and most knowledgeable would have major problems with themselves, their program, and their patients. Since even those sophisticated in the field are not agreed on what a treatment center should be or do, whom it should or can treat, what methods of treatment are optimal, or even workable for what kind of children, confusion in policy as well as practice abounds. One area of debate, for example, concerns the inclusion of a school program and to what extent it should be considered intrinsic to the total treatment program.

Bayside Treatment Center went through every extreme and every phase of the present state of professional bewilderment. It went through every phase of financial uncertainty. During this Pilgrim's Progress, staff changes were so many, so costly, and so traumatic to adults and children alike that the only constant was a state of emergency.

History of Bayside

Bayside Center was the result of a merger of three hitherto separate institutions. The original center, occupying a beautiful eighteen-acre tract of land, had been set up a hundred years ago to care for neglected children and had become a treatment residence for those emotionally disturbed. The second institution, day-care treatment center begun immediately after World War II, had concentrated on group work and individual therapy for children. Before the merger developed, it had a tutorial program and a recently introduced school program. The third institution had been a traditional, privately run, community supported clinic, offering the usual multiple clinic services.

The merger had not come about easily and had left many scars, owing to major staff changes and disagreements. The kind of school program to be established was one of the issues which caused bitter feelings. When our consultation began, Dr. Moss, the psychiatrist who had directed the clinic, was over-all director. The former director of the residence, a psychologist, was treatment program director. The school program which was, after a struggle, seen as part of total milieu treatment was in the hands of the teachers from the former day-care center, who had had supervision from me on a private basis for two years before the merger. In addition, the school program included one teacher lent by the city to the combined center, who, although under the local school system, was able to join in staff meetings of the center and have consultation with me.

Our hopes that a relatively stable organization would be operating by the time we began work at Bayside were illusory: There was a continuing state of flux and confusion throughout the two years of our consultation. Inevitably the organizational difficulties set the tone for the way psycho-education consultation progressed. One of the basic tenets of our consultation method was to try to perform the services requested by the organization, to take a place as we found it. To do what Bayside wanted us to do and what was needed meant becoming involved in forming policy, which was never part of our intent. Yet, given this quaking structure, we had to deal with administrative planning and the smoothing of ruffled feathers, with programming and the picking up of broken pieces—as well as with the job of psycho-education consultation as we saw it.

The following excerpts or summaries our consultation records reflect sometimes incredible chaos, with the result that in some ways the consultant's job became nearly as frustrating as those with whom he consulted.

The Teachers: (1) Vi

Vi had come to the day center two years before the merger. She had had training in group dynamics and some teaching experience, but none with disturbed children. She had a natural empathy, was intelligent, eager, and quick to learn. By the time of the merger she had made herself into a competent special education teacher. Characteristically, she had been hired in desperation, at a time of crisis, and because she would accept low pay for a half-time job. Her job was a full-time one within a year, but her salary did not go up in proportion to the increased time given nor to the additional skills Vi learned by hard work and at personal expense.

By the time consultation began she had become a full-time "head teacher" with full (though shamefully low) salary. Her rise was due to great initiative and because she was, by nature, an innovator. Vi planned hundreds of programs that would give the school greater flexibility and importance. She introduced new ideas, such as incorporating muscular coordination training as part of reading training, and used group work as the core of her teaching. Many of her plans were unrealistic, but many others were imaginative, sound, and constructive, and some were incorporated into the Center's program. But she was also a fighter and at one time or another got into everybody's hair. Vi eventually left the Center, as she had come to it, in a cloud of bitterness. The Center was angry that she left in mid-term. She left because, among other reasons, for a year and a half she had been asking for a raise which, if met, would still have been lower than the city school teacher on the staff was getting. The year before, Vi had warned the Center that if the raise was not granted, she would have to resign. Characteristically, they failed to meet the raise, although they did make promises and occasionally raised her salary by small fractions, and yet to hire a new teacher the next term, they had to pay $1,000 more than Vi had asked.

I mention Vi's conditions of employment because this was an area where I, the psycho-education consultant, fought hard and furiously with the administration for a better, less bargain-basement attitude so common in private institutions toward professional salaries. Teachers at a treatment center are asked to give more time than public school teachers, attend more meetings, suffer more supervision. They often are asked, indeed should be asked, to do research and record taking. And they often work, as at Bayside, eleven months of the year. But they do not get the same holidays, they rarely get better pay than public school teachers, and many of them have no tenure. The consultant's rationale for intervention in such basic employment practices is the necessity of emphasizing the professional respect owed teaching by the higher-status professions on an interdisciplinary staff. I wanted to educate the other professions, but I also wanted to counteract the teachers' low-man-on-the-totem-pole attitude by helping them learn to negotiate for themselves.

Excerpt 1

Vi stated her bitterness in this way as she left: "By now I don't even want them to offer me a raise. I spent a year with your help, educating the uneducable therapist. I spent another year educating another therapist about a school program. I've spent two more fighting one group-worker. I've got through to Director Stanley and somewhat to Roger and I'm not going to educate Dr. Avery. I'm finished; I need another set-up."

One expects a show of separation anxiety in any place where a dedicated teacher has to leave her class. In centers such as this, staff turnover is tragically high. The consultant needs to be aware of the effects on the children.

Excerpt 2

Vi felt very strongly about Dick. She was insightful but over-protective to some degree; a better word would be possessive. She tends to be possessive about her whole group of kids. This possessiveness has its assets as well as its pitfalls: She really does better and more thoughtfully with them than others with less involvement. The atmosphere she creates is healthier than the group-work atmosphere which she tries so hard to help her children avoid. Also it is clear to me that much of her exclusiveness with her group is intensified because she is planning to leave, and she is guiltily and anxiously concerned in planning every little thing so that she will leave herself behind, so to speak.

The Teachers: (2) Dot

Dot was hired a year and a half before our consultation began. She was a well-trained nursery school teacher. Like many nursery school teachers she had skills in arts and crafts, nature study, and the use of a variety of materials. Being a good nursery school teacher she could accept infantile behavior; she understood rivalry, difficulty in sharing, short attention span, quick changes in mood and interest, tempers and tears, battling and biting, confusion of fantasy and fact. Thus, though she had had no specific training with disturbed children nor with the academic teaching of children above kindergarten age before coming to Bayside, her attitudes, understanding, and interests gave her an excellent set for the handling of these children. It has been found by many that nursery school–trained teachers often make superior teachers with the disturbed child. At first Dot was assigned to work within a group, more or less as assistant to the group worker, who carried on a kind of Axline play-group activity for the major part of the day. Under these conditions, school work was never differentiated from group work for these children nor separated from the free group activity. Differentiation of environment is a prime aspect of learning, more or less native to the ordinary child but causing great difficulty for the emotionally disturbed. So, in the midst of teaching problems and problems in the relations between group workers and child therapists, as the program changed and changed again, Dot and Vi, with my help, began to develop a small group-school program separated from group work.

Dot and Vi both found it difficult to get staff to pick up troubled or troublesome children who temporarily could not behave themselves at school. Both encountered difficulty with child therapists who sabotaged school by ignoring school hours, or by taking a child out of school *in medias res,* or by not helping him take school seriously. Each tried valiantly and in her own way (Vi aggressively, Dot passively) and yet both failed to work out all their school problems with the directors, group workers, and therapists. They struggled to work out problems with one person only to find him gone the next month, then they tried again with the new ones who proved to be equally well-intentioned but equally ignorant of educational goals and methods. Dot and Vi used consultation to air their frustrations, to clarify their views, and to discuss plans that could be put into effect regardless of who turned out to be their bosses or colleagues at any given moment.

To combat confusion, Vi inaugurated a pattern: Dot assisted as second teacher during Vi's class period, picking up children who needed to work separately or differently from the group, or who needed to be bounced from the school group entirely. She stayed in the background except when called upon for a crisis in which Life Space Interviewing techniques might be used or tutoring sessions begun. A half-hour conference to discuss individual children and the course of the day in Vi's group followed the class period. Then Vi assisted Dot's group in precisely the same way for an hour, with a similar half-hour conference period following.

In essence, this was the beginning of an active school program at Bayside. *It was initiated by the teachers.* Though difficulties in relationship and methods often occurred, these women, with assistance from me, not only learned to work with each other and to respect each other, but were able to learn from each other. Vi learned a great deal about materials and something about games and projects as well as how to approach other staff without antagonizing them. Dot learned some group dynamics from Vi, as well as some academic skills in reading and writing and physical coordination training. She also learned to face her own hostile feelings better, to come out with her feelings and be braver about things she wanted to fight for. Both became more comfortable with handling groups of disturbed children, and both defined for themselves what school for those children *ought* to be. As they became aware of the kind of help they needed and wanted, they were able to make optimal use of our time together. Time was allotted for both individual consultation and joint sessions.

Most of their criticism about the unstructured, over-permissive group work was valid and confirmed by all the directors in succession, but only after the final, total reorganization, under a new, experienced program director, and with the help of our consultation methods was group work structured and coordinated within the school program. Then school became the focal activity—the healthier the child, the longer his school day. In time, when Vi wanted to lengthen her school group she became comfortable enough to do so alone, while

Dot got a school room of her own and taught a few individual children as well as a science group.

Excerpt 3

This is an example of helping a teacher to understand some dynamics and to handle curriculum in special ways when teaching a troubled child.

"We talked of another child, Jim, who would fly into a rage when given a pencil without an eraser. As Dot described Jim's terror of being anything but absolutely right, we began to understand his frustrations with certain other school tasks. In the reader, 'Nip, the Bear,' for instance, the word 'kitten' was not in the text. In using his workbook, he would check questions that had 'yes' and 'no' answers, but would not write a 'kitten is a baby cat' because the word 'kitten' was not there for him to see first. His deep need for certainty, allowing no margin for error, was something we had to accept at that time. Dot agreed to give him enough safety in himself so that he could eventually move out into an imperfect world. I suggested the use of a magic slate where mistakes vanish. I also suggested that, for a while, she might skip those irritating adult remarks, such as 'You're allowed to make a mistake,' when right now he can't allow himself any errors. We decided that Dot, herself, would become his authority when the text fails him, until he gains sufficient security in himself to take a chance."

Excerpt 4. An Example of Staff Relations Affecting Teaching

"Dot told me how difficult she had found Vi to work with, how she always felt steam-rollered by Vi, how she resented taking on Vi's children and having to deal with them when she felt Vi had not turned them over to her for the science work in good shape. We first talked briefly about the difficulties between the two teachers. Then we talked about Dot's feelings of dislike for this science project from the start. Although she liked to teach science, she had never done it with this age group before. She felt she had been forced into it by the directors. She was feeling pushed to do more than she wanted to do all the time. We talked about how two of Vi's three charges who were residence children were at this time in terrible shape because of residence staff trouble. We agreed that, although Dot had a perfect right not to like everything about Vi, it was at least possible she was blaming Vi for frustrations that belonged to the whole set-up. We discussed how some motor activity or recess between Vi's reading class and science could help these hyper-active, short-attention-span children get to work and what kind of science projects might be appropriate."

The Tutor: Della

There had always been a need for a remedial tutor in the Center. Some children's emotional disturbance, while hampering their learning skills and making it impossible for them to stay in school, did not prevent their learning in a one-to-one tutoring relation. Others could only learn when one or more remedial methods were sufficiently modified to fit their short concentration span, their compulsive and perfectionistic needs, or their proneness to perseverate. Others simply could not attend any school during their initial stay at the Center and had to be introduced gradually to the notion of school by individual work, either with their own teacher or with a tutor. Still other children lived in residence and were able to attend regular public school classes, but needed remedial tutoring to improve their skills, or help with their homework before frustration made it impossible for them to work at all.

Della was the remedial tutor. She had been trained in a rigid method of remedial work. When she first came she felt too insecure to modify, expand, or alter this method. Yet, in my experience, any given remedial method must be modified to be used with genuinely disturbed children. Through our consulting sessions she became most able in using many methods eclectically according to a child's current needs. Her confidence and her success with the children rose accordingly. Della's confidence was further boosted when Dot proposed taking on a group of four, then five, then six children, only if Della would be her assistant in the groups and if Della would become the Life Space Interviewer when bouncing (see Appendix B) was necessary—and it often was. Not only did Della learn Dot's methods, but she found she had a great deal to contribute to Dot and the group in planning the more academically focused projects or those parts of any project where basic learning skills could be used. In addition, with specific help from me, she was introduced both to academic testing techniques and to the Life Space Interview concept and method. She caught on quickly and was able to deepen her insight and observation by practicing Life Space Interviews.

Excerpt 5. An Example of Curriculum Needs with a Disturbed Child

"Della discussed a tutoring case, a fellow called Ben from the residence who attends the nearby public school, but who will not write or read or do anything but draw. He draws everything—drawing is a kind of speech for him. He talks with a pencil in his hand. He has been much praised by everyone in the unit and on the staff for his great drawing talent, and Della can't get him to do anything but draw things. She spoke of how, in final frustration, she had taken the pencil out of his hand and said, 'Well, I'm here to help you with reading and spelling, but I can't if you're just going to play with the pencil and draw.' Ben got down to some short, real work for the first time. We talked over this whole incident and I suggested from her cue that he had so much praise for his art work, and so little praise in everything else, that he had just given up the notion that he had any way to communicate except by drawing. It was fine to praise him for his drawing skill, but she might serve the boy very well by saying he was capable of doing other things too. In her room during tutoring periods, they would not draw but would concentrate on what they were supposed to be doing. I advised her to remove props and distracting objects and use other, non-pencil means of teaching reading and spelling, such as finger feelings, eye focus on the blackboard, visual memory of words, sounding phonics and to keep away from the seduction of pencils, pens, and drawings. There ensued a fight not only with Ben but with the psychiatric staff whom Della unwillingly had to go against; Della had to bounce Ben once, whereupon he came back to Della and for two solid tutoring hours, without pencil or drawing, did phonics, visual memory, and learned his spelling words as required by the public school. Since then he has been working; his reading level increased two years in four months."

Excerpt 6. An Example of Life Space Interview Technique

"Della and I analyzed a Life Space Interview session in detail because I wanted to help her see what to look for before and after: to hear what the child was saying and to try to understand what had gone on before he had been bounced or had left the room. In this instance, the child had been kicked out of class for stealing the keys to the bathroom. When he had completed a piece of assigned work, he stole the keys and locked the bathroom and stayed outside. By reading the records and talking with people working with the boy, we found that he is having a hard time keeping away from water-play, which has been a long and severe preoccupation with him, and which has been curtailed in group-work. The boy had been pleased that he had finished his school job. He had seen the open bathroom door and that tempting sink and toilet, and at a period of transition it could be guessed that he was trying to use the key for ego support, granted that he did so in a disturbing way. Della had missed this but quickly understood once it was pointed out."

Excerpt 7. The Therapeutic "Bounce"
from the Classroom

"I asked for details on the child Della and Dot were most concerned about 'bouncing' from the class this week: Mike is a fellow with a low frustration level and no controls who had been able to tell Della he had to go out for a bit in order not to blow up. Della handled this acutely and let him go, notwithstanding some guilt in doing so—was it a ruse, a case of malingering? We worked this out in the light of the facts, and she realized that Mike was really trying to believe her words: 'Tell me before you go to pieces, and then you won't have to go to pieces.' I told Della she and Mike should be proud of Mike's new step and should not hesitate to let him try it out for size. Not to do so would be damaging to Mike's own self-concept and his trust."

Mary

Mary, a teacher in the city's public school system, was in her own hierarchy and had her own supervisor. She had been on loan to the residence for two years before psycho-education consultation and before the merger.

Mary taught a group when the children seemed in shape to learn in a group; otherwise she took one or two children for half-hour periods. A woman in her late fifties, with long years of teaching behind her, she was thoroughly familiar with school routines, materials, texts, and curriculum. Having been in special education (where she taught children who were hospitalized for physical reasons) she could accept abnormality, irritability, and need for attention. But she was not familiar with nor at first did she feel comfortable with the emotionally disturbed. The supervising system under which she worked was not one in which she felt free to air self-doubts, questions of success or failure, or questions of one's own feelings. She tried to find progress whether or not it existed in order to make the child, herself, and the system comfortable; but she herself often honestly doubted its presence.

When Mary became frustrated or anxious she got sick. She didn't *play* sick, she got colds and stomach aches, complained of the drafts in the building and the extra load of work. She was a conscientious, compulsive woman, who had to fuss about the position of a chair or a book out of place, but the children liked her and respected her. When they could maintain themselves, they did well with her if only for brief periods of daily time.

Psycho-education consultation was planned at the same time that one of the major reorganizations at the Center was to take place. Mary's supervisor from the city and I conferred many times to plan a sensible school program for Bayside. The administration allowed for Mary's continuing supervision by the city and also invited her, if she wished, to avail herself of individual consultation with me. The other teachers thought that Mary, loaded down with meetings by both Bayside and the school system, would not relish attending more. Not knowing Mary at the time, I tended to agree. She attended all group meetings and stayed as long as she could.

One day, having arranged a schedule of individual sessions with each of the other teachers, I was ready to close the meeting. Mary spoke up, saying, "And when is my time?" The other teachers, who had been sure that Mary would not want this kind of consultation, showed their surprise. I explained that this individual session was voluntary. "I know," said Mary. "When can I have time?" Thus started regular sessions with Mary. So eager was she, that when time was short because of this or that emergency, she actively protested or would seek me out for make-up time.

The Genius-Type Child

Our relation was fostered by my good fortune in being able to help her considerably in the handling of one boy, partly by the accident of my knowing his family, partly because of a particular interest of my own in the disturbed, genius-type child who, because he has a very high I.Q. and has been dubbed genius, is expected and expects himself to know everything magically without effort, without ever having to work, without ever being allowed to make stupid mistakes, without the need to learn the basics, the routines, the details of the essential first steps to knowledge. She was told by the social worker who saw this boy's mother that this nine-year-old genius needed stimulation—Latin or Greek, geometry or algebra, to enrich his program so that he would not be bored. Mary knew that though this child read at a very advanced level, he could not and would not write, and though he did arithmetic in his head (often wrong) he could not and would not do his work step by step, and though he understood the concepts, he was ignorant of the arithmetic process, and refused ever to commit himself on paper. I completely supported Mary's feelings (which she had not dared express to the social worker) that he needed limits, clear directions, and simple tasks successfully completed far more than he needed geometry or Greek at nine years of age. Though her instinct had been right, she had feared saying this because underneath she was afraid she was unable to teach high-school-level subjects, and therefore, wasn't sure her objections were based on valid grounds. When I pointed out what a terrible burden was being placed on this fellow by making him perform in a grandiose fashion, further separating him from ordinary mortals with ordinary learning tasks, and never helping him to see one small task well done, she was intensely relieved. We mapped out a weekly program for this child, giving him tasks and subject matter that would meet his actual need for limits, allow him the margin in learning to make errors, so that he would gain gradual, solid, unflamboyant, sure learning growth. The boy flourished under this plan and his behavior in school relaxed. With his experience of increasing success, he began to have a feeling that he had a right to be a nine-year-old and did not have to be a nineteen-year-old in nine-year-old clothing.

This case clinched our relationship. After working on it Mary felt safe to talk with me of her difficulties with one group worker who, she felt, disrupted the children and played into their pathology by her well-meaning probing, shouting, and interpreting. Mary talked about her anxiety, created by the atmosphere of ever-shifting personnel at Bayside and her concern over how anxious the children in her class became each time another staff member left—which (for one period of time) was virtually every other week. We made a joke about how staff work time had increased by the need to have a farewell party every week of late for each departing staff member. She began with me to recognize and to relate her illnesses to the periods of stress at school (interestingly enough, though this period was a winter when everyone tended to be ill, Mary's illnesses and absences lessened). She was able more and more to be her good-humored self, competent in what she knew, firm about not taking on what she didn't know, open to learning, and accepting of the children.

Consulting with Non-Education-Trained Directors at a Treatment Center

Since at Bayside so much work was done with the series of directors, it could be said that their role in setting tone, delineating atmosphere, and making final decisions was similar to that of a principal receiving psycho-education consultation, as described in previous chapters. To an extent this is true. However, there is a significant difference probably common to most treatment centers. Only the last director after the final merger could be considered an expert in education. Consultation with all other directors involved a great deal more education on Education, and much more interpretation of why certain methods, subject matter, material, timing, texts, etc., were selected than would be necessary with an educationally sophisticated principal who had requested consultation. On the other hand, all the directors' understanding of psychodynamics and psychopathology usually made it unnecessary to explain or bring out this kind of information. Their need was for help in relating their understanding of dynamics to specific problems in learning, classroom behavior, etc. The blind spot that many professionals in the psychological disciplines have in regard to school and learning makes them separate school and the rest of life. Some psychiatrists, psychologists, and social workers arrogate to themselves operations of a child's id and ego. Consciously or unconsciously, they often regard school as that "evil society" from which they must protect children, or help the children "to take" much as one takes castor oil. Thus, school and teacher can be set up in children's minds as representing superego, the very last thing to be incorporated into treatment. Fortunately, increasingly professional literature, theory, and experience have been instilling the idea—which good educators know—that school and teachers must serve the ego functions and that to do so (even with well children and certainly with sick ones) both id and superego must be cared for at various times. The primary function of education may be said to be ego development, i.e., helping a child to grow, to expand and deepen the use of himself through increased skills and knowledge, in order to help him cope with his world, his culture, and himself. Many clinicians are giving lip service to this idea and some believe it; others are able to act upon it; but not a few have unconscious if not conscious sets against it.

Essential Understandings in a Treatment Center

These attitudes make life in a treatment center difficult for teachers, who tend to look on the psychiatric director as the fount of all wisdom and who think of him as a school superintendent if not a school principal. They wish to go to him for the kind of help he cannot give as well as the kind he may be able to give. They are surprised at his often primitive notions about school and since he has, in addition to authority, the halo of status, they lose confidence in their own profession and feel inadequate to teach—in which case they often quit or become in defense more psychiatric than any psychiatrist, thus losing their own professional sea legs. In such a setting the consultant spends a good portion of his time interpreting one discipline to another, trying to use the language of each, and finally trying to bring them to a common understanding.

What Is Teaching? What Is Therapy?

Another area of severe conflict that invariably arises between disciplines in a clinical setting is defining the boundaries of therapy and teaching. It is a plain truth that since language, the expressive arts, games, and the manipulation of material are used in both disciplines there will be overlapping. A teacher may find herself being therapeutic through her teaching or doing or saying the same thing one might say in a therapy session, and a therapist may often legitimately teach. Many people feel the difference lies in the amount and quality of interpretation: While a therapist might say, "You broke my pencil because you were mad," a teacher might let the thought go unspoken even though he knew the reason for the pencil breaking. Yet a teacher, especially in a treatment center, might very well make such a statement or might say to a child who does not need infantilizing, "But I'm your teacher, not your mother. You do not need to sit on my lap at school now." The therapist might most appropriately say, "Let's go to the *World Book* and find out if you're right about eclipses," even though research and reference-book hunting are teacher tasks.

The least arbitrary way to distinguish therapy from teaching is not so much the use of materials or words, but in defining roles. In essence, a therapist who is clear about his role conveys to the child, "In therapy, you may feel free to talk about anything and, within limits, do or say anything, while at school you may not *always* wander about the room—many times you must sit at your desk and the *teacher* will tell you what subject you are to be concerned with or will decide if what you want to talk about and how you say it is appropriate to school. In therapy, for a while, you may swear and it is tax exempt—nothing will happen. At school it doesn't do to swear; if you do you must take the consequences. In therapy you may tear up reams of paper. At school, now that you are

ready, you use paper for other things. *Both* teacher and therapist hope you will soon care enough about what you do so that
you will not need to tear up your papers." In this way psychiatrists and therapists and group workers can have their roles
operationally defined for the child and for themselves and
need not waste so much energy worrying about overlapping
of functions. But to get this concept across to interdisciplinary staff takes months of time, thought, and effort. This is especially true since so many times the issue is *not* one of therapy
versus teaching, but whether what was done was the optimal
way to handle the child at *that* moment, by *that* individual,
no matter what the setting. "Would it be better to say it differently or not to say it at all?" "Is this an activity you stop or
is this one to let go on?" "Do I hold the child now, or do I let
him get himself in a rage?" Then it becomes a question of
whether it is good or poor therapy, good or poor teaching,
good or poor technique, more than what person in what role
should do or say a certain thing.

   Thus it is a major task of consultation with all disciplines,
separately and together, to interpret and clarify legitimate
theoretical conflicts, the red-herring issues, and the fuzziness
of conceptualization.

Interdisciplinary Group Meetings

   The gap between disciplines was bridged somewhat by the consultant who, dizzied by trips back and forth
between group worker, teacher, program director, and psychiatrist director, decided that these things had to be brought
up in an interdisciplinary group meeting. Therefore, I arranged a schedule where first of all I would see the program
director in order to see what new changes in program, personnel, resignations, salary, time schedule, had occurred during the week and which things had to be relayed to the teachers. I then saw the teachers in a group to discuss things concerning all of them. After this I saw each teacher individually
for a half-hour to discuss whatever concerned that teacher
most. After the individual conferences there was a general

case-conference of the entire staff, including the clinic and
their social workers who saw the parents of the school children. Then I inaugurated a weekly meeting between group
workers and staff, which would include the directors when
they could attend.

Policy Meeting: "The Big Four"

Finally, during the year of constant stress, there
developed what was called the Big Four meeting. This meeting was inaugurated by the over-all director, Dr. Moss, an
able and well-intentioned man upon whom all administrative,
interpersonal, financial, and clinical burdens fell from all
units of the merged center. He valiantly tried to juggle all
aspects of his administrative problems. As with all such tasks,
the results generally satisfied no one and displeased many. In
order to clear some lines of communication, as well as to get
some help in making decisions, he asked the current program
director, the group work consultant, and me (as consultant)
to meet with him. It was here at the Big Four meeting that the
question of indecent salaries and hideous personnel practices
were taken up. Both consultants repeatedly insisted on getting
good, adequately paid new staff to fill vacancies, and under-
scored the importance of supporting present staff so that they,
too, would not fall apart and again present the children with
more disorganization and consequent increase of separation
anxiety.

One difficulty I had as consultant, growing out of my attendance at the Big Four meeting, was the question of what
I could, or could not, relay back to the teachers. The discussions held often directly affected the teachers, and I was intensely uncomfortable letting these teachers plan ahead in
one direction when I knew the whole program was about to be
changed in a quite different direction. I handled this by trying to get the two directors to be open, or as open as was appropriate, or to let me be open with the teachers. Occasionally, I took a chance on my own responsibility of telling the
teachers some of these decisions directly affecting them or

their work. When I did this, I reported to the Big Four that I had done so. Another solution for me was not to do anything, a kind of counter-transference disease caught from the organization itself. I began to realize that what was definitely decided Tuesday afternoon would certainly be changed before Friday anyway, so that telling the teachers would, in these instances, only confuse them further. I learned to wait to say something, with or without permission, until the probability of its happening was overwhelming. Although the idea of holding these meetings was to determine over-all policy and program, in actual fact the emergencies were so acute from week to week that by necessity most of what was done was to try to deal with the distress of the day. We searched for some solution to the lack of staff, low morale, and consequent wild acting-out of the children, which in turn made for mounting anxieties, frantic decisions, lower morale, and consequent staff turnover.

Included here are a few excerpts concerning staff feelings, crises of various kinds, hiring and firing methods, administrative policies, and individual problems.

At the various meetings I used myself largely to clarify what I felt were basic problems at the Center, regardless of who was leaving or staying: lack of communication, the seeming sense of helplessness with higher-ups that made the decisions, the lack of higher-ups with whom one could communicate in time about decisions, old, pre-merger bitternesses coming out on one side or another. It was clear that staff were using the children's anxiety as a means to express their own anxiety and resentment. Once, a high-powered meeting was called during Christmas vacation by Dr. Moss to discuss the need for more meetings—everyone was supposed to come.

Excerpt 8. An Example of a Staff Meeting and Time of Crisis

"Then came the staff meeting. It seems that things at the residence have fallen apart to a major degree. There they have three new, naïve, untrained workers as staff helpers. All old staff left together in a group with the departure of the former directors. There was no gradual moving in and out. As a result the children were extremely upset, since there were only the head people left who could handle their anxieties, and they were the only people who were familiar with the children and their problems. Too frequently these people were not able to be on the spot. The children were acting out by running away, vandalism, physical assaults. Director Moss started off the meeting by inquiring into the multiple causes of the severe acting-out. Two therapists held forth in an analytical, philosophical jargon about the nature of pain. The new program director said how the children should learn to behave better—only this was clothed in psychiatric sheep's clothing. Dr. Moss asked for my opinion. I said that considering the fact that we were dealing with disturbed children, and disturbed, untrained staff, and disturbed old staff members who had been through many frustrating and anxious times, it was hardly to be wondered at that things at the residence were a mess. Indeed, the kids were, by acting out, saying something about their lack of security, their unsureness about new staff, their feelings of loss and lostness. I asked what was being done about training new staff members before they came on duty, and what plans there were for intensive in-service training in their first few weeks. I asked why three new staff members had been added all at once and, finally, why add fuel to the fire of over-all uncertainty by continuing to have these upset children go home for weekends. This was explained as necessary because of lack of staff. I suggested the radical possibility of shutting down the residence for a week or so to orient new staff and give them the individual dynamics of the kids they would be dealing with so that, for example, they might know about a child who hates to be physically handled and should therefore only be touched when absolutely necessary, or about another child who needs and likes physical handling and should be held when he becomes too upset to hold himself in check.

"Dr. Moss outlined the children's problems, why they were

there, what staff was doing about treating their problems in
the way of daily new-staff meetings, extra supervision, etc.
He made an excellent presentation of the facts. Thus things
were brought back to sanity, and then the issue that was clearly the major irritant came out—the lack of inter-staff communication. Dr. Moss said the school program was working
fine even with these upset kids, partly because of the planning
and partly because the school staff had learned to communicate with group workers. He added that this was untrue in
the rest of the outfit including the residence children who go
to the public school."

Excerpt 9. Group Atmosphere and a
Period of Unrest

"The farewell luncheon for the departing directors was held in the staff board room; very large and full
of people. People tended to sit in a given place and talk to
their neighbors and never stir, as at an unsuccessful cocktail
party. This whole sociogram was symbolic of the interpersonal relationships obtaining in Bayside. In this gathering
there were not only the teachers, group workers, and residence staff (of which only two remain) but the social workers, parent therapists, and secretaries from the clinic. Someone came in whom I had never seen before, a music therapist.
I didn't know we had one. Moreover, she was supposedly a
music therapist for the school—this I had never heard of. I
was glad that someone like this existed, for heaven knows the
program is thin and could use more of the art therapist's time
and a music therapist too, only it turned out that she really
wasn't with the school because they never had had money to
pay her. Typical. A thesaurus was given to departing Director
Stanley, accompanied by a speech about two seconds long; a
book of stories to the departing Assistant Director Roger and
a one-second speech with nasty overtones. Then there were
great expressions of love from everybody to everybody that
sounded embarrassingly phony. There was a distinct feeling
of relief when the whole thing was over, the clinic staff me-

andered out, and the rest of us got together for my group meeting."

Excerpt 10. Panic Reaction of Staff.
The Hiring and Firing of Featherwhaite

"The whole procedure of hiring and firing an unqualified staff member was so typical of exactly what goes on that, aside from being an incredible series of incidents that ought to be recorded for posterity, it is worth reporting. Bayside was in a panic because since Vi had left, and the assistant director had left, and one group worker had left, the children were acting up and acting out simultaneously. The group workers were overworked, tired, and anxious. Dr. Avery, the new program director, was terrified of the boys who kept being bounced from everything. In an understandable panic she hired a male teacher named Featherwhaite and set him to work the very next day. He had not been given even one day to observe the plant, or the kids, or the groups, or the school classes—i.e., Dot and Della's group—or Mary's individual tutoring. He was given no knowledge, or even verbal summary, about the individual boys he was to teach, no time to look at records, nothing. When I asked the program director if he had been allowed to read the records, I was told, 'Of course not.' He could be trusted to deal with the kids, but not to read the records! He was given two boys who had had Vi before, missed her terribly, and were in a sad state. Along with these two boys, he was given three other absolutely wild ones. One of the boys, it is well known, can't stand another boy in the group; another boy had just been expelled from public school for impossible behavior and was feeling his failure bitterly, acting out in a violent, disorganized, desperate, homeless fashion; the third had had three new stepfathers in three years and was threatened by any new male at any time. Lovely grouping!

"The teacher, who is rather tall, absolutely bald, about thirtyish, very pale, watery-eyed, and wan, quite feminine and tentative (a Featherwhaitish sort of a person), was about as equipped to handle these kids (even if he had been given time to observe) as a five-year-old child. He had no program and gave the boys material to make *girls' costumes!* They rebelled and gave him what for, and I mean they really gave him a hard time.

"I arrived for my Tuesday at Bayside. Featherwhaite didn't appear for his scheduled conference alone with me. All I heard from Mary, from Dot and Della and from the art therapist, was Featherwhaite and how ghastly everything was, and how the boys were running wild and the group workers were going mad picking up the pieces that were left from Featherwhaite's mishandling. Dr. Avery kept saying the only reason the kids were anxious was because they were told by the staff that they were suffering because of all the loss of staff.

"Anyway, at the group meeting I've inaugurated, Featherwhaite came late. I had never before set eyes on him. He walked in, looking distinctly red around his bald head. He was introduced and, before I had a chance to say hello, he began talking at a great rate—clearly to fend off anyone who might say anything to him. When I finally got a word in edgewise, he began to say how 'naughty' the boys were and, as a matter of fact, the reason he was late and couldn't come to the individual conference with me was because he had to wash the mercurochrome off his head. The mercurochrome was on his head, he explained, because Arthur had written 'fuck' with it on his bald spot. Now, he is tall and Arthur is small and I could think of absolutely nothing to say, wondering how it could have happened. Finally I said, 'Arthur writes very slowly, how could he manage to write on your head?' 'Oh,' he said, 'I bent down.' I gulped. He said, 'I'm not very good at setting limits.' There seemed nothing whatsoever to say. I then began to talk of Arthur and his troubles to try to get Featherwhaite less uncomfortable and asked if he knew what the kids were like. He didn't. We gave thumbnail sketches of each of his kids; we talked about programming and limit-setting. It was all useless. To complete the story—and I swear it's true —the next week (his last) at my conference with Featherwhaite, he bragged to me that he didn't let Arthur write on his head this week; only Peter had written with chalk on the seat of his pants while he was standing at the blackboard! He was incompetent to handle, to program, to plan. He was afraid of the boys and was attacked by all the rest of the staff. He should not have been hired in the first place. It was unfair to him, the children, and the rest of the staff. But even if he had been better, it is criminally destructive to launch a new staff member into a program without orientation. After two weeks, when all the group workers threatened to resign if Featherwhaite stayed, he was fired. I talked at length about what had happened, about impulsive hiring, working with the teachers of disturbed and disturbing children, in an attempt to prevent future disasters of like nature. The only good thing that emerged from the incident was similar to the tale of the rabbi who advises his parishioner who complains of the hell in his cottage, containing a wife, six children, a mother-in-law, dog, cat, and a goat, to get rid of the goat. When the man does so, he is so relieved at the absence of the goat, he no longer complains of the others. Featherwhaite was Bayside's goat."

Excerpt 11. An Example of Regathering of Forces

"Actually things are better at this place now. Somehow, entropy was stopped and some new organizational force has set in. The staff is in better shape and the kids follow along. Perhaps the theory of a counter-irritant, namely Featherwhaite, may have served the purpose. But though a group worker has resigned (we do have to have our weekly resignation) she won't leave till June, so it's not an immediate personnel change with which to confront the kids. But there's a semblance of order in the place. It may not be gorgeous order but it is a relief to see something. Director Avery, who has gained in skill and miraculously achieved rapport with her unhappy and weary staff, put it to me in a rather lovely way. She said, 'Now, I think I can get sick. I didn't dare get sick for the past two months.' "

After a full school year of weekly psycho-education consultation had been going on, the final merger of Bayside with a city institution occurred. The merger was explained to the staff. Those members who wished to stay on were for the most part encouraged to do so. Some staff members left then, others left later, but many remained, especially during the rest of that year.

A new program director, Dr. George, took over the following year. He was well trained for such a job, sophisticated in education for the disturbed and in psychological understanding and management of disturbed children and anxiety-ridden staff alike. He brought with him an excellent assistant trained in Life Space Interviewing at the University of Michigan (one of the few places this is done intensively). He reorganized the group work, focused activity around the school program, hired two new teachers with my help. Although the year's consultation program was over, I agreed to consult with the teaching staff every other week.

Soon after the beginning of less intensive, alternate-week, shorter-period psycho-education consultation in the fall of 1962, it became apparent it was no longer necessary to participate in policy decisions. Director George planned the program, altered it to fit current needs, and communicated his decisions to the entire staff. He could support morale, interpret and clarify the anxiety of the staff that was aroused by new decisions and new plans. He, or his assistant, took over the group meetings I had inaugurated, and his over-all chief, a psychoanalyst of note in the area, determined policy in frequent joint meetings. This made the channels of communication more direct and less confusing. Director George tried to make himself available to staff on call. This is never totally possible, but was achieved more than is customary. He and his assistant attempted to handle bounces from classroom or groups by Life Space Interview techniques, in which he was very skillful. Dot, Della, and a new teacher, Grace, were given small classroom groups that lasted a good portion of the morning. When the children were not in school they remained as a unit and went to the group room. Here each group of children had its own group worker, who was assigned to work closely with their teacher. Children were bounced from school to the group worker, who either used Life Space Interviewing with them, or turned them over to Director George, depending on the situation. Staff turnover was reduced from extreme numbers to the usual amount of comings and goings. Consultation became a more normal process.

This abbreviated account of consultation in a land of chaos finally molded into order should indicate the problems of the consultant in any setting which is in turmoil.

6

Forest Knoll:
A Cooperative Nursery
School

I found there were great differences in my role as consultant at the elementary school and at the cooperative nursery school.* For one thing, I had taught nursery school myself for a number of years and was thoroughly familiar with techniques, scheduling, and procedures. This was a great advantage at Forest Knoll, where the two teachers were both relatively new at their jobs and interested in learning some group techniques which they felt they lacked. We found that on-the-spot training was a more effective way than didactic courses for teachers to learn. It left them more able to put newly acquired skills into practice. Therefore my own skills and experience made me particularly comfortable and, I felt, more specifically useful in the nursery school. Since children in elementary school are older, they have more experience in group living, are less spontaneous in acting out their problems, and have to grapple with academic achievement in addition to learning to live in a group. In the nursery school, inter-

---

* Mrs. Claire M. Bloomberg was the consultant at Forest Knoll for one year. She had taught in both private and cooperative nursery schools and supervised many nursery school teachers before taking on the role of psycho-education consultant. Her experience was particularly appropriate for consultation at the chosen nursery school. The "I" in the subsequent pages of this chapter refers to Mrs. Bloomberg.

185

relations between individuals and groups are, in a sense, as pure a culture as one can find already institutionalized. From the point of view of psycho-education consultation the greatest difference lay in the fact that in the nursery I was free to observe, demonstrate, even participate a bit in just two groups for a whole morning, and then consult with just two teachers for an hour afterward, while in the elementary school my time and energies were spread over a much larger population. The result was that in the nursery school I was able to develop a much more intensive relationship with the two teachers than with any one teacher in the elementary school. We rapidly got to the point of looking at and discussing personality problems as they impinged on professional tasks. I made it clear from the start that I was neither qualified to function as a therapist nor was consultation a substitute for therapy. I wanted to help them sort out and become aware of those areas of personality which influenced their teaching.

Differences between a Cooperative and a Private Nursery School

Forest Knoll differed markedly from the private nursery schools with which I was familiar. The greatest difference lay in the mother's participation at school as teacher-helper, and the effect this had on the mother, the teachers, and the children. For the mother, this meant that she had to learn to accept the demands of her own child for special attention while at the same time being helpful with the other children and maintaining a cooperative relationship with the teacher. For a competitive mother, it was often difficult not to get caught up in comparing her child with the children of other participating mothers. For the teacher, it meant that she was constantly under the scrutiny of the mothers and often felt criticized for her handling of a particular child or for her whole philosophy in managing the group. Since there were many points of view among the mothers regarding the role of discipline in the school, or the amount of learning that should go on, the teacher often had to content herself with the feeling that she was only able to please some of the people some of the time, which I suppose is the lot of most of us, at best. In addition, the presence of a mother in school often makes it embarrassing or even impossible for a teacher to discipline her child at the particular time when he most needs it. For the children, the presence of the mothers was in general a good thing, in that it enabled them to learn to get along with many different adult females at a time when they were expanding their horizons. However, the school was thereby pervaded by an atmosphere of home, and this made the movement outward more difficult for some children. Finally, for some, it was very difficult to get over the feeling that they wanted their mothers all to themselves on the mother's participation days, with the result that, particularly in the beginning of the year, there were tantrums and outbursts of jealousy when a mother paid attention to children other than her own.

For the teachers, the presence of the mothers meant that they not only had a critical audience every day, but that, since some of the mothers were members of the administrative board, they were therefore employers as well. This created a somewhat anomalous situation, where the teacher was called upon to please the board at the same time that she "trained" them in nursery-school philosophy and techniques. In this small and intimate situation, each teacher had also to maintain a good relationship with her colleague so that they might function together smoothly and present a united front to the board.

Another area of possible difficulty in a cooperative nursery school is that of the interpersonal relationships among the participating mothers. Happily, such difficulties were noticeably minimal at Forest Knoll, though I have seen schools where the mothers were competing for power, or jealously protecting their children or themselves to such a degree that certain ones could not be scheduled to participate on the same day. It is not uncommon to see mothers try to play off the teachers against one another, not too differently from the way children play off teachers or parents. It is much more difficult to handle the parents' needs to enter into this kind of defeating game than to cope with children who use less subtle methods. As consultant, I was prepared to have to help the teachers deal with this kind of strain and tension, and I was glad that it was not necessary to devote the time and energy needed for this task when there were so many others to work on.

Role of the Psycho-Education Consultant

From what has been said, a cooperative nursery school is a potential breeding ground for all sorts of complicated and interwoven interpersonal difficulties. In this kind of school the teacher must walk a tightrope if she is to function effectively. Though the consultant comes in as an outsider she, too, can get caught up in the crosscurrents of relationships in the school if she is not careful. Since I saw my function primarily as one of being helpful to the teachers, I made it plain that I was there for consultation with *them* and not with individual parents. Any mother who wanted my opinion about her child could talk it over with the teacher, and the teacher could bring it up in our periods of discussion. Several times, at the invitation of the teachers, I sat in on parent-teacher conferences, though I tried to keep my participation at a minimum and intervened only when I felt I could demonstrate something about interviewing techniques that might be of future value to the teacher. In an early meeting with the parents of the school, when I was explaining my role and how I would function, the question of my availability to the board was raised. Here again, I stressed the fact that I was there primarily for the teachers, but would be available for discussions of policy with the board provided the teachers were present.

There was an additional problem for me as consultant in a nursery school which grew out of my background and personality. This was the fact that, particularly at the beginning of the year, I had a tremendous desire to interact with the children and had to bend over backward not to start teaching again. To make matters worse, since I appeared once a week, the children looked upon me as another participating mother and often approached me to ask for help with clothing, to be taken to the bathroom, or simply to engage in conversation with me. It became clear after a few weeks that my bending over backward was a most stringent and artificial device, and I relaxed and allowed myself the pleasure of being more natural with the children. As I got to know the teachers better and became more involved with their problems and identified with them, the fear that I would become competitive or seem to be in competition with them for the children abated and I found myself concentrating my attention on *them,* with the result that I was less tempted to revert to my old and thoroughly familiar role.

The Teachers and the Course of Consultation

The two teachers at Forest Knoll had come into the school together at the beginning of the year before, each with a background of working with children, but neither having been trained as a nursery-school teacher. Jane, the director, was a social worker who had worked in a treatment center with emotionally disturbed children in a group. Mary had been trained as a recreation worker and had taught in a private nursery school before coming to the cooperative. As a result, both felt somewhat insecure and tentative in school.

In our first conference, they were anxious to know what I would or could do for them and how I saw my job. I pointed out that this was the first time we had tried psycho-education consultation in a nursery school and that we would be working things out as we went along, but said that in general I was there to meet their needs, and asked how they thought they could best use me. Jane responded that she had personal problems and would like to use me as a therapist, smiling when she said this, and I answered that I was not there to function as a therapist even if I were trained for that, which

I was not. I could and would help her to look at the personal problems which affected her teaching. At this point Mary remarked that she felt the same need and would be glad of the opportunity for more self-knowledge. The fact that the question of how and when personality difficulties affect the teaching task and the children one teaches arose in our first conference is in striking contrast to my work with teachers in elementary schools, where personal problems were the last thing to be brought to consultation, if, indeed, they were ever discussed. The partial explanation for this, I think, lies in the atmosphere of the public school system, with its hierarchical and bureaucratic defensiveness. A more comprehensive explanation can be found in the differences in training for teaching on the two levels. There is a great deal more emphasis on interpersonal relationships in the training of nursery-school teachers than in that of elementary-school teachers, and they are consequently much more aware of the impact of their own personalities on the children they teach. This apparent undefensiveness on the part of Jane and Mary was most welcome to me because of my conviction that to be a good teacher one must have self-awareness and the humility to look at what one brings to the classroom situation.

However, my over-directness and my firm belief that "The truth shall make you free" led me to the mistake of wading in too fast. I had brought up Jane's greatest area of professional difficulty, that of setting limits, during the first conference. She had backed away from it, and we spent the next four conferences alternately skirting it and hitting it head on. By the end of the fifth conference she acknowledged this as her problem and was ready to work on it and did so with increasing comfort until, several months later, she could make the statement that she felt absolutely comfortable about having me there and didn't care if I came on good days or bad days.

Though Mary shared to some extent Jane's problem in setting limits, for her the need was for help in the handling of parents, particularly parent conferences, and she brought up her anxiety on this score very early in our sessions. While I actually participated in only one parent conference, at her request, there were many times in the course of the year when I worked with both teachers, singly and together, to help them prepare for a conference or to clarify their goals in relation to their talks with a mother about her child.

An interesting pattern emerges from my work with these two teachers which could probably not be repeated in a less intensive relationship. We got right down to the most important business in the consultative process, that of establishing relationships, during the preliminary conference, and worked on it intensively for five sessions with all of us looking at what we brought to the situation, with me using supervisory consultative help to grapple with my problems in it. No matter what background and training one brings to a job, there are always situations in which one's own problems get tangled up in one's functioning. When this happens, an uninvolved and understanding outsider can often point up these problems in a way that will clarify the blind spots we all use for self-protection from time to time. At this time the co-director of our consultation project helped me to see that I was pushing too hard and too fast, and to understand why I was doing it. After that it was easy to gear the consultative process to the teachers' needs and not to mine.

From the fifth conference, things went much more smoothly, with some hesitancies of course, but with a steady increase in openness to the point where we could spend all our time on the problems that presented themselves without having to worry about being careful of each other—just as a figure skater, once he is sure of his balance on the ice, can go on to the more intricate business of learning figures.

This is illustrated by the consultations with Jane. Although frank in our first encounter, when she had asked for help with personal problems that got in the way of her job, being human she had to retreat a bit when I took her at her word and attacked her major problem of limit-setting.

First conference: "The teachers asked what I had noticed in the school that needed changing. I told them that I

believed some of the children had been asking for limits and
had been either ignored or channeled into other things when
it looked as if they required head-on confrontation. I gave a
specific instance of a child in Jane's group who had been kicking his heels on the floor during the reading of the story. Jane
said she hadn't noticed this. I said I felt the child had been
getting more and more anxious about his behavior as the story
progressed and should have been stopped. Jane said then that
I had gone to the nub of her problem, that she had an awful
time saying no to a child, that she could stop actual physical
mayhem but that she couldn't really be direct about stopping
a child when his behavior was only slightly disruptive. Having been this open, she now backed away and said she had
been taking a course in child development in which the in-
structor had said that certain kinds of misbehavior were peculiar to certain stages of development, and therefore she had
ignored certain misdeeds. I replied that the fact that a piece
of behavior might be normal at an age helped us to understand it but didn't mean that it shouldn't be corrected or handled, that normal growth always foreshadowed the next stage
of development, and that for a child to be helped to grow he
needed an adult to point the way. Specifically, I said I felt
this child had been acting out a four-year-old need to defy,
that the next step was his learning to control that need for
the sake of the group, and that my observations told me he
had been anxious about what he was doing—his anxiety was
an indicator that it was time to stop this behavior. I added that
setting the limit needn't be punitive, that he had been wearing new cowboy boots and telling him to stop might well have
been accompanied by an invitation to come to the front of
the room and show his new boots to the rest of the children.
Though Jane saw the point she remarked that I must not
underestimate her ability to control the group—a clear sign
to me that I had gone too far too fast."

Second conference: "Since I felt I had barged in too fast
the week before, I started our conference by saying that on
thinking it over I felt that I had been too definite and opin-

ionated with too little humility the week before. Before I could finish the two teachers looked at each other. Jane smiled a funny smile and said, 'I told Mary after you left that I felt I had been too defensive.' I replied that if she had it was my fault: I really couldn't tell on the basis of one observation that she was too permissive and should have waited until after many more observations. I said that I was often too quick and too direct about things. Apparently she had felt attacked but I wanted her to know I didn't feel attacking when I made criticism, that I was pointing out what I saw from the point of view of someone who knew what the problems of teaching in a cooperative were. She replied that I had been too fast for her but that she knew she had asked for it and that I was indeed right about her being too permissive." (We then had a long discussion of specific incidents that had arisen that morning, including several in which one little girl had been defying her.)

My notes continue: "The whole discussion led us back to limits again, and because I really felt comfortable by now I gently brought up the case of Sara. Jane acknowledged that Sara had annoyed her all morning. I said I thought she had been begging for limits and that although Jane had stopped her at one point by telling her she was acting like a baby, this put all the responsibility on the child to stop herself when what she actually needed was the support of firmness from Jane. She saw this immediately and we went over the whole of Sara's behavior and how it could have been handled, how each time the child didn't get the boundary for behavior that she needed she went on to some other way of defying. Jane and I both felt good about this discussion."

Third conference: "Jane said it is terribly hard for her to stop a child doing something because for her to do so is equivalent to getting mad and that seemed awful, for an adult to get out of control was bad for the child. My first impulse was to point out that stopping a child doesn't necessarily mean getting mad, but I suddenly felt I had to tackle what seemed most important, so I asked what was wrong with getting mad.

This started a long conversation. Like so many of us, Jane is terribly afraid of anger. Perhaps, she said, it's because if she really got mad it might get out of control, so she had to stop herself from showing any anger. I asked if perhaps she felt she had no right to be mad, ever. We talked at great length. I delivered several homilies concerning the teapot that boiled over because it couldn't let off a little steam now and then. I went on to say that I thought children needed to face the reality of life, which included people who were angry sometimes. Jane listened intently but kept shaking her head. This is a hard one for her and will take all year to get at."

As we sat down for the fourth conference, I sensed a great reluctance on the part of the teachers to begin. With gentle probing I discovered that they were upset because they thought my presence caused a new competitiveness in their relationship. Jane had been angry after last week's conference because she thought she had talked too much. Further questioning brought out that she actually felt she had been picked on as the "bad girl with a problem" and Mary had not been. Jane had felt angry with me afterward. "Jane began to speak again about her inability to get mad, and I said, 'Well, now, what are we going to do about this? I can try to keep from wading into your problem areas, but you really do ask me for this. As you know, something like this can't really be gotten at completely without going into your life before this and exploring your psyche to see why it is so hard for you, and I have no business in that area. I'm not trained for it and it's not my job. However, it is my job to point out very directly that I think this issue is one which is fundamental to teaching, especially preschool teaching, and it does get in your way as a teacher.' Jane said she knew that. She was always worried whether she had made each morning the best possible morning—had she gotten mad, had she handled the kids correctly? To this I replied that such high standards are impossible to maintain and asked her if she knew anyone who could 'improve each shining morning.' Then she said perhaps the thing that was wrong in our consultation setup was trying to have conferences with all

three in the group; perhaps it would be better to talk about
things that were this deep and fundamental in separate sessions. I said I was willing to do this any time they wanted and
that I would leave it to them to decide when we would have
single sessions and when we would have joint conferences."
(This is in interesting contrast to the usefulness of staff groups
in other settings. It is undoubtedly because three constitutes
a triangle, not a group, and too many things can get played
out one against another in a group of two with one leader.)

The fifth session started out as a joint conference, during
which Jane and I again discussed Sara's behavior that morning and her need for control. I outlined a very definite plan for
handling this child, since Jane had asked me just exactly how
I would have stopped Sara. This pleased her. I was pleased
because Jane challenged me several times during the course
of the conference, at one time pointing out a piece of behavior that I had missed in my observations. I accepted her cor-
rection, knowing there was some hostility in it but also feeling glad that Jane could now express criticism during the
conference time instead of telling me later that she had been
angry. When Mary had to leave for a parent conference, Jane
and I arranged individual conferences for the next two weeks.
Jane said, "It will be much better for me when I can have
time alone with you. I know I invite you to go deeply into
things that bother me and then withdraw. I lay myself bare
and you are very easy to open up to." I smiled and said that
I really didn't see that she was laying bare such terrible things
about herself, to which she replied that she knew that she always had to make the least of herself, but that she was now a
great deal more comfortable when I was at school, and she
wanted me to know that I had been a real help to her in making her think about the meaning behind daily classroom
events.

The next week I had a conference alone with Mary since
Jane was sick and out of school. The following week I had a
conference alone with Jane which I think was crucial in getting us to the point where the relationship was easy for both

of us and consultation could progress in a fundamentally constructive way although there were always small reservations on Jane's part. On rereading my notes it is clear to me that something happened on both sides: I was opening up to Jane as much as she was to me. I had let her know early in our consultations that the inability to set limits had been one of my problems with my own child. However, during my observations on the morning of this seventh conference, I suddenly became aware that I not only wanted Jane to be able to set limits for the children, I also wanted her to do it in *my* way. I knew that each person must be allowed to evolve his own style of teaching and managing a group and yet I had been acting as if I had *the* way to do these things. My notes for the morning read, "There was little kicking up and Jane handled it when it happened, not as decisively as I would have liked to see but it was her way and it worked. She seemed much more comfortable about having me there than she had ever been before." No wonder!

In our conference alone, Jane started out by telling me how much easier she felt about my observing her and then wanted to discuss an upcoming parent conference. She was very anxious about this conference because she felt critical of the mother's attitude toward her child. She asked me to do some role-playing with her so that she could be more comfortable about just what she was going to say. This we did. Then, "Jane said how uncomfortable it made her to be 'critical,' and I said I thought she equated criticism with hostility. There was constructive criticism and in a sense that was what a conference was supposed to be for. I thought this was a parallel with how she felt about setting limits: There was no law that either limit-setting or criticism had to be hostile. Here she got very anxious and defensive. I said, 'You are feeling criticized,' and she said, 'Yes, that's it. I have a terrible time taking criticism and that's why I can't face this parent conference.' I agreed I was being critical in a way, but it wasn't with the idea that she had to accept everything I said but only that which she could use. I tried to imply that there was a parallel of her anxiety about her role as consultant to the parent and mine with her. I stopped then to let her make her own connections concerning the consequent anxiety. When I left I thought she was feeling a great deal more comfortable about the conference with the parent and about me in general. I thought about this a lot later, and I think perhaps what has happened is that I have somehow grown more genuinely respectful of her way of doing things differently from mine. I don't know how this happened but at any rate she seems to be reacting to it. The interaction between Jane and myself was a microcosmic demonstration of the very problem we were working on: Can consultants make statements that seem critical without making the consultee feel judged, rejected, or angry?

From this time on, Jane worked steadily at evolving her own way of stopping undesirable behavior in the group. She almost never acted as soon as I would have in a particular situation, nor did she hit things head on as often as I would have, but the group came to know that it could depend on her to take the responsibility for setting limits and that was the important point.

This kind of working through of difficulties in teaching, particularly those which stem from a teacher's own personality and background, was certainly optimally possible in a nursery school where there was time and opportunity for intensive consultation and observation. It may be objected that Jane's own background and experience had made her much more open to this sort of consultation than most public school teachers would be. This is true to an extent, yet my further experience tells me there are many teachers in public schools who are able to use this kind of intensive consultation and would want to do so, if only time allowed. It would certainly take more time before results began to show, but I sincerely think, on the basis of my experience at Clements Elementary School, that it would have been very possible.

The importance of intensive consultation to nursery-school teachers cannot be overestimated. They are dealing with young children at a most malleable period. They have a unique opportunity, second only to that of the parents, to influence the course of personality development. Sara is a case in point. At the time when I was working with Jane, Sara's home life was disrupted by the fact that her brother was very ill, her mother was upset and guilty about having to spend so much of her time with the brother, and consequently was experiencing great difficulty in stopping Sara's antisocial behavior. As the child grew more upset she acted out more, with attendant guilt and an exacerbation of behavior problems. Thus a vicious cycle of guilt and acting-out piled upon more guilt was building up at home for the child. When Sara first came to school that fall, she found a teacher who was reacting to her behavior in almost the same way as her mother was doing at home. Had Jane not been able to change her way of handling Sara she might have become just one more factor in over-determining the creation of vicious cycles of behavior revolving around misdeeds and guilt and more misdeeds and more guilt. As it was, Jane was able to see the child's crying need to be stopped and to alleviate her anxiety while in school, at the same time that her insights from her experiences with Sara enabled her to help the mother change her response to the child at home.

This is only one example of what attendance at nursery school can do to influence the mental health of young children. At a time when large sums of money are being directed into an attack on poverty and disadvantage and the problems in living that go along with them, it is no accident that many programs have been directed at getting underprivileged children into school at an early age. Much emphasis has been placed, in these programs, on the prevention of learning problems later in life through curricula which are aimed at increasing cognitive functioning. This is certainly important and can be shown to have a direct influence on the child's later mental health.

It can also be shown that these programs influence mental

health because they present the opportunity for early recognition and diagnosis of problems when the child's personality is still fluid and relatively undefended by neurotic patterns. What has been underemphasized, in my opinion, is the opportunity presented in nursery school to work these problems out without the need, at least in some cases, to resort to individual outside professional help, which is scarce, expensive, and often not optimal treatment. If the nursery-school teacher can be aware of what has gone on in a child's home, and if she can interact with him in a way that is different from what he is used to, when what he is used to is damaging to his growth, change can often result at this early stage of development. Indeed it is not clear how much of the improvement shown by underprivileged children's functioning after exposure to especially tailored nursery-school programs is the result of the curriculum and how much has come about as the result of being handled in a way that increases the child's self-respect and feelings of adequacy. Both changes in curriculum and understanding of the child's background and needs are necessary if we are to attack the problems of underprivileged children, and it makes little difference which is more important. The salient fact is that nursery-school attendance can be most influential in affecting the course of personality development and learning potential of a young child.

Other Uses of Consultation

I have mentioned Jane's problem in setting limits and Mary's trouble with parents because I felt that these were the two major areas of greatest concern for them. When I had lunch with them the following year and asked them which had been the most productive area of consultation for each of them, they corroborated my feeling that among all the others we had gone into, these two were the most satisfying for each of them.

During the course of our consultation, however, we covered many other areas.

Over and over again we went into the dynamics of a child's behavior and tried to interpret it in the light of what is known about child development in general and what we knew in particular about that child and his family. We discussed ways of handling behavior and how it affected both the child and his group. For example: I stressed the differences among children in rates of physical development and was able to make them see that Donald, who was unable to use the jungle gym except in the most tentative and careful way, was actually less physically ready for it than his well-coordinated and adventurous age-mate Jim. Because we knew his family background, including the fact that his father was an athlete and hoped and longed for a physically agile son, we were able to plan for Donald to have small successes on the jungle gym. We gave him much encouragement without pushing him and with the verbal assurance that he, too, would be able to climb when his legs were longer. In the meantime we planned that his teacher would communicate our plan of action to his parents and would underscore the fact that the child was not yet physically ready for this task and that pushing him would only result in making him feel inadequate and would inhibit any attempt to go as far with it as he was presently able to do.

We had many discussions about the goals of nursery-school education and what we were trying to give these children. We discussed ways of observing a child's behavior, and I demonstrated some of them by keeping running notes on a particular child for half an hour one morning and then going over the notes with the teachers in the consultation time. We spent much time on techniques of handling a group and the use of space and schedule to affect the temper of a group. We discussed how certain members of the group went about helping or using other members. In the four-year-old group I made concrete suggestions about the use of music, group discussions, group play with rhyming, and the reading of stories and then demonstrated these techniques at Jane's request. All of these were areas that might have concerned any nursery-school teacher.

Consultation to the Administration at the School

There was one other area which, because it is so peculiar to a cooperative, should be mentioned—that of the relationship of the cooperative teacher to the president and board of the school. From my own experience as a teacher in such a situation, I know that unless the teacher is able to provide an educational philosophy for the school and to express it and defend it firmly vis-à-vis her administrative board, there will be no continuity of philosophy in the school, and standards will go out the window. This is because the board will always represent a variety of views as to the purpose of nursery-school education and as to the point at which standards must be sacrificed to expediency, usually financial expediency. I had observed at Forest Knoll that the teachers, because they were relatively new to their jobs and not specifically trained for them, were somewhat hesitant to assert their views. Consequently, when a situation arose in which teachers were called upon to meet with the board and discuss a problem involving school standards, they were delighted when the president suggested that I be invited to participate in the meeting. They felt they needed support, not because they were unsure about what was best for the school to do, but because they felt unable to express their point of view in a convincing way. Since both were intelligent and articulate women, I felt that their need for support arose because of an over-humility about their previous training, a knowledge that acceptance of their point of view would mean some financial difficulty for the school, and the feeling that if they didn't convince the board they were somehow failing the school and themselves.

Despite the disadvantage of duality in her relationship to her administrative board, the teacher-director in a cooperative nursery school has the great advantage of being able to deal directly and immediately with the board of her school when she wants to raise issues of policy, even though she has to deal with role confusion because she is both policy maker and employee. The principal of a public school, on the other hand, is working within the framework of a policy handed down to her by the administration, and it is difficult for her to make her point of view known through the channels of the school hierarchy.

Summary

The cooperative nursery school is the ideal situation in which to offer psycho-education consultation. The teachers in such a school are much more oriented toward thinking in terms of the mental health of their pupils than are elementary-school teachers, who have the additional burden of an academic curriculum to carry. Because of training and experience they are more aware of their own personality structure as it impinges upon their teaching. They are dealing with children of a very malleable age and are challenged by that very malleability. They are able to observe parent-child relationships at first hand and to use their observations to help the parents guide their children. The consultant uses her time to observe and consult with only two or three teachers, which enables her to establish a much more intensive relationship than would be possible in a larger school situation. This also gives her time to become thoroughly familiar with each child, his background, and his relationship to his mother, so that she is much better prepared to be useful to the teachers in discussing the children. If, as in this case, the consultant has actually worked in the same kind of school, she has an additional advantage of familiarity to bring to her job. This experience is certainly not a prerequisite to being able to help nursery-school teachers, but I should think that this kind of consultation would be infinitely more difficult without at least some group experience, even if it were with older children.

As opposed to other nursery schools, the cooperative presents some pitfalls to be avoided if consultation is to be productive. The consultant must keep her focus on the teachers as her consultees. This does not mean she may never be available to the board and the administration of the school, or even to individual parents in special cases, but it does mean that the teachers must be included in any such consultations so that they may be completely free of the fear that the consultant will discuss them or report on their problems to others. In a small, tight cooperative group, with all the personalities involved, there will invariably be some who will approach a consultant and attempt to use her against another member of the group, be it teacher or another mother, in a hostile and gossipy way. Here the consultant must be absolutely firm about her role as helper to the teachers and direct in her refusal to be drawn into any conversations about them, about the other mothers, or about the problems of any particular child in the school.

There is no doubt in my mind that the experience at Forest Knoll demonstrated that consultation can be extremely useful in a cooperative nursery school. The only doubts I have about its general applicability arise from the budgetary problems which are usual in cooperative nursery schools. Money could be set aside for such a consultant, or someone from a neighboring clinic or research program might volunteer. Otherwise, the only way I can think of it being generally used is pooling of resources by three or four cooperatives to share a consultant to do just this kind of consultation on a weekly basis. I do think, however, that this experience in intensive consultation has demonstrated to me the absolute necessity of periods of such intensive consultation for all teachers, and particularly for new teachers regardless of the level of teaching—elementary, junior high, senior high, or nursery school —if they are to develop the kind of security, competence, and feeling of professional adequacy that is the background of good teaching in any school. Bank Street College in New York City has been working with new teachers in this way. My experience has convinced me that opportunity to develop an undefensive, open relationship with someone who is familiar with the situation in which the teacher finds herself, and to talk over problems as they arise, is the best possible in-service training for good teaching.

It is also imperative that thought be given to including consultation of this sort in Head Start and similar programs at settlement houses and schools where aides are used as teacher helpers. Sometimes these aides are educated middle-class people not professionally trained. Sometimes they are high-school graduates or high-school dropouts. Both groups have potential usefulness. Each needs different kinds of help both for themselves and to work with the professional teacher on the job. The teachers likewise need help in working with aides, much as they needed help at Forest Knoll with the participating mothers. Regular, intensive consultation is a possible fruitful answer.

7

Problems of
Initiating Programs

Having talked at length with the Superintendent of Pupil Appraisal and Psychological Services of the District of Columbia Public Schools, Dr. Irene Hypps, who had helped us in our original project and was enthusiastic about our goals, we approached the Agnes and Eugene Meyer Foundation for a grant enabling us to acquaint the psychologists in the Psychological Services Department with our methods and to train ten or more of those psychologists for consultation work.

We initiated our program between the fall of 1964 and February 1, 1966, with the permission of the Superintendent of Schools, Dr. Carl Hansen. This chapter describes the difficulties of introducing the consultation method into a system where general procedure and policy had been rooted in traditional methods of individual diagnosis, and where the psychologists are seen primarily as testers and evaluators, responsible more for the placement of a child than as a potential arm of service to teachers, counselors, and principals.

To move into a complex bureaucratic system and to bring about change is a herculean task. To some extent, unless one can implement one's plan with freedom and authority, the roadblocks that we encountered would be likely to occur any-where. But these can be removed with time, patience, and skill. Therefore, should anyone, or any group, wish to try, we offer the following warnings in the hope that some of the frustrating and hampering problems we ran into might be avoided, or at least diminished.

Inertia

Inertia is the force most operative in bureaucracy. Until a greater force can change the direction of the forces in operation, it would seem that the old will go on forever. This implies that if the job to be done is to change from traditional, individual diagnostic to over-all consultant service, the only way to do it is to see that a force greater than that already operating can be put into motion.

In this we partially failed. We believed that the loud pleas of teachers, principals, counselors, children, and parents for more comprehensive services would be force enough to up-root traditional attitudes, procedures, and policies—especially if the school psychologists were given the tools to demonstrate such services. This was done and it did work: Many of the school psychologists whom we trained were often very talented as consultants—dedicated, imaginative, and knowledgeable. But to counter inertia an even greater force is necessary—absolutely established and clearly stated *authority* to proceed. Those in charge must communicate clearly to those on all lower echelons that such-and-such a policy will be tried out for such-and-such a time. This dictum must be frequently reiterated from the seats of authority. In school systems the "boss" (whoever that boss may be in the hierarchy) is a more magical word than "president" or "union leader," and his word has the inexorable quality of a general's to a private.

Outside Events—Personnel Changes

By establishing the interest and approval of the Superintendent of Schools and of the Special Services Department, we thought we had achieved the needed aura. We were

naïve. To make things more ambiguous, there were personnel changes during the year and a half of our project. The
Superintendent of Special Services, with whom we had dealt
most closely, resigned and a temporary superintendent was
appointed. After four more months the temporary appointment was made permanent.* Although she wished us well
and tried to cooperate, there were many conflicts and insecurities during the new superintendent's first six months of
office, preventing her from launching a new program. Her
newness to the role, her original uncertain status, along with
many other changes and new programs (brought about in
part by the poverty program and federal interests, as well as
by local insistence and pressure from citizen groups) made
the period very difficult, no matter how well disposed she was
toward us. We felt she was never truly convinced that the Superintendent of Schools really wanted her to go ahead with
our program. Understandably she was unsure of the reaction
to anything more that was new. Therefore her containment
of this program into a kind of possibly contagious ward was
thoroughly understandable, but it made it difficult for us to
work most effectively. We had to reassure, placate, compromise, and do what I call pretzel thinking and acting to an extent where sometimes we felt our goals were so watered down
that we wondered if they still existed.

Changes in staff and changes in over-all policy occur in any
system. What can be done? We should have spent far more
preliminary time with the Superintendent of Schools and all
his subordinate superintendents. We did not do this because
he, like the other superintendents, was a busy, pressured man
and couldn't be expected to be involved in every experiment.
We didn't do this because the original Superintendent of
Special Services understandably didn't want to spend time
winning over the other superintendents to an experiment
which she was "trying out for size." She had told us that in
her own bailiwick she had authority, and therefore she want-

---

* Mrs. Aileen Davis, Superintendent of Pupil Personnel of the District of
Columbia schools.

ed us to begin only where she knew she held authority. Because we felt that to work in a bureaucracy we had to do everything we could to go along with the powers that be, it made sense to us not to push further. But it certainly was not the most effective way.

Time

Under other circumstances we would have asked for a full year to orient and indoctrinate the policy makers, the principals, and the counselors, before putting our method into effect. The period of joint familiarization and planning would have been well worth the time and money spent.

Any change takes more time than is usually allotted for it. But fund-granting institutions reasonably want to see results and grant applicants hesitate to ask for enough time for fear that the whole project will be refused or that they might be accused of gold-bricking or of spending money without measurable results for too long. These attitudes add to an already virulent American penchant for rushing into things with maximal enthusiasm and minimal preparation, based on the assumption that frantic activity must be equivalent to efficient endeavor. But, without everyone concerned substantially aware of what is being attempted and why, the misunderstandings and the doubts natural to bringing about change multiply in geometrical progression.

Paranoia

Paranoia seems to be an inevitable accompaniment to any task whenever one group is getting information not shared by another group. This is true even if the information is for the acknowledged and accepted use of the total group. This phenomenon, familiar as it is to those aware of the behavior of groups, got in our way countless times.

For example: We met with the total group of school psychologists once a week for one semester and once a month thereafter. From this total group, twelve psychologists volunteered for more intensive training. Ten were accepted,

the other two having been disallowed by the department because they were on temporary status. Some members in the
large group made no bones about suspecting the motives of
members of the small group. Many of them ambiguously expressed doubts about the research staff's motives and competence, or about the acceptability to the school system of what
was being done. In turn, another smaller group, the Superintendent of Special Services and her assistants, worried about
what was being said in the small group. We set up regular
meetings with the high-level group to alleviate the most distorted notions of what was going on and why. Since these were
busy people we hesitated to ask for too many meetings, yet
too few appeared to be even more disastrous to the project.
Much time, which must be planned for, is consumed in dealing with natural inter-group paranoia.

We had less trouble with our small group of psychologists
because we became trusted by being as open, honest, and direct as possible. Yet, even here, at the beginning, suspicions
appeared concerning the fear of our potential betrayal of
them to the higher-ups or our possible breaches of confidence
to school personnel. We tried to handle this as carefully as
possible and to bring everything we could out into the open.
But we were not always successful.

Instances of group paranoia cannot be avoided. But when
anticipated, pathways of communication can be opened up
and one can elicit hidden concerns and help overcome them
by bringing them to light.

Professional Self-Esteem and Morale

Low morale and low professional self-esteem in a
department make change even more difficult than might be
expected. It is true that every work group has its malcontents
and complainers. But, where there are too many issues which
result in making a professional group feel put upon, morale
will fall so low as to make even the changes they themselves
desire hard to attain.

This department was not unique among school systems.

Many school psychologists and social workers are, or feel themselves, underpaid, overloaded with cases, and burdened with time-consuming clerical tasks. Many school psychologists feel that they are not given a say in their own fates or in matters concerning school policies where they might have skill, information, or good judgment to contribute.

At worst, highly trained professional staff are too often treated like bad school children. They are scolded for every minute not actually engaged in tasks on the job, even though to function well in their jobs requires time to think quietly, time to talk with, meet with, or help each other. The small group of psychologists, and later an additional small group who joined us, came to realize that whatever else we could not do, or failed to do, we at least treated them respectfully, but this took an amount of time and energy beyond what would have been necessary if the morale had been higher to start with and if professionals had been able to use their independent minds and sensitivities. If good morale is lacking, building it up becomes a necessary task in order to introduce change.

This is a fascinating subject of inquiry in itself. It would be well worth investigating the extent to which a school system bureaucracy infantilizes staff so that the lack of initiative, the dependency (often hostile), the lack of spirit for experimentation, innovation, and imagination not only cripple the professional growth of individual members but also paralyze programs and their evaluation, deaden communication, and carry over to a point where students are infantilized. As Erik Erikson pointed out recently, this is a particularly serious educational error in dealing with a minority group (representing a large percentage of this school population) which is already severely handicapped in functioning and development. It would not be inaccurate to set up the hypothesis that, while all bureaucracy may fall into this trap to some extent, a school system, whose methods are predicated on the expected conformity of its population, is even more prone to this immobilizing practice.

Compromise

We wanted to train school psychologists to act as consultants to the school. The Special Services Department, for good reasons of its own, wanted some in-service training of assistant principals so that they and the psychologists could work better together. We were asked to begin our project by holding a series of six lecture-centered workshops for all assistant principals and psychologists in the system. This seemed important and not inappropriate to our goals (although given our choice we would not have wanted to begin with any one professional group on a large scale before getting to know the psychologists much better). This was of immediate concern to the department, and so we agreed.

We did not think that a series of lectures would at best do anything more than break ground for further work. When we found out that the psychologists we were to work with would have nothing or little to do with the assistant principals whom we were addressing, we were exceedingly frustrated, feeling that we had been seduced into going along with a type of program we disapprove of, wherein people are stimulated and aroused, given covert, if not overt, promises that help will come—and then it doesn't. We were still more upset when we found that the psychologists had not, as we had thought, been told of our plans and projected program and were thrust into these workshops not knowing we were talking for them, not at them. Thus, they believed that we were lecturing to them on a level of sophistication below their own, and we had, before we ever started, innocently committed this prime sin.

Everyone knows that to introduce a program into any community system one must perform undesirable tasks in order to do the things one wants to. But to what extent? At what cost? Beyond what point is there diminishing, or even negative results? In this case there were some minor gains and, certainly, through it the major problems of the department were opened up to us. We were able to work the difficulty through to some extent. Was the compromise worth it?

Later we had a number of group meetings. A large one included all the school psychologists. The department head requested that this be well structured, to which we conceded by having one staff member give the structured part and the other staff member give the free discussion part. The lecture, probably in part because of the antagonism raised by the workshops cited above, was not unanimously welcomed, though some gains were made. We finally held this large meeting once a month instead of once a week and published the material instead of delivering it. If we had done it in the way we had originally planned, the same material could have been conveyed to a series of small groups informally. In fact, we later asked for an increase of small groups conducted in this fashion; we were able to inaugurate some of them although time was too short to do as much as we wished. The preordained large meetings were another questionable compromise which we are not sure we should have acceded to.

By the late spring of the first year, the one small group with which we had worked wanted to continue the following fall so much that we agreed and, on department request, added a second group. We were assured and reassured that the original group of school psychologists would be able to keep their project schools—i.e., the one school at which each had chosen to give weekly consultation of the kind described in these pages —so that they and the selected schools could profit by continuity of service in a relationship just launched. The second group was to pair six school psychologists with counselors in the schools they would select for consultation, so that some of the services initiated by the psychologists through consultation could be implemented and carried on during the week by the counselor, insofar as that position allowed. This notion was suggested by the Superintendent of Schools on hearing about our procedures and the new Superintendent of Special Services and her assistant eagerly agreed.

We returned to work in the fall to find that an emergency city-wide program of testing had been called into immediate effect for new placement purposes, that new staff had been added in a rush through poverty program funds, that the greatly enlarged department had been divided up into four teams, each headed by a clinical psychologist, each to serve a geographical quadrant of the city. In many ways we considered this a good change, in the direction we liked, for better service. We were, however, dismayed to find that not one of our original group had been assigned his original project school and that both our groups had to be completely switched. The old group now was changed to six of our previously trained people, plus one new psychologist, each with new choices of project schools they were not directly acquainted with. These six psychologists chose schools with counselors and brought the counselors to the new group to work jointly with us. The second group was made up of members of one complete team of six psychologists and a leader representing one geographical quadrant. Some of these psychologists were new to our program, and some were familiar with it.

On the whole, this arrangement worked well, but we wondered how flexible we could be and still achieve our purposes. Where draw the line at what one can or will do and still work toward the goal? This is a problem for anyone without complete authority to bring about changes.

The results of our study are not yet digested by the system over a period of time long enough to predict outcomes. We think, being optimists, consultation can be introduced into the school system. We think we have in part done it; we do not know how well, and we have grave doubts about whether this is the best way to do it. Certainly it is happier working as a group independently from outside the school—whether in a grant-supported group such as ours, city mental health clinics such as I, for one, have been supervising, or a private group hired by the schools, such as some nearby cities have suggested they might do. There are, withal, some advantages in having a school system maintain its own consultative service if, and only if, consultants are clearly and definitely not in, or not considered in, the traditional school supervisory role. The advantages are an inevitable involvement in the interests of the system, a knowledge of its working, and shared

experience that makes the washing of soiled linen less hor-
rendous and the question of confidentiality less an issue (although in some cases it becomes more of one).

In our minds it is worth doing, in order to give better psychological services and provide a better climate of learning
for children and staff. But if it is to be effective, there is certainly a better way of doing it than that which we took
through force of circumstance.

This being the case, let us share with the reader what seems
to us an ideal way of introducing consultation into a school
system as the major type of service. The material quoted here
comes from Dr. H. N. Blackwell of Canada, who inaugurated
in the schools of London, Ontario, a complete comprehensive
program of psychological services in which consultation is one
focal method.

In 1964, after our original reports of consultation were
distributed, we received material from Dr. Blackwell, who
had become Director of the Department of Psychological Services of London, a community of about 40,000 pupils with
about 1,200 teachers. When Dr. Blackwell took on the directorship, he insisted that the first year of his activities would
center on a comprehensive survey of the needs of the school
system which could be met by psychological services. He was
in a unique position since, up to his appointment, there had
been no psychological service department in the system.
Therefore, although he needed acceptance for his ideas from
the Board of Education, the administrative and teaching staff,
he had little dead wood to brush away.

The material quoted below all comes from letters and seminar material Dr. Blackwell sent us in 1964.

After six months of surveying the school system as it existed and familiarizing himself with schools and personnel,
the sequence of his program development was as follows:

1. He asserted: "Any programme of psychological services
must come from the people on the firing line who face the

daily difficulties and problems which these services must be tailored to meet. Consequently, while I reserve the right to recommend strongly the way that such services will be provided, I am most concerned that the problems themselves be defined by school personnel. Individual interviews with principals, vice-principals, guidance heads, special education teachers, administrative staff at Head Office, and other specialized service representatives within the system have been held. A wealth of valuable material, partly the result of my reassurance to them about the confidential nature of the content of our conversations, has been accumulated and organized for consideration of both priority and impact when we decide finally on the services which are to be provided."

2. He formed useful liaisons with community agencies: "About as much time has been spent with the various agency representatives of the community in the field of mental health, most of whom I had known prior to leaving this City three years ago. Most of our discussions have centered around my attempt to understand thoroughly the actual work circumstances and the functions of each individual within the agencies. In many ways I have been able to raise issues concerning the needs for clearer and closer communication with school personnel, more effective liaison generally with the schools, and have proposed alternative methods of programme organization within the agency which might lead to a more efficient working relationship with the schools. Up to now this has been a rocky road, but despite the anxiety which my suggestions have provoked, many of them have been tried successfully by the agency directors."

3. While the survey of needs was going on, emergencies within the schools occurred. Dr. Blackwell inaugurated emergency first aid until the designed program was put into effect: "In the matter of 'putting out fires,' it reached proportions which almost torpedoed my survey of the school system. As a consequence, in conjunction with the guidance director, a Directory of Mental Health Services in the London Area was

created and distributed to all school officials who are in a position where demands are made upon them for information concerning sources of specialized aid for any particular student. The use of this Directory has resulted in a dramatic drop in demands for immediate help or information by these people. We know for sure that it has been used extensively by the school personnel in advising parents and others about the treatment resources within our community."

4. In order to bring community and school in closer working relation and to get rid of the antagonism between city mental health agencies and schools, so common in many communities, Dr. Blackwell organized a workshop on teenagers for representatives of the mental health field, the secondary-school principals, assistant principals, guidance personnel, and central office administrative staff.

"Knowing that the mental health people had at least four active committees working on the problem of the need for more adequate treatment facilities for teenagers in the community, as a participant in their planning groups I recommended that they meet with the secondary school people in order to share with them their concerns for this particular population of patients and to exchange ideas on either the creation of new treatment resources or the many ways of improving the services offered by the resources we already have here. After all, the school people are those who see the condition in its incubation stage, far in advance of the presenting symptoms as they appear when the adolescent goes to the clinic for assistance. I was able to persuade them that the school personnel could be viewed as an excellent resource group who would be indispensable in any planning which had a preventive flavour. Consequently, I organized a Workshop to be held at the Education Centre and composed a letter which was signed by the Director of Education and by the local president of the Canadian Mental Health Association, inviting approximately 72 people to attend the Workshop. The final attendance was 96. . . .

'One item may be of particular interest to you. For our

buzz groups,* as you will note, two reporters were used. The representative of the schools was assigned the job of reporting the group discussion content which had to do with the mental health field. The representative of the mental health field was asked to report the content relating to the school situation. This worked out amazingly well, I'm sure contributed to clarity of communication, in many cases resulted in empathic comments and suggestions from each group for the other, and finally resulted in a two-hour tape of the afternoon plenary session, which I have summarized, containing 90 points of issue and of recommendation.... I feel that, as a service, this is one significant contribution I have made to the school system and to the mental health field since coming here. Without any doubt, the channels of communication were cleared, mutual understanding of each other's work circumstances and problem situations in dealing with these teenagers was developed, the strategically selected group leaders who were able to dig deep enough to elicit some pretty open expressions of discontent, if not hostility, were also able to make use of this negative effect constructively, and to enlist the cooperative efforts of both groups in looking at the problem from the point of view of solution rather than complaint."

5. Working with the Board of Education on plans:"I was recruited here with the specific instruction of the Director of Education that this programme should be developed 'without haste.' It was implied that I should 'nose around,' take my time, plan thoroughly, be sure and avoid error, and provide the school system with something that would be the most efficacious and reasonable programme of psychological services possible. However, curiously the pressures came not from the community or the schools so much as the Board on myself and the Director of Education, to expedite matters of programme development and to institute services at the earliest possible time within the schools. A sequence of three events, involving summaries which I had prepared for the Director

---

* "Buzz groups" are small subgroups that form out of a large group to discuss issues of particular interest to the participants.

of Education, seemed to gain the kinds of concessions which I felt were in the best interests of the schools so far as the programme was concerned. . . .

"We are blessed with trustees who have foresight and flexibility. Not one of them had anticipated such an anomalous proposal as I had made. My fears that tradition would prevail were soon dispelled by the Board's endorsement of this broader concept of services. In terms of simple politics, by this endorsement they were hooked in the sense of being compelled to go along with any further plans I proposed which were consistent with these terms of reference. You will note that they differ little from the kinds of convictions expressed in the literature which I have received from your group. Actually, I have worked in a community mental health programme in Minnesota over the last two years or so, and the community mental health approach is the model I have used to try and formulate a psychological programme within the community of the schools."

6. In order to implement the program Dr. Blackwell wisely considered the question of salaries in order to attract competent people. He presented a summary to the Director of Education who would in turn present it to the Board of Trustees at a budget meeting on the basis that if the proposed program were accepted the price had to be paid for the appropriate staff.

"This summary is written in a very dogmatic and forthright manner representative of the characteristic communication between the Director of Education and myself. He wants opinions, proposals, and above all facts to back them up. Apparently the Board of Trustees resembles this man in this respect. The ten points presented here were considered at length prior to the Board meeting, at which time only token resistance in the form of about three questions related to specific functions and potential lack of staff cooperation were raised. This Board, not known for its extreme generosity, endorsed the recommendations and instructed me to take action on recruitment. Frankly, I feel this is a premature rather than a precocious development. There is so much left to know about our schools before I can be completely realistic in the kinds of decisions made about programme details."

To paraphrase Dr. Blackwell's recommendation for recruitment of appropriate staff for the Department of Psychological Services, he suggests ten points to be considered.

1. That the chief staff members be mature persons with advanced postgraduate training in psychology and from five to ten years of diversified experience in mental health work and work with children.

2., 3., and 4. Salary rates must be high enough to attract competent people. If standards are lowered, the whole program can be jeopardized. A minimal starting salary of $10,000 to $11,000 is suggested. Yearly increments with a flexible ceiling are urged.

5. It is proposed that ultimately there be a psychologist for each secondary school and its area feeder schools beginning with kindergarten up through high school.

6., 7., and 8. If too few appropriate applicants can be recruited, the idea is not to fill the staff with inferior quality but for the time being to hire only those that are good and to double the workload until such a time as appropriate applicants are found. The board must understand that the number of psychologists hired at first will be added to so that the personnel picture will not be frozen. Rigidity in keeping outmoded salary scales or number of personnel must be avoided.

9. As for the difficulty of comparing educators' and psychologists' salaries, Dr. Blackwell believes that, considering the academic qualifications for psychologists, the additional training required, the variety of highly specialized skills they command, and the responsibilities to be handled, an income comparable to administrative positions in the school system is justified.

10. Dr. Blackwell's last point is a plea for realistic apprais-

al of current and future needs and for the realization that a half-done job is often a not-done job.

The above material illustrates how any school system, if it desires, can incorporate over-all consultative service of the kind directly appropriate to its needs. This kind of intelligent planning and communication makes workable what only seems possible in less thorough and imaginative approaches. The kinds of cooperation needed can only be enlisted by competent people who are skilled in orienting those holding responsible positions so that administrators may become hospitable to new ideas if they serve the purpose better than did the old. We do not know precisely how Dr. Blackwell's program has worked. We hear from him, from time to time, enough to know it is in process and appears to be working most effectively.

To summarize the material from this chapter: Granted that comprehensive consultative services are a useful way to create a healthy climate for learning in the schools, how is putting the service into effect best accomplished?

1. One can come from outside as a separate agency whether supported by the community, grants, or indirectly through mental health clinics, etc. This is a happy way to operate and it works, but it may not fully cover the entire school system.

2. One can be an outside agency or group specifically hired by the school system to do this job, thus keeping existing departments separate from this service. This is a method untried by us but intriguing in its possibilities.

3. One can, as did we, move into a school system as trainers of one group of people who can in time apply these methods as a focal service. This can be done if the difficulties we pointed out are considered and dealt with. It is probably the most likely method. It is also, probably, the most frustrating.

4. One can plan ahead as did Dr. Blackwell, given the support of a Board of Education, given time, and given his skill. In this event, a truly comprehensive service can emerge as a fine example of good community psychiatry and good education.

Any one of these methods of introducing consultation is worth the doing. It is a tool necessary to the healthy growth of a school, its students, and its staff.

Appendix A

Need for Consultation as Expressed by Two Diaries of First-Year Teachers

In the course of our three-year consultation program described in the preceding chapters, we became aware of certain recurring, persistent, unanswered needs that teachers, experienced and inexperienced, skillful or unskillful, had in common. These needs, then as now, are not being met by most present in-service training programs or graduate schools in education. From our material we believe there are four assumptions that underlie in-service training needs of teachers at all levels in all settings. (1) All school personnel, including master teachers and administrators, need some help, support, and consultation at regular intervals. (2) A teacher may have a great deal of factual knowledge and be skillful in the use of some techniques, but may be unable to apply insight and understanding in the classroom. (3) A teacher may have a high degree of understanding and insight but lack the book learning and mastery of teaching skills to do the best job. (4) A teacher may have varying degrees of knowledge and understanding without being able to use one or both attributes to advantage because of her particular professional or personal situation. Each of these four premises is vividly supported in the excerpts from the following diaries.

Concern over the high resignation rate of teaching staff, especially among new teachers, is widespread at a time when teachers are scarce and the need great. The high rate of loss is not explained by salary, marriage, or pregnancy. We have a great deal of data from old and new teachers alike to substantiate the fact that the underlying cause is more likely to be a sense of inadequacy to deal with behavior or discipline problems, a sense of professional isolation, and a lack of support for professional growth. The diaries underline these facts. Consultation appears to be one answer.

In the course of collecting and analyzing our data from daily consultation reports or logs, we collected five diaries of first-year teachers to determine where the needs for in-service training were and how, or if, consultation could help. The diaries were made in five different settings, geographically removed from each other and from the schools in which we consulted. They covered elementary, junior, and senior high schools. Two schools were in extremely low economic areas (both urban), one was rural and suburban, two were lower-middle-class suburban. None of the diarists had any consultation program in their schools or any help from specialists. One had a psychologically sophisticated and strong principal, one had an exceptionally skillful department head. Both were helped by these people, but this did not take the place of the services a consultant could have offered. We gave the diarists one principle to follow: They were told the diaries were useless to us if they were not strictly honest. We wanted their observations, subjective experiences, failures and successes with themselves, their children, colleagues, and superiors. All of the diarists did just that. The two diarists whose selections are included here had by far the most difficult settings—one elementary school and one senior high school, both with a goodly number of slow learners, both with inter-racial problems. Both diarists suffered from culture shock. The high school diary may sound like *Up the Down Staircase* by Bel Kaufman, but it was written before the book, and the similarity derives from the distressing conditions existing in the secondary schools. Both of these talented teachers resigned after their year of teaching. Happily, both returned to teaching after a year's recovery in systems far removed from those in which they had had their first experience, one of which had regular consultations built in.

First Diary

The following excerpts come from a talented young white teacher who unquestionably had the worst experience of any of our diarists. It should be made clear that this teacher chose a slum school in a large recently integrated city. Being devoted to principles of civil rights and inter-racial education, she was pleased to be placed in a school with a large Negro population, though displeased at the de facto distribution: There was no white pupil and she was one of only two white teachers. She had minimal difficulty with her colleagues but a great deal of difficulty with the white principal, who was unpopular with all teachers. The diary might be called "A Principal's Power to Destroy."

Some of the issues in this diary focus on present-day problems: the slow learner, the children of poverty, the verbally disadvantaged, the living together of races, the patterns of child management. The diary delivers the clear message that all groups, minority as well as majority, have remarkable myths about each other which arouse incredulity and surprise and shock in the object of the myth, regardless of race. This young teacher had great humanity, which is not to say that she was not angered, taken aback, and hurt by the irrational myths of Negroes about whites, just as she was indignant over the white irrationalities in relation to Negroes. This culture shock, whether racial, economic, or rural-versus-urban, must be taken into account in school life where people have to live together in order to learn together. Consultation, especially with a consultant who is aware of these problems, could have alleviated some of the strain and made a more ready soil for acceptance and learning on all sides.

January 2

First day back after a long vacation. The school had been cleaned while we were away. The sight was refreshing. My holiday spirit was doused within five minutes. As I walked into the office to sign in, my principal greeted me with "Happy New Year, and before I forget to tell you, you must make plans for taking a reading methods course next semester." I was taken aback when she launched into a discussion of my various deficiencies, and I suppose she meant to be kind when she finished her talk by saying, "You know, I do want you to do well. You are an intelligent girl."

I feel that I should explain my defensive attitude toward this morning's encounter. My principal has often had talks with me about my progress. The result leaves me empty, hurt and somewhat resentful. I find that harsh criticism is often confusing. It results in a reaction more personal than professional. Let me give examples: Today I had playground duty for 12:30–1:00. (Lunch hour is from 12:00 to 1:00.) At 12:25 one of my students came into the classroom in obvious pain from a bloody and swollen lip. She had been "whipped" by one of the boys in the junior high school across the street as she was returning from having lunch at home. My immediate duty was to care for the child, her wound and her upset state. I took my eye from the clock and did what I could to comfort the child. It took a bit of doing. Also, there were five children in the classroom eating their lunch. They had to be supervised at all times, according to the plan of operation. At 12:30 they were to be dismissed for supervised free play. Because of the accident and subsequent veering from the time schedule, we got outside at 12:40, ten minutes late. I took my stand on duty and within three minutes my principal . . . "You have a professional duty to be on time. During the time you were not here an accident could have occurred. The children lunching in your room have been deprived of valuable play time." "But . . ." I said. And she said, "Speak to me after three if you must." My immediate reaction was that of frustration, then resentment, then five boys began fighting and on to the next issue. . . .

January 3   (Issue of the Specialist)

We had a faculty meeting today. I looked forward to it because the speaker was a Reading Expert. I found her talk helpful. She spoke with feeling and obvious knowledge of her subject. She spoke mainly about comprehension of reading. I was especially interested because I have a third-grade class, which, according to special reading tests, is primarily on a pre-primer level. Comprehension is a bad problem with these children. Their level of retention is very low and their attention span rarely exceeds fifteen minutes. This is trying when two forty-minute reading periods are called for. At the end of this talk we were requested to ask questions. I responded by saying that I found my pupils could not use any words they "learned" during reading unless they were in direct reference to the story they were reading at that particular time. As a result, their vocabulary barely increased and new words were forgotten as soon as they went on to the next subject. I explained that I tried to incorporate these "new" words throughout the day no matter what we were working on and made special efforts to play "fun" games with said words. At this point the specialist asked me what techniques I used and commented on "constructive originality." Her main suggestion was that I go even slower with the lessons. I was in the midst of thanking her when my principal began to speak. She said, "Miss B., I noticed that your children responded beautifully the day I put their reading directions on the board. They sat on the edge of their seats with enthusiasm and knew they had to read to get anywhere. Try that. Does anyone else have a question?" Frankly I was ready to walk out. Then I thought maybe I had missed the point of what she was saying. I still have not figured it out. These children cannot read on a pre-primer level, much less directions from a blackboard. I have found that written directions with these children produce confusion and bland expressions. Whether her comment is relevant or not, it just doesn't work that way. Further, the morning she took over my class (while I was at a demonstration) the children related that they had done some arithmetic and had then gone to see two movies in the auditorium. They expressly asked to have reading that afternoon as they had none that day.

January 5

Until recently I had the horrible fear that nothing I was teaching was sticking with my "slow" third-graders (I.Q. range from below 70 to 83).

The first advisory of school, for science, I did a unit on Plants and Animals. This was a failure. I could not strike up interest and acquired results were almost nonexistent. I felt bad about this because my intuition led me to believe that science, because it can be quite dramatic and tangible, would be a good point of contact and gain of knowledge with these (retarded) children.

In preparation for my next unit in science I decided to do some careful fieldwork and planning. My curriculum guide showed a unit on Astronomy. I felt this was one of the most exciting units, but since it included names of planets, abstract concepts, new concepts (for these children), I was hesitant. I almost decided to give up the idea, and then on second thought decided to casually mention some of the planets the next day during science. Bingo! These "slow" learners threw questions at me right and left, wanted to know how to spell certain words (names of planets, gravity, universe, space), and for almost the first time I had the interest of all of them.

The next day they begged for science. I dared not veer from the omnipotent Plan, so I managed to stifle their enthusiasm until after lunch. When the time came I was completely overjoyed to find that on their own volition, three-quarters of the class not only knew all nine planets but knew how to spell their names.

We set up our unit together, lining up what our objectives

were and projects we wanted to do. Since then we have been very successful and these slow third-graders have been working (in science only) on at least a fourth-grade level. (This is amazing when reading levels are on a pre-primer, primer, and first-grade level.)

Today my principal observed in my room. She came in during the middle of science and we had rocketed ourselves into the heart of Uranus. They had already dictated a story about Uranus to me, which I in turn had put on the blackboard. (The children and I had decided to do a story about each planet when we had learned enough about it. This was the sixth week of the unit and we were on the seventh planet.) Each time they orally construct a story I put it on the board. They have eagerly requested to copy the story and make a Planet Book. Since "handwriting" follows science on the Plan, I felt this permissible. When paper was being passed the principal walked in, sat down at my desk, and during her stay walked around, checked over the room, spoke quietly to some of the children, gave me a "dirty" look, and left.

The next time I saw her was at 4:00 as I was checking out. She called across the office (with two other teachers present), "That was a brutal assignment you handed out." I couldn't believe she was speaking to me. When she called me over for a conference, I knew a rise in blood pressure was in store. She ranted about how some teachers kill time with paper work, how they don't check the level of their pupils, and how this deprived the children. I sat there patiently until her spiel ended and then, because I could not contain my feelings of frustration, let her know exactly why I was doing that unit. At this point she began coughing and before I knew it we were talking about the weather.

(Colleagues and Culture Shock)

I get to school early so that I can get the blackboards set up and use the duplicating machine without having to wait in line. This morning when I got to the machine room another teacher was there. I often met her there. This

was just about our only contact. We usually had brief anecdotal exchanges while working the machine. This morning
she said she had heard I had a visitor Friday afternoon. She
was referring to my principal's visit. It seems that being observed by the principal or supervisor is "hot news." She then
went on to say, in no uncertain terms, what she thought of people who observed late on a Friday afternoon. Then she said,
"Sometimes you don't know what to expect from those stupid
white people." She and I realized what she had said at exactly the same time. Then she turned on her heel and left.

I should explain that there are only three "white people"
in the school: the principal, another new teacher, and me.

January 9

"Corporal punishment is forbidden" is one of
the things emphasized for all teachers, new and old.

Because I got a ride back to my school I arrived a bit before
the noon bell had rung. As I walked through my building I
passed a room in which I noted the children were sitting like
angels. There was perfect order, and from what I could hear,
as I stood in amazement, nothing much was going on. I could
hardly believe it. Such order! I had had very little contact
with the teacher in that room but with this display I was determined to get some advice and hints from this teacher.

(The Cost of Order and Quiet)

Since I was not on duty from 12:30 to 1:00, I
went down to visit Mrs. X. She, I knew, had been teaching
for about fifteen years. I was hungry for her advice. I stepped
in and excused myself for disturbing her lunch. (I have found
that at my school teachers hate and resent being bothered
during lunch by either teachers or pupils.) I explained how
impressed I had been with the conduct in her room and admitted that I did have quite a disciplinary problem and would
appreciate her valuable advice. She looked up at me and
said that there was nothing to it. "Nothing to it!" I exclaimed.

To me it was amazing. She said, "Honey, when I say nothing to it, I mean it." I said, "Perhaps it comes with experience." "No," she said. "It's easy. If they act up, take them one by one into the cloakroom and beat the hell out of them; it works every time. Just don't leave marks." I must have shown my shock. Then she said, "Don't worry about getting caught, because it's your word against theirs." I excused myself and left.

January 11   (Teacher-Parent Interview)

Today my principal came into the room at 11:30, just as we were getting ready for our phono-visual game. She called me over to explain that an enraged mother was here about me. She claimed that I had choked and beaten her daughter. My principal suggested that she would take over my class while I spoke to the woman. I was told she was waiting for me, with bated breath, in the clinic. I went in, and there she was, fury fuming. She let go. According to her daughter, I had taken two hands, picked her up by the neck while squeezing, dropped her, and beaten her with a stick. Oddly enough, I was relieved to hear that. It was so extreme that to disprove it on a friendly basis would be easily done.

We talked about it for a while and then I suggested that Melissa (the child) come in and join us. I also suggested that upon the child's entrance I would inform her gently that we wanted the utmost truth. Her mother welcomed the idea. The child stalked in. The air by this time was relaxed, the child was glad to see her mother, etc.

Before I knew what had happened, the child's mother had grabbed her and, as she shook the child violently, screamed at her. I acted as referee and had the child released. There was something a bit too ironic involved.

We quieted down a bit. Melissa came running over to me, grabbed on desperately, and began sobbing. She spoke but I could not distinguish her words. Soon the sobbing subsided and she apologized to me for "telling a story." "Miss B., I'm sorry. Miss B., on the way home James beat me up. I told my mother you did it. I'm sorry, I'm sorry." I told her it was all right and dismissed her. Upon her exit her mother said, "I'm going to beat that girl." She apologized to me. I asked her if she would let me handle the situation. She was grateful and said, "Miss B., anytime you want that child, she's yours."

January 16

I had sent a note home to a mother whose child was acting intolerably in class. Having had no contact with the woman, it was my hope that through our combined efforts we could help solve some of the youngster's disciplinary problems. I wrote a note to that effect. As I have learned, unless I ask for the parent's signature on the note, and to have it returned, it will hardly reach its destination.

The next day no signed note appeared. At lunchtime I asked Jessamine where it was. She told me her mother didn't want to sign my "old note." I asked if she had read it. "Yes, Miss B., she read it and she didn't like it neither." I said something to the effect that no parent wants to hear that her daughter has been misbehaving. "No, Miss B., my mother doesn't like you. She called you something bad." I could imagine what it was, so I tried veering from that angle—to no avail. "Miss B., my mother said you was a stupid white shit." I hardly had time for a reaction, when she continued: "But I told her I didn't think you was stupid."

January 17

Two supervisors visit our building—one for the upper grades and one for the lower grades. We can expect them at least once a month without fail. Some teachers claim that they have not been visited yet.

I have been told by many teachers that when the supervisor comes into the room, first continue what you are doing as if no one had appeared—ignore her presence. However, there was one suggestion given by the majority and that was "Keep going on, but smile, honey, smile."

January 18 (*Slow Learner*)

Today the reading specialist came into my room to speak to me briefly. A few weeks ago all teachers were requested to submit the names of those children who needed special help in reading. I submitted the names of nine children. When the reading specialist appeared she requested the I.Q.'s of the children I had recommended to her. She claimed she had tested these children and could hardly believe the results, hence she wanted to know more about them. I showed her the cumulative records. She said that if she hadn't tested these children herself she wouldn't have believed it. She told me she could not spend time on those "worthless" cases. I said, "If you can't work with them, can you suggest something for me do do?" She said, "Honey, I'm so busy testing now. Maybe when I'm through I can help." She then went on to tell me to be sure to keep a list of the names of the children in my room. She said, "Ten years from now you'll see their faces in the newspaper and they'll be held up in jail for the biggest crimes in this area." With that she began laughing and saying she had never seen such a "homely" bunch. Her parting words were: "Good luck to you, honey. You need it!"

Tuesday, January 23 (*Culture Shock*)

Today I had nine children staying for lunch; they were sitting in groups of three. I was sitting at my desk doing some paper work. Each group of children had a different conversation going. One group was talking about how "nasty" Ted's mother was, another about snow, and a third about television. I was hardly paying attention until someone yelled out, "That dirty white doctor!" Then I listened. The children all merged conversation and a great buzz and chatter went on about a program many of them had seen the night before. Apparently it was a program about health research and the topic was eye disease. The children said it was "all in the hospital." Then they talked about white doctors killing babies and lifting their eyes open when they (the babies) wanted them closed. Then one said, "My mama says white peoples is murderers." Another said, "You know the truth too." A third started to whisper and they all got into a huddle. Then two of them came up to me and the bolder of the two said, "Miss B., do you kill babies?" I said no. Then one of the children, sitting down, said to another, "I guess she ain't all white."

January 25

At 3:00 today the rain was pouring down. Not all of the children came to school equipped for such weather. I decided to hold back the children with no coats, boots, or hats until the rain subsided. The children didn't seem to mind. While they were waiting in the room a few asked if they could do some odds and ends. I said I'd be happy to have them help and we had quite a cheerful time dusting and washing boards and cleaning up in general. By 3:30 the rain had stopped and, just as I was about to tell the children to get ready to go, a parent, whom I had never seen before, came in to get John. I introduced myself to her politely and this was her response in front of about ten children: "You whites will use us niggers to clean up all you got no matter how you go about doing it." I started to tell her that these boys and girls were not equipped to go out in that downpour and had volunteered their help. She interrupted me by saying, "Don't tell me. I knows how you whites operate. You get on us niggers and ride our backsides off. Come on, John. Get yourself out of here. I'm gonna wop you for staying in here."

January 26

Today the children were dismissed at 12:15. From then until 3:30 we teachers were to tally up our roll books, as it was the last day of the semester. The roll books must be absolutely accurate. The figures from each book are combined to make the building report. There are many cross-checks for accuracy and an error shows up as a crime. For each child you must figure each of the following: sessions enrolled, sessions attended, sessions absent, sessions tardy. After this is figured you get a total for each category, which in turn goes on the Teachers' Report to the Superintendent.

Each teacher has a checker and is a checker. My "partner" is an experienced teacher (by that I mean that she has been doing reports like this for fifteen years). We began our work at 12:30 and were through by 1:15. We were all given a list of things to do if we finished our books early, so there were few idle moments.

At one point I walked down the hall to speak to a teacher. She had a visual-aids guide I wanted to borrow. She was sitting and eating lunch with four other teachers. She asked if I had my roll book completed. I told her I had. I asked her the same. As I asked, a giggle began from all the room. I asked what was funny. She said she could tell I was a new teacher because I had waited until today to do my book. Without thinking I said I didn't know how it could be done earlier since it included today's attendance. She said, "If you want them absent, mark them absent; if you want them present, mark them present. If they're tardy that's less time to worry with them. Don't mark it though, it's one less column to add." She went on to say that her roll book included today just like mine only it was completed two weeks ago. "Catch on, honey. That's the way to move in this system."

Tuesday, January 30

I had a beautiful experience today. I wish I could relate the feeling I had. Larry came into school early. He wanted to help pass out papers and get the room set up. He told me that it was his birthday last weekend and that his "father" had given him five dollars. Larry lives with guardians, as his father is unknown and his mother has been institutionalized. He refers to his guardians as parents; they seem to take good care of him. He is always clean and, though a devil, knows how to be polite and sweet. Larry had just celebrated his tenth birthday.

I asked Larry what he had done with his money. He said

he spent one dollar and was saving four. He asked me if I would hold it for him. I, of course, said that I would. Larry then showed me what he had purchased with his dollar: a set of fish models and a model skin-diver. I admired them. Then he said when he bought it he hid it under his bed because he didn't want his "mother" to see it when she was home over the weekend. He said he was going to play with it when he got home from school each day because she would be at work. He went on: "I got home on Monday and it wasn't there. I didn't know where it was till later." I said, "Where was it?" He said, "Miss B., that night my mother gave me a present at supper for my birthday. Miss B., she gave me my own fish set." I said, "What did you do?" He said, "Miss B., I thanked her and pretended I never saw it before. She ain't got much money, Miss B., and we just let her think she bought it." I almost cried. I looked at him and said, "Larry, you are the sweetest little man I know." He said, "Miss B., you is something!" I said, "So are you!" Larry began passing papers.

Friday, February 2   (A Special Problem)

I have a child in my room whom I feel is definitely a candidate for psychiatric aid. She is probably the most hostile little girl I have seen. Lisa and I have been working together since September. She shows signs of progress only because she has made a conscious and mature effort toward improving herself.

Today Lisa asked if she might stay after school to help with straightening out the room. I welcomed her. There were two other children here also. By 3:30 their chores were completed and I excused them. Lisa claimed she wanted to see me privately. I told her to wait until the others had left. Then I went over to her; she was sitting at her desk. She beckoned as I approached. When I was standing right over her, as she apparently wanted, instantaneously she pulled a large rock out of her desk and dropped it on my foot. Before I could wink she was gone.

I wasn't exactly sure how to handle this but I thought I

would play it by ear on Monday. Lately Lisa has been sweet to me and this last note was a surprise.

(Monday) Today before I could even say "Good morning," Lisa threw the attached note at me. I think it explains itself. "I want to see if you be my friend   you are"

February 7   (Faculty Meeting)

Most of our faculty meetings have a specific topic or are conducted by a "specialist" of some sort. The meetings begin at 3:15 and are over between 4:00 and 4:30.

At our meeting today there was no special speaker. Our principal began by telling us, "Today is a fortunate day for those who thought they'd be here late. I have only a few announcements and we'll be through . . . fini."

I can't begin to count how many words were spoken but so many pertained to almost nothing. The predominant characteristic was redundancy. To make a long story short, we were there until 4:45 and our principal was the only one to speak.

February 8   (Violence as Discipline)

I dismissed most of my children at 3:00 today, though about six children voluntarily remained to complete some things which had to be done around the room. We were working on a bulletin board. Suddenly there was the hair-raising scream of a child. Next there was a sound of a slashing whip and another such scream. My children and I dropped what was in our hands and ran to the classroom door. The noises continued and sounded as if they were coming from the teachers' room. I ran to the room and tore open the door. There was a child screaming, a strange woman, and a teacher . . . I was asked to leave and the teacher came toward me as if to back me up and shut the door. I refused. I said that woman was to hand over the whip to me or I would send for the police. She dropped the whip to the floor. The child ran to me and literally clung with all her might. She had huge welts on her arms and legs. I took her out into the corridor and asked what was happening. The strange woman was the child's mother, who claimed she beat her because she "weren't no good in school." I told her that if she knew what was good for her she'd take the child home and care for her. She promised she would. I then told the teacher that unless she wanted serious action taken that had better never happen again. She said she hadn't touched the child. I told her in no uncertain terms that that would not save her job. She broke down and cried and said she didn't know why she had let that happen. She promised to go to the child's house on her way home to make sure the child was all right, and if any more danger seemed likely, to take the child away to officials. She cried and cried and promised she would do what she could. She also promised this would never happen again and thanked me for intervening.

I went back to my room and calmed myself down by calming my six frightened, crying children.

February 12

At lunchtime Bill asked me if he could get me some lunch from the store. I told him I would love a Dixie cup of vanilla ice cream. He was delighted, then he looked puzzled. "Miss B., they come in two sizes"—one was small, the other large. I told him I'd like the large. I gave him a quarter and told him he could have a nickel of the change for himself. He said, "Miss B., I am going to get you the best ice cream there is." I thanked him and off he went. About twenty minutes passed. Bill hadn't returned and was cutting off his eating time. Then he appeared with a large shopping bag and a smile from ear to ear. He had a wonderful twinkle in his eye and was obviously overjoyed and bursting to share his delight. "Bill, what in the world have you got in that huge bag?" He laughed and laughed and told me to close my eyes. I did. There was a great rustling, giggling, a big kiss on my cheek, and a clatter of running feet. I opened my eyes and there, on my desk, was Bill's delight and surprise—a half gallon of ice cream.

February 13

We were having a relay race today during recess. One of my children suddenly yelled, "Miss B., someone just threw a milk carton out of the window." There on the playground was an empty milk carton. I looked up to see where it could have possibly come from. Hardly had I raised my head when "Crash!" I got a full milk carton on the head which dropped to the ground with a substantial splash and I was half covered with milk. Another teacher was sharing the playground. I asked him if he wouldn't mind taking my children up with him. He agreed.

One of my children pointed to the second-floor window from which the loaded missile was heaved. I had a splitting headache. I made a bee-line for the second floor. I located the room but it was empty. I went next door. It was empty also. They were all at recess in the central playground.

I was quite upset. It was a combination of physical pain and, for many reasons, hurt feelings and also the feeling of "what do I do from here?" I went to the office. The principal was not there. She was due back in ten minutes. "Please tell her I would appreciate it if she would come up to my room. I consider it an emergency."

Twenty minutes later she appeared. "Miss B., an emergency?" I said, "Yes." "Well, before we talk let's get the trash up off the floor." I was stunned. All I said was, "Would you please watch my class for a minute?" I left, went into the teachers' room, and had a good cry. I came back. She said quite curtly, "Miss B., I don't understand." I said, "Yes, I know, thank you anyway."

I need not go into the frustration and humiliation of that. I decided it would be much easier to handle the situation as I saw best. I spoke to the teacher who used the designated room. She found the culprit and sent him in. I told him he was to go straight home at lunchtime and get his mother. He did. His mother was very upset about this, gentle and cooperative. She explained, "Joe just doesn't like white people." Then she said, "I don't mind you whites but my boy, he does."

I felt I should give my principal an explanation. Honestly speaking, I never wanted to see her again. I have learned that procedure is procedure and if wind of this had gotten back to her without my explanation things would get sticky (stickier?). I walked into the office at 12:45. She was eating lunch.

"Miss Farmer, excuse me."

"Certainly, but aren't you on duty?"

"No, I'm not."

"Are you sure?"

"Thank you."

EXIT

February 14

This morning during arithmetic we were finally getting somewhere. We were looking at various concepts of "ten" which is a "must" for the children to learn. The lesson was going well. Roseanne decided she didn't feel like working. How did I find this out? She simply stood up and announced it. This brought down everything and the lesson was shot. I assigned the follow-up work and, while the children were busy, took Roseanne to the side. She was belligerent and nasty, disrespectful and totally unresponsive in any positive sense. When she cockily told me that she couldn't stand me or my room, I asked if she would rather go next door for a while. This incident had thrown me a bit and her attitude clashed with any ideas of progress. She went next door and frankly it was a relief. The teacher next door is a strong person and has told me I could send any problem over to him. This is a reciprocal understanding. We are supposed to send problem children to the office but I am frankly disgusted with that policy. The children love to go to the office. Their principal gives them all kinds of fun games to play and sends them around with messages from room to room.

At lunchtime (ha!) I was having a conference with the psychologist about my friend Lisa. In came my principal. She was angry and started yelling at me from the door, that is how I knew she was there. Roseanne had reported that the other teacher had slapped her. The mother had called. I was told (in front of five children and the psychologist) that sometimes I didn't have the brains God gave me, that all children should be sent to her, that I had an easy class and had a nerve loading my problems onto any other teacher. Her final words were, "When Roseanne comes in send her to me, and you had better watch your step."

The psychologist looked at me and I at her. I was on the verge of tears from frustration. She said, "Some people will kick a dying dog." She left. The 1:00 bell rang. Children returned. Roseanne's older brother came in threatening to "break your neck."

February 20

Melissa came up to my desk crying, crying, crying. She could hardly speak. It was such a sad cry that if she hadn't started speaking the tears would have come to my eyes. She told me that some child told her she had "dirty ol' bubble-gum clothes." I really try to keep up with the phrases but that was one on me. It was obviously the height of insult, though. I asked Melissa to try to be more specific and tell me why he had said that. She reported that the boy picked on her ("He's meddlin' with me"); her sweater was torn and ripped at the neck. I had a bag of some small items I no longer needed and among them was a white cotton collar to snap around the neck over a sweater. I told Melissa to close her eyes, that I had a surprise for her. When Melissa saw the collar she actually changed from a pauper to a princess.

"Miss B., you white teachers are wonderful. I'm so glad you are my teacher."

February 26　(Parent and Culture Shock)

Today we got out of school at 11:00 for the Col. J. Glenn parade. At 11:15 one of my children came upstairs crying her eyes out. I tried to calm her down and her story was this: Her mother had said she wanted to kill all the white people she could. She said the parade was for a white man and "all the niggers" were left out in the rain. She said she first wanted to kill her daughter's teacher (me) because I was white and was sending the "niggers" out in the rain while I stayed in the "nice warm school."

My little girl said she did not care if her mother killed all the white people, but she didn't want her to kill me. "Miss B., I tried to tell her you was good to us and was like a nigger yourself."

March 1   (Problem Pupils)
I have playground duty this week from 12:30 to 1:00.

This morning I had a great deal of trouble with one of my "problem" pupils, Lisa, whom I have already written about on February 2. Lisa's actions in class this morning were intolerable and made classroom living and learning most unfortunate and uncomfortable. She continued to "meddle" with all of those around her, was belligerent, and refused to do her work. She demanded attention and, at times when she had more trouble than usual getting it from me and her peers, she threw jars against the wall, sang, ran around the room, and kicked spare chairs around.

I would have called for help from the office but I find that aid most ineffective. Any child I've ever sent to the office for bad behavior has been next seen delivering messages from room to room. As a result, the children, either knowing directly or by report, love going to the office.

Somehow, we made it until noon, though my nerves felt shattered. At noon I tried speaking to Lisa. She would not utter a word. Since I had duty in a few minutes (and God help the teacher late for duty!) and since Lisa hadn't had any lunch, I dismissed her to get something to eat. Then she spoke. "No one is home and there ain't no food." I gave her some change and sent her on her way. I went on to duty. At about ten minutes before one, three of my girls came running up to me as if a tiger were pursuing their hides. "Miss B., watch out! Lisa has a knife. It's real big and she said she's gonna slit you up." I saw Lisa watching the report eagerly from around the corner. I beckoned Lisa to me. She came with no hesitation. I hadn't said a word when Lisa blurted out, "I ain't gonna slit you up, Miss B." (When this was reported Lisa was not within hearing distance. Her immediate reaction told me she had a knife and some intention—remote or no, passing or not.) I calmly and simply said, "Lisa, may I please have the knife?" She looked all around her, obviously uneasy with so many of her peers about. I said we could go in if she wanted. She said she did. We walked in, Lisa stomping her feet and muttering. We had just gotten inside the building when along came my principal. She said, "What's the trouble?" I didn't want to say first, "Lisa has a knife," because that is far from complete, so I said, "Lisa and I are solving some problems." I hoped that this answer would be bland enough so that Lisa and I could handle this unaccompanied. I've been working hard with Lisa and felt that I could handle this without bringing in others. Lisa trusts me and I felt that she was confused enough. My principal then said curtly, "Miss B., you have duty this week, don't you?" I said I had. She said, "Then get out there! I'll take Lisa." I said I could handle it. She said, "Obviously not, if you can't even take the responsibility of noon-time duty!"

Again, I can't express my humiliation. This is the second day in a row of this. I've never been so discouraged.

March 2

As I wrote yesterday, Lisa had been taken out of my hands and I didn't see her for the rest of the day. As is par for the course, she spent the afternoon delivering messages, which is a thrill for these children.

This morning Lisa appeared. She came into the room and as she entered "tripped" by my desk and fell. I mark "tripped" because the floor was clear. I ran over to help her

up. She said, "That's all right, Miss B., I don't care if I dies."
She then ran out to the cloakroom. When the bell sounded
she came in and sat at her desk. She didn't do a bit of work
but was relatively quiet. She drew pictures and looked
through library books.

At noon I went to the office to check my mail, as I didn't
have a chance earlier that morning. In my mailbox was a note.
I am sure my principal requested having it written because
it sounds too stilted for a note from the Lisa I know. My principal has not said a word to me about it. It galls me as I feel
that in an issue like this there should be consultation and
communication. I resent this. No contact about the issue, just
humiliation, which far from solves anything.

The note read: "Miss B.

                I am sorry that I would not give you the
                Knife to you.
                from Lisa Bernice Taylor"

Today I went to have a conference with my principal at
12:30 about Lisa.

I told her the reason I wanted to speak to her was that Lisa
and I had worked hard together, and I wanted to know what
action had been taken or would be taken concerning the episode with the knife. My principal had just about kicked me
out of the office when it happened and made no mention of
ever communicating with me about it. When I told her why
I had come she drew back and said that it was over and done
with, but if I wanted to get the parents in I could. She then
asked me if I knew the *real* reason Lisa had the knife. I told
her I felt I did know the real reason, as Lisa had revealed it
without my asking her. She then launched into a tirade, the
gist of which being that teachers are "just too busy to seek the
truth" and are too ready to condemn the children.

The story she had heard was that Lisa saw a young child
with a knife, about to cut himself. "Lisa was brave enough to
save and protect the child." I asked where she got this story.

She said, "From Lisa, of course." I later asked Lisa about this story, which had changed her from devil to angel. She said, "It wasn't true but Miss Farmer likes stories."

March 6   (Parent-Teacher Interview)

I have mentioned Mrs. C., Jessamine's mother, on January 16. Since last meeting we have had three involved conversations. She has changed radically (thank God). She keeps in touch with me and I with her. I never dreamed this would be possible since she and I had had such miserable run-ins.

Four days ago I sent a note home to Mrs. C., telling her that Jessamine had been causing trouble in the classroom. The next day Mrs. C. was at my door ready to "kill that child" for disturbing one of my classes. Then she asked me how I felt about children playing together and if that helped them to work together. I said I believed that there was definite correlation. She said, enthusiastically, that she wanted to help me and thought of starting a sewing club to promote playing and working together. I couldn't believe my ears. This very same woman, a matter of weeks ago, had literally threatened my life. Somehow, through our conferences, a tremendous change was made.

To get back: The next day Jessamine reported that her mother was getting a note ready for me and today I received the following:

"Dear Miss B. I am Sorry to have to keep Jessamine out of school but it cannot be helped. What we were talking about Friday. I will be up there Tuesday or Wednesday and find out how many girls that I can get to come and try and learn."

March 8

During recess today we played a relay game. The bell rang and, as we were getting into line, a child from another room smashed into me and half crushed my right foot. It was an accident to be sure, but (unfortunately) when the child immediately turned around and gave me a very "dirty" look, I had suspicions about it. There was more than met the eye involved. I pursued the young man (I knew his name, as he has quite a vivid reputation). His immediate reaction was "I did nothing to you." This was ridiculous. He had looked back and given a deliberate reaction. I explained that I knew it was an accident, but we should excuse ourselves when we *see* that we have hurt someone. His reaction, and I'll never forget the venomous emotion and the spite displayed: "I ain't sorry to your white face for nothing." At this point his teacher yelled for him and that ended that, except for the look he gave me as he turned the corner.

March 9   (Supervisor Support—Like Aspects of Good Consultation)

This morning my principal approached me and said, "Miss B., I do not like what has been going on in your room, and since Miss G. will be here I'm going to send her up to straighten the situation up." I tried to ask her what she was referring to when she said, "What was going on in your room," but she is a busy lady and cannot be kept from her duties.

I inquired about Miss G., and it seems that she is in charge of a corps of supervisors and has a great deal to do with the Elementary School Curriculum. I was a bit edgy about the whole thing, I must admit. Actually I was frightened. I anticipated her arrival all morning, but she never came. I was beginning to feel a bit relieved after our lunch hour when suddenly she appeared, standing in my doorway. I have no idea how long she had been there. I walked over to her, extended my hand, and she said, "Miss B., the working climate in your room is lovely and your room certainly seems to reflect the many interests of your children. I'm so happy to see this."

I thanked her and told her how much I appreciated the kind things she had said. She said, as she left, "The thanks goes to you."

March 12   (Contrast)

Unbelievable—the entire incident, that is. This morning we had a good arithmetic lesson. There was good response and something was definitely accomplished. After the lesson I have some follow-up work to be done by each child at his seat. We had just gotten into that when my principal came into the room with a new child. I had just finished walking around the room, checking the written work as it was being done, and at this exact moment was walking back to my desk to put the Bible on it. I had forgotten to return it earlier. The conversation went like this (by the way, the new child was left standing in the middle of the room):

"Miss B., you have no business back at your desk. You can't just pile written work on these children and call that teaching."

"Miss Farmer, we just finished our oral lesson with our books."

"Are you sure?"

"Yes, I am sure."

"Miss B., you have no business of your own to do during school time. There is no excuse for you being at your desk."

"Miss Farmer, I had just checked the progress of the papers and, on my way around, dropped the Bible off on my desk."

"Miss B., I don't want to hear your alibis. No supervisor would fall for that either. Now, I haven't got the time for this. Here is your new girl" ... blah, blah, blah.

March 16   (The Role of the Specialist)

The art specialist, a visiting teacher, made her rounds today. It so happened that all of our bulletin boards were up to date and were, to be frank, quite attractive. We have a bulletin board for each of our different areas of study.

Some teachers put up the boards themselves. I choose to do it with the children, my part being guidance. When a new board goes up, the children can take honest pride in "their" work, for their work is genuinely on display. We have fun with the boards and the children like to decorate their own room.

The art specialist stepped in. I had once signed up to have her give my class a lesson but, as it was a complete fiasco, I never signed up for her again. However, there she was. She walked right in, meandered about the room, and said that no room should display more than one "art medium" at a time. I didn't quite get the phrase and asked her what she meant. She went around in circles, flinging in nasty cracks as she went along. She went on and on. I was getting more and more angry, as I was in the midst of an important lesson and was in no frame of mind, after ten minutes of her insults, to be polite. She finally looked ready to stop and said, "Also, Miss B., the basic color combinations in here are dreadful. Room 13 must be color-blind." I got furious and though it was tactless and disrespectful, I said: "The day I want *your* views on aesthetics I'll call for you. Until that time, kindly leave my room." God knows how far my words will go and what the results will be.

March 20

Today at about 2:00 I heard a huge crash and then the shattering of glass. I was in my room with the children, who became startled. Our doors were closed, so I went to open them and see what had happened.

Standing in the cloakroom of the now vacant room across the hall were two boys. The other classes in my wing had gone down to the rest room. I stepped across the hall to see what had happened and if anyone was hurt. Just as I approached I heard that familiar clicking of heels and knew my principal was nearby. I continued my investigation and after finding no one was hurt I called the boys into my room. As we crossed the hall, there she stood. She took a look at me, shook her head negatively, pursed her lips, and then said at the front of my classroom, "Boys and girls, the next time Miss B. leaves her class we'll have to give her a bad report card, won't we?" She glared at me as she spoke. The children must have sensed something and, flatly, together replied: "No, Miss Farmer."

March 22   (*Home and School*)

One of my children has been absent for four days. None of the children had seen him for all the days he had been gone. I was a bit concerned and sent a note to his home with one of the children living on his street.

I got a note back from the child's mother the next day which said, "Mind you God Dam Business."

I submitted a report to the attendance officer but, before receiving her findings, the child returned with a thick bandage on his head. I immediately asked what had happened. He told me his mama told him not to dare tell me. Later in the day he said, "Do you promise you won't tell Mama if I tell you?" I promised him, then he said, "My mama had a party with them rough men, and the next time I woke up I had this white thing on my head."

Luckily it was the doctor's day at school and I sent him in. Truly, the child had been hit over the head with something at least as heavy as a baseball bat.

March 27

I met with my principal today during lunch. She came up to my room and started off by saying that according to my plan book she saw I had been working on "borrowing" for well over a week. She said that when she took my class she was horrified to see that not one knew how to borrow. I tried many times to stop her and tell her we were *not* working on subtraction at all, but on "carrying in addition." I couldn't get through; that line was busy. She went off into a tirade on how weak I was in teaching arithmetic and how the children had been so terribly deprived. She said, "Only one thing to your credit: They know their addition very well." Then she said, "Most of them are repeaters though and probably learned that last year." At that point I got furious. I really stamped my foot and half-yelled, "Wait a minute." She stopped short. I told her that if she cared to look at my plan book again she would see it said we had been working on "carrying in addition" and not "borrowing in subtraction." I also said these children came to me not knowing the first thing about "carrying," and that is why I had spent a week on it. I opened my plan book and very deliberately pointed to the word "carrying" each time it appeared. "Excuse me," she said, and left.

March 29   (Problems)

Another story about Lisa: It all began at 1:30 when Lisa pinched the child behind her. I just caught the recoil of her hand, and the next thing I knew there was a raging fight. The two girls tore at each other mercilessly. To give a better idea of the forces involved, in breaking the fight up my stockings were run, my dress torn, and my hair, piled atop my head, gradually slid down the side of my face. Lisa had a scratch on the side of her face (bleeding slightly) and May found she was missing a nicely plaited braid which lay on the floor, as a result of which she had a miserable headache and a raw spot on her head.

As calmly as possible, I separated the howling ladies, one on this side of the room and one on the other, clear across the way. Next, May raced toward Lisa, Lisa ducked, and in so doing tapped Martin (the most temperamental, defensive, and disturbed child in my class). He jumped up and, before I could run, had pounded Lisa onto the floor and had lifted a chair. Luckily I caught it, yelled for the male teacher next door, and it literally took the two of us to separate them. I had never seen such a fight in my life. They weren't yelling or muttering at each other, but growling and using "sophisticated dirty tactics" toward each other, each aware of sexual sensitivities.

(Attempt to Communicate)

At 3:00 I related this incident to my principal, who sat there quietly and took in every word. Her first comment: "Well, Miss B., you should have known better than to let a male teacher near Lisa." My mouth dropped. She then said she'd bring in a psychology book on male-female hostilities. I picked myself up and between my teeth muttered, "Good afternoon."

March 30

The teacher next door has been out of school for three days, and today is the fourth. The children have gone absolutely wild. This afternoon I literally rescued the substitute. Furniture was being thrown around the room, all were yelling and screaming, the substitute was being maltreated, name-calling no respect, the target for chalk, pencils, and crayons. I walked in to try to help; the substitute was almost in tears. I told her to go into my room and I would calm them down. This gesture took time and effort, but after twenty minutes the children were "down." I went back to my room and the substitute went back to hers. Within two minutes the children were completely wild again. I asked the substitute if she wanted me to send for the principal. She wanted me to and claimed she was going to walk out. I sent my messenger down to the office, asking the principal to please come up. I received the following reply:

"Miss B. You mind your class and let the substitute mind hers. I'm sure she can manage on her own."

April 10   (Contrast: Principal and Supervisor)

Today my principal observed in my room for well over an hour. I find it a most unpleasant ordeal. I guess I find it so displeasing because I hate and dread the conference which will follow. She'll talk, and I'll listen while gnashing my teeth because of her condescending and negative approach.

Luckily it didn't happen that way because she caught me in the hall during lunchtime. So, instead of stretching her complaints into an hour's session, she compressed it into ten juicy, detestable minutes. To make a long story short, she didn't like a damn thing she saw, including my manner, my way with the children, my procedure. I guess that doesn't leave much.

While she was there I had had an arithmetic lesson on "carrying" in addition. She said she didn't see how even an intelligent adult could have understood from my "methods approach." I told her I had checked the follow-up work the children had done, and maybe three or four out of thirty-three had a couple of errors in the work they did on their own. She told me I had better start facing both truth and facts. She turned on her heel, and I stood there as she plodded down the hall.

April 11

I had an enlightening experience today. My supervisor stepped in at precisely the time my principal had yesterday. She saw almost the same work being done and, at the end of the arithmetic lesson, asked me to give the children a bit of extra seat-work to do so we could talk. I did so.

She did most of the talking and gave me high, high praise. She said she knew I loved the children, and she could feel their sense of freedom and their love for me. She told me I had a rare gift with children, that the lesson was beautifully conveyed, and I could not have been more precise. I felt like telling her that only twenty-four hours ago I was condemned for the exact lesson. She went on and on. It embarrasses me to write her high praise any more. About fifteen minutes of this and she left. As she stepped out she said, "Miss B., may I thank you for an encouraging and heartening hour and a half. Please call on me for anything you might need."

April 12

Today my principal told me she had heard excellent reports from my supervisor yesterday. She told me she was very pleased to hear the news but also added that supervisors come in at tricky times. Rarely is it a good hour; frequently it is a bad hour. She laughed, then she added, "You were lucky." I looked at her, smiled, and left.

April 12

I can't help showing off the experience I had today. There are parts ... one is that of my principal and the other is that of a child in my room, Jane Lov. The only part my principal knows is her own and the only part Jane knows is her own. I know them both and now will relate them.

Today at lunchtime my principal asked me how a child in my room was doing. She wanted to know about Jane. This child was entered in my room perhaps six to eight weeks ago. I said she was doing very well and was indeed an "added" pleasure to my room. I went on to praise her manners and cleanliness and to tell of her fast and positive adjustment in my class. My principal kept a skeptical eye on me, and I sensed trouble of some sort. Then it came out: "Miss B., I want the truth about Jane." That bothered my integrity a bit and I said, "I have given you the truth." I admit my tone was not too pleasant. "Well," says she, "the children report you've beaten her." I said, "Miss Farmer, I can only tell you what I know. Jane and I are far from in conflict in our relationship." Says she, "I hope you are speaking the truth." She walked away.

The bell rang. I went back to my room and we carried on until 3:00. At this time Jane asked if I would please read something she had worked on during her free time this morning. This is what it said:

To Miss B.

  Look inside

  please

For me

  I like Miss B. she is Kind and true so Every day I look at her she is Kind and gay I like Miss B. I no you do too.

    And now

    My story

    is all

    told

  I like you Miss B.

    I like you

April 17

My principal sat in my room for forty solid minutes. The only indication I could derive from her reactions were negative nods every so often.

As she was leaving she said, "I know one Miss who will be unhappy on rating day."

April 18

"Miss B., your vacation is coming up soon. I hope you are not planning to go anywhere. You have plenty of planning to do. Remember your rating."

"Thank you for your suggestion, Miss Farmer. I am leaving but will manage to get some work in."

April 19

Today was the last day of school and tomorrow Easter vacation begins. As I left the building today at 3:30, my principal took me by the arm and said, "Miss B., there are two courses at summer school which are a must for you. Where will you take them? One is Arithmetic Methods and the other is Phono-Visual Methods."

Between my teeth I told her I would think about it *now* that I was on my vacation.

Thank God for Easter!

After Easter

The children bring in their money for cookies every day. Though milk time is at 10:30, they ask me if I will hold their money for them. Also, some ask me to hold their lunch money.

This morning I had exactly forty-five cents in change. I was quite busy and put it on top of my desk only for ten minutes. When I went to put it in my wallet, it was gone.

I went to the front of the room and told the children that I wanted their help, that I had lost forty-five cents, which is a lot of money, and I would be very happy if they could help me find it.

Nothing turned up all day. At 3:30 the children were dismissed. I had clerical work to do and stayed after school to do it. At 3:30 on the dot I heard a shuffling in the cloakroom. I went to see who it might be. There was Johnnie, one of my boys. He looked terribly embarrassed and edgy. I thought I knew what was up, and I wanted to help Johnnie be honest. I told him I was happy to see him and asked him if he would straighten the chairs out in the room. He smiled and began. I continued my work. Suddenly, there he was next to me, his hand on my arm. "Miss B., I have something for you—here!" and with a grand gesture, forty-five cents was produced. Says Johnnie: "I found it earlier today but wanted to wait and wait so you would have a nice surprise to go home with." I put my hand in his, thanked him, and before I knew it he had flown.

This morning I walked into this:

"Miss B., you give me a solid headache."

"Miss Farmer, what have I done?"

"I'm busy now."

I felt badly at noon today. I know I took that incident out on my children. The woman galls me at times. This time especially.

May

We had our class party today. I provided most of the goodies, save for a few the children had brought in. After the party was over, Lisa came up to me and handed me a bag. She told me to open it up, which I did. Inside was an apron. "Miss B., I don't want you to get your party dresses dirty when you work at this school."

May

"Miss B., do you believe in the Kingdom of God?"

"Why do you ask?"

"My mama says only us 'Negras' go to heaven. My mama says the Devil's white, and he takes in all them ol' white folks."

"What white folks?"

"He takes in all them crackers, that's all them white folks."

"Will he take me?"

"I don't think so, Miss B., I hardly know you is white!"

May   (Culture Shock—and Information)

"Miss B., where are you going this summer?"

I asked Lucy why she wanted to know. Lucy was an amazing child all year. She never once did a thing wrong, did all of her work, and was always sweet and kind. She said she wanted to know where I would be so that she could visit me. I told her I was going to be far away, in Maine. She simply shook her head and left.

The next day Lucy came up to me sadly and said she found out where Maine was. Then she said, "Maine is in the North and there ain't no niggers there."

May   (Handling Larry)

Larry was absent yesterday. Today, when he showed up, grinning like a Cheshire cat and with clean white tennis shoes on, I knew exactly why we hadn't seen him.

I have written about Larry before. He's a sweet, lovable child. He's got a twinkle in his eyes, a beautiful smile, and is a little devil. I jokingly call him Mr. Bullfrog sometimes, because when he gets righteous he swells himself up and beams.

I asked Larry why he was absent yesterday. "Miss B.," he said (and there stood Mr. Bullfrog!) "I, I couldn't make it to school yesterday because, well, because, if you wants the truff . . . I, I, well I had a heart attack."

I looked at Larry and he at me, and we both suddenly roared. I couldn't have kept a straight face if I tried. He knew exactly the situation. Then I pulled him over to me and whispered in his ear, "I'm awfully glad someone thought of getting you tennis shoes as a get-well present." He looked at me and a great grin came over his face. Then he said: "Shoot, a man can't get away with nothin' these days."

May　*(Principal and Crisis)*

Two children got into a terrible fight in our classroom. I grabbed one of them. The child was absolutely hysterical. He called me a "big fat white motha." I grabbed him by the arm and sat him down. He grabbed at me and then spit. I took him by both arms and sat him down. I sent one of my children to get Miss Farmer. She came about twenty minutes later. By this time the child was sobbing bitterly. I had my hand on his shoulder patting it. She had barely entered the room when she yelled out, "The School System forbids any teacher to spit on or to attack a child."

I said, "Miss Farmer, that was not the situation."

She said, "Let's forget it. Your teaching efforts aren't worth the talk."

I said, "Miss Farmer, it is fortunate for both you and me that I am using will power." She stalked out.

I had a visit from one of my children's mothers today. She said she had to hurry but had one favor to ask. It was: If her child passed or failed she didn't care, just so he didn't have another white teacher. She said she didn't want to be mean but it was bad for her child to be "mixing." She said, "The people been kept together for a long time and there ain't no need to start trouble now."

(Resignation)

Yesterday I told my principal that I was resigning from the School System. I gave her my reason, that I was getting married this summer and would be in New England for at least a year. She was quite cordial about it, but today as I was leaving the building she grabbed me by the arm and said sternly: "You may be leaving here, but remember—you'll never make it if you shirk on your job now."

May　*(Discipline Interference)*

Today was rainy. It lasted all morning and all afternoon. It is my week for being on duty during lunch recess.

The policy for inclement weather recess is to have the children go down to the playroom. It is wild. The children yell, scream, fight, throw things, call each other names, etc. All teachers dread rainy-day recess.

Today got particularly out of hand. At one point I demanded absolute silence and was preparing to tell the children they would have to go back to their rooms if this continued. Just at that point Miss Farmer appeared. She poked me in the shoulder and said, "In the public schools we abhor tyrants." I said, "Excuse me," and I left.

At the end of recess my children returned to their room. "We don't like that ol' Miss Farmer." I asked them why. "For the whole recess she made us stand in the playroom facing the wall."

(Clerks)

The final roll books have been completed, a mammoth job which must be done accurately at a time of excitement and tension. I felt great relief yesterday after mine had passed my checker's eye and then had passed through the eyes of the roll book committee. Then it goes to the principal. She goes through all roll book reports and consolidates them. Woe unto the poor soul who makes an error. God help them.

When I went home last night I was a bit concerned that my principal would find an error. I walked in this morning to a livid woman. In an outraged voice she yelled: "Miss B! What am I to you? Your trash man! I can't spend all my time picking up after your sloppy habits! You should take on adult responsibilities if you're trying to be an adult!"

I said, "Miss Farmer, what is it I have done?"

She said, "Look!" and from the back of my roll book produced two small slips of paper with two names and addresses of children who had entered my room late this year. I just looked at her and said, "Excuse me, please, I have work to do."

June

The final day of school. We had to hand in all completed forms and clean up the rooms. This is followed by a luncheon given by the P.T.A. mothers. After this is a teachers' meeting.

At the end of the meeting Miss Farmer said she had a few important announcements to make. She named one teacher who would not be back because she was going to experience one of "God's greatest blessings to women." She was going to have a baby. The teacher was then presented with a small gift. Next she announced that another teacher was going to Europe. She gave her a small gift. Then she said, "I know there is something else . . . Yes, Miss B. is getting married, but getting married is getting married and anyone can do that . . ."

At this point a teacher stood up and simply said, "Obviously, *not everyone* can get married."

Second Diary

The following diary is that of a talented young high-school teacher. After receiving her master of arts in education at Harvard, she accepted a post as an English teacher in a lower-middle-class school in an industrial suburb of a large city.

The town in which my school is situated is lower-middle-class and has fallen some—socio-economically—in the last few years. The students are primarily of Italian and Polish origin. By and large there is a measure of good old cultural deprivation among the students. Certainly there is little scholarly or humanistic concern. The vocational emphasis is heavy. Although the guidance department claims that 50 per cent of the students go to college, I am quite sure that the figure is closer to 30 per cent of our 1700 students. The average I.Q. is just about an even 100 according to the California, Otis, and Binet administered at various times in the students' career. English, of course, tends to have big problems because all students must take English to graduate. Our students are forced to be there, and we are faced with teaching unwilling and sometimes unable students. The groups are supposed to be homogeneously arranged, but there is often juggling because of programming difficulties.

The school is brand-new this fall. Layout and classroom design are quite good. My room is a little too small, but it is pleasant, facing on a very pretty interior court. I have five classes: a slow, a medium, and a fast junior class, a medium and a slow senior class. The average class size is about 27 or 28, which makes my total load about 135 students. Too many, I feel, to do an adequate job, especially with the writing program. I spend literally half of my time correcting the compositions I require weekly.

An Instance Where Consultation Could Have Helped

In my fourth-period class, a so-called "normal" senior class, I have been having trouble. In the first place, I think "normal" is not quite an adequate description. There are at least five or six kids I would consider subnormal, at least as far as English skills, reading rate, writing, etc., are concerned. There is also an over-preponderance of wise guys. I made a mistake at the beginning when I was amused rather than firm and I'm paying for it now. I'm over a barrel. There is an undercurrent of obscenity that goes on, just barely sub rosa. I can't really hear, but neither can I ignore. Of course, as I am young and female, these older boys are out to see how much they can get away with and so they tease all the time. I either have to ignore the undercurrent and its occasional outbursts or acknowledge that I know exactly what is going on, giving the boys the pleasure of teasing. I tried ignoring and feigning ignorance, but I could not take the disruption in the class, so I tried another alternative—sending the boys out of the room—realizing that this was sidestepping the problem. In any event, this did no good, as administrative support is negligible. A cryptic note from the assistant principal saying, "Al and I have discussed the matter," is the only action I have gotten. Of course, it's also true that I don't know exactly what they could do either.

On the subject of administrative support, I heard some teachers at lunch today complaining that the assistant principal (called Little Napoleon) never does anything and it's better for the teacher to call the kid's parents in.

Anyway, Dick, one of the chief wise guys, whom I sent to the office yesterday in desperation, came in this morning and said, looking as if he meant it, "I'm sorry about yesterday, Miss Clovis." I'm afraid I may have made a bad mistake in response to this; I made him go to Little Napoleon for a note saying he had been to the office yesterday. Maybe trust rather than mistrust would have been the right thing. Anyway he did come back with the note and was very good for the rest of the period, even responding often to questions. I did let him speak quite a few times, remembering my Harvard psych classes about rewarding positive behavior.

There are several other real problems in this class. Mike sits and baits me constantly. I tried the friendly "You're not letting me do my job" sort of approach—with little success. I have yet to figure the way to quiet him down. Unfortunately he is funny and, of course, the rest of the class loves it. Ted is a brighter, more sensitive kid than most, but he is plump, and was, according to his records, once really badly overweight. He finds it necessary to be right in the center of acceptance. He feels bad about it, though, and tries to woo me by telling me about a short story he is writing. I have encouraged him to bring it in, but he hasn't so far. Joe is my only success so far. He started out as prima donna of the wise guys, but he wasn't ever nasty about it. You can really tell the difference between when it's aimed at you and when it isn't. Joe wasn't an aimer, but he was damned annoying. Anyway I talked to him several times, saying that, not being humorless myself, I did appreciate his humor, but that it had become a question of his having the class or my having it, and he would have to cut it out. One day I found out that he was doing work in the print ship and mentioned kiddingly that I'd love some stationery. He said he'd make me some, and after making sure it was O.K., I said, "Fine." He has been angelic ever since. About once a day he consults with me about type size, spacing, paper size, etc. In fact, I think that's probably the key. Today, Dick having returned chastened and the class being more subdued than usual, we made some headway in *The Ugly American*. I didn't quite understand how the "ugly American" hero of the book constructed his pump system, so I asked some of the boys and, I admit shame-facedly, to my surprise, they have made a complete and de-tailed explanation—"they" meaning my trouble-makers—even with diagrams. I think if I could lose some of my intel-lectual snobbery I could handle this class better. These boys know about mechanics and motors; perhaps I should find a way to utilize this better. On the other hand, the girls were quite bored. This is always the problem in a class where my aim has to be content.

October 17   The Department Head as a Consultant

Great staff meeting for the English faculty to-day. I always come away fired with enthusiasm, which un-fortunately wilts a bit under the day's occupation. Every new technique is at our disposal, at least theoretically, and Joan is doing an excellent job of trying to utilize all resources. The camaradarie of the department is such that the meeting lasted one and three-quarter hours quite voluntarily—unusual for teachers.

(Time and Planning)

I have been working hard to present some really hot-shot lessons on Puritanism and also an introduction to poetry. It is disappointing, however, to find that things never go as well as planned. I find I consistently overestimate my classes, even the slow ones. I was talking to one teacher about the fact that, although I know how to plan good lessons, I find it almost impossible in practice because of the time factor, and there always seems to be at least one kid ready to blow in even the hottest-shottest lesson. She assured me that it all shakes down after a while and that once materials are built up the planning becomes easier. In the course of the conversation I found I was the only one with five separate preparations besides having one of the heaviest student loads. Maybe this is part of the reason I see myself as so much more disorganized than most of my fellow teachers. I do, at the moment, have some 200 papers, tests, and quizzes to correct. Of course, maybe I just am disorganized. In any event, I almost always find it difficult to know exactly where I am and what I'm doing despite lesson plans and unit plans. There simply seem to be too many factors to juggle. I'm sure the disorganization which reflects itself in, if not inconsistency, at least some inconstancy of routine, is somewhat responsible for generalized discipline problems. I'd like to hold everything tight—just the mechanics of roll taking, test giving, homework checking, assignment giving—but I don't seem to be able to.

> *(Special Consultation Needed to Deal with Classroom Crisis)*

After a foul day, what with the constant tension on the part of students and me, the dessert came when Laura in my last-period class had an epileptic fit in class. I knew she was epileptic, but had not been warned that she frequently has attacks in class. I was scared to death. However, I don't think it was visible to the kids. Luckily it wasn't either severe or prolonged, and as soon as she was O.K. I went on, knees a-tremble, with my class. Interestingly, I had been in the middle of trying to get the class to imagine themselves as Puritans, having described the belief, setting, church, etc., and was about to launch into "Sinners in the Hands of an Angry God" when the attack came. The girl next to Laura said, "This happens to her in church pretty often." All sorts of associations started in my mind; I wondered if I should read the sermon, especially this one, but I did and it was O.K. Good grief, perhaps I have a Mohammed.

November 2   A Bad Day—Need for Consultation

This was the day! Problems have been mounting in the cafeteria. Because this is the first time the kids have not been able to go out for lunch, they are extremely resentful. The setup for eating is two dining rooms of 300 students, with three teachers; this is hardly adequate, especially as we are blessed with a fairly large number of tough-guy troublemakers. There is usually incredible noise, mess, throwing of things, pushing, teasing, etc., and once a kitchen knife was thrown. There has been virtually no control. The teachers in charge have tried everything, including conferences with students, permissiveness, and authoritarianism. The administration has been no help. Gus brought ten boys into the office; they had been chanting obscenities ensemble. Little Napoleon, the bantam rooster, ex gym teacher, assistant principal, looks at all ten, says, "Did you do it?" They say, "No." He says to Gus, "See, none of them will admit it," and dismisses them, leaving Gus waving in the breeze. Anyway today a whole trayful of garbage was spilled on a girl who refused to say who had done it. Pandemonium ensued. Little Napoleon whipped in and accused Gus and Joe, two eminently capable men, of being incapable, irresponsible, and at fault for all the trouble in the cafeteria. Both Gus and Joe were understandably livid. Evidently this is not unheard of from this man; there are many teachers who are terribly dissatisfied with the lack of support teachers are given, and there is a movement afoot to do something about it. Joe did speak to the principal, but to no avail. It should be interesting to see if Little Napoleon shapes up or if teacher spirit gives out first.

November 7

Fourth period I walked into my class, quasi-unprepared, and spied the Superintendent of Schools lurking in a corner. This is my big, tough-guy class, and I was really scared. Once again, however, I was pleased to note that if a class likes you they are amazingly nice when they know you're being observed. They were angelic. Mr. Price, the Superintendent, stayed about twenty-five minutes and then walked out with nary a word, nor was there any note from him or anything else. I'm a bit annoyed as I feel he should acknowledge his visitation, and I use the word in its primeval sense, in some way.

November 13

Today marks the end of a grueling several days. Registers—involving hours of computation and little squares —and quarterly grades were both due today. One wonders what the dames in the office are paid for. I handed in my register, having spent literally hours trying to make it come out even, and settled down to finish up my grades during my free period. I find grading terribly difficult and arbitrary, and I was most unhappy. In walks Miss Moon, and pounces on me, literally yelling at me that my register was so faulty that she couldn't check it. I am quite ready to tell her where to put her, rather my, register, but I restrained myself, feeling angry and humiliated. Finally, with sympathy and help from some other teachers, I was able to correct the mistakes, I hope. I have to give the thing back to Miss Moon tomorrow. I went into my last-period class feeling bedraggled, and in pops little repulsive Mrs. Setter. In her loudest voice she informs me that I must take some materials to Mrs. Foote, who lives miles out of my way; Mrs. Foote has pneumonia. I am annoyed by the demand and irritated by her obtrusive interruption to my class. She goes out, but returns within the moment to inform me, loudly, that I should be careful of it because Mrs. Foote's register is in there. I now feel about two years old, which is not so hot for teaching.

November 15

This morning five of the boys from my advanced class came to see me to complain. I had announced, foolishly I guess, that there had been no marks over 85. These kids were really angry. I'm going to keep them out of college; I'm the only one who marks this way; my standards are impossible. I was very much upset about this visit. I decided to bring up the issue in class, and I gave my point of view: I had always resented the low standards, and I believed in academic excellence, which I do, and I believed they were all capable of meeting my standards. What surprised me most was the real anger I faced. I suppose it is good that they feel free enough to express it, but it is not easy to take, especially when the guidance department is on my back, too, in regard to marking this particular class. I simply do not understand why bright kids should be guaranteed an excellent mark, which is the predominant practice. It seems to me that it should be just the opposite. I hope I can withstand the pressures.

Right after the delegation left, and I was feeling a little shaky, in walked Miss Moon again. Rather she stormed in and told me there were some thirteen errors still in my register. I was ready to weep.

The finale to the day was when two college teacher-education students walked in on my very slow class, unexpectedly. Had I known, I would have prepared the kids. Usually they like to behave well for visitors, but I didn't know and the kids were awful. They even threw paper airplanes when I wasn't looking. In short, a most horrible day.

November 21   (*Day before Holiday*)

Half-day today because of the Thanksgiving Holiday, and it was awful. Everyone—students, teachers, everyone—sat waiting for freedom. I drove my two brightest boys into the city after school because they wanted to go to a matinee. They said how much they enjoyed my class, its freedom, and especially the sense of free inquiry. I, of course, felt great, although they did get in a few digs about my grading system.

November 28   (Too Many Trouble-Makers)

Today my normal (slow-normal, I would say) seniors finally got me. The annoyance was so insidious, so skillful that I cracked. If it were one or two only, I could handle it, but there are a number of first-rate hell-raisers and, despite the fact that they are as separated as I can get them, the collusion is obvious. Dick will pretend he is throwing something at Saul on the other side of the room. I tell Dick to pick it up, thinking that he is throwing chalk. There is nothing for him to pick up. I am at a loss. I turn my back to write on the board and Saul really does throw chalk. I have no recourse. These boys are too deeply anti-school for me to really interest them. The best I can do is amuse them, and I can't do that—I risk bedlam.

Anyway, I finally went to pieces and screamed, realizing even as I did it that it was entirely the wrong thing to do. I did manage to have one boy, Art, removed from the class for at least two weeks. I don't usually have real personality problems with kids. Even Dick doesn't dislike me; he's just a universal nuisance. Art can't stand me, and I fear it's mutual. He was sitting in the back of the room egging on John, who had been mercifully quiet. I said, rather gently, "Art, cut it out," to which Art responds, "I wasn't doin' nothin'. Why do you always pick on me? You just be quiet until I do something." I icily sent him to the office and, for once, got some support. I don't like that kid, but I was not picking on him, so I felt justified.

November 29   What Makes One Group Go and Another Falter?

My nasty seniors were docile today. I was very quiet and very cold, and it settled them down pretty well. But my slow juniors, the class with an 85 I.Q. average, was impossible. I was attempting to have each of them choose one out of five books for the second part of a scholastic unit we are using called *Moments of Decision*. There were not enough books for everyone to have what he wanted. All hell broke loose. Half were screaming that I wasn't fair; half were snatching books from other people. When that settled down, they began trading, which would have been O.K. up to a point, but it didn't stop. I became so exasperated I was really about to cry, and I couldn't calm them down. I'd get things quieted down, but the minute I started to do anything there was bedlam again. I was at my wit's end. I've never been so glad to hear a bell in my life.

I don't understand why I get along so very well with my slow seniors and not the slow juniors. I wonder whether the difference is with me or with them.

Tomorrow I'm going to give normal and fast juniors the same writings that the English faculty corrected and let them grade them and make comments. It should be interesting.

December 5   Why Did It Work?
(Gratification: A Place for Recognition)

Today I tried a new idea I had about teaching vocabulary, and I was very pleased with the result. I made mimeo sheets with the words and two sentences using each of the words. I had the kids read the sentences and write down their guess as to the meaning. Then I had them look it up and finally use it in a sentence themselves. Then I went around the room and had some of the sentences read. Finally, I started a sort of round-robin story, and each kid had to add a sentence using a vocabulary word. It was very successful. The kids enjoyed it and really began using the words.

(Motivation. Meaning What? Consultation?)

In my fast class we had a superb class on *Billy Budd*. They did a magnificent job with the allegory, the symbolism, and the conflict of justice and mercy.

A very nice day. The fact is my classes have been almost tractable, except my slow juniors. I find I have so very little patience with them. I feel a little the way a collie herding sheep must feel; I get four in line and two more act up. I finally sent a boy who was passing out obscenities in the back of the room to the office, but without any result. He merely came back and started the same thing again. I'm beginning to agree with my colleague Gus that motivation is the key, but that at this age very little external motivation is functional These really slow kids have simply had too many bad experiences with school to be anything but distrustful of ANYTHING I propose.

December 12   (English and Mental Health)

In preparation for my poetry unit I decided to make use of music and pictures. My idea was to show how tone, volume, pitch, rhythm, pictures, etc., can evoke different responses. I intended to do it only in my normal and fast junior class, but the interest in the phonograph and records was so high I decided to adapt it for my slow classes and my messy seniors. I asked these classes to simply relax, listen to the music, and then write down whatever story, picture, or idea they might have. I hoped at least to point out that language can have an emotional effect. My slow classes loved it but didn't get anything very concrete. I used some Gregorian chants, a cool jazz record by Amhad Jamal, and Van Cliburn's inimitable rendition of Tchaikovsky's Concerto No. 1 in B flat. In my messy senior class I asked for a little more developed reaction to the music. I got a troublesome response from Saul. I have been aware that Saul is a strange boy, bright and fairly dangerous. I looked up his record and found some vague story about his having broken into a biology lab during his sophomore year. It seems Saul and a cohort, now in a mental hospital, had a big thing going about medical experimentations and death. They had a lab, surgical equipment, and animals. The real psycho used to plague the biology teacher for information about autopsies and about obtaining a cadaver for himself. He and Saul used to run experiments together. During a week when the biology teacher was out sick, Saul and friend broke into the school at night and took strychnine and curare from the room. Later both boys were found with the drugs, but Saul's family hired a fancy lawyer and got him completely exonerated. In view of all this I find his two papers, the first about the music and the second about two pictures, more than a little disconcerting. Here is certainly a place where some good professional help would be useful. Saul likes me, but I'm scared to try to handle this at all.

I was interested, by the way, in how mistrustful many of the students were of my little games. Lots of them said things like, "Why don't you just bring a couch?" or "Do we get ink blots tomorrow?"

January 4   Reading Level and What to Do about It

I am somewhat worried about some of the boys in that messy senior class, one especially, Wayne. Evidently Wayne is a reformed rowdy, at least he is very good in my class, despite past history. He has been complaining that he just can't read *Madame Curie* and I think it's legitimate. I talked to the head of my department, Joan, about it and, for the first time, was somewhat disappointed in her reaction. First she messed around about substituting another book, and then she decided that Wayne and several of the others do not belong in a normal class and they really cannot do the reading.

Speaking of reading, using *The Hidden Persuaders*, the book assigned for my slow seniors, is ridiculous. They are absolutely incapable of reading it on their own, so I have to read it to them. This is particularly difficult when the book begins discussing prunes as laxatives, Maidenform Bra ads, perfume as an extension of libido, and the Cadillac as phallic symbol. This is just too much for these kids, and for me, too, for that matter.

(A Trouble-Maker)   How to Handle a Positive Move

About a week ago I had trouble with Ted and arranged for him to talk with Ric, the one guidance person for whom I have any respect. I don't know what Ric said, but Ted came back the next day and asked me if I thought he was mean and vicious. I sort of ignored this. But all week he has been pestering me, so today I suggested he come in to see me. I was not anxious for the confrontation, since Ted is difficult anyway and I would be at the disadvantage of whatever Ric had said. A little to my surprise he showed up at the appointed time. It turns out that Ric quoted to Ted something he overheard me say to Gus in the lunchroom, something about the difference between directed and non-directed goading in which I mentioned that Ted was often directly and maliciously a teaser. All I could say to Ted was that I did feel that he directed a great deal of his misbehavior at me and that, being human, when I was treated like that I became angry. I never can be sure of Ted's reactions. He is lovely and perceptive when he has you as a lone audience, but the minute other people intervene, and he has to share, he is extremely unreliable. He stayed for a long time and wanted to talk and talk, but I decided to leave (a) because I had to, but (b) because I'm afraid it would be all too easy to become ensnarled in Ted's insidious "best buddies" net. For instance, he was assuring me that if the situation in class (he's in with my messy seniors) ever developed in a rumble, Walt, who is fond of me, would lead the auto mechanics boys to my defense. Comforting as I found this, I still had the impression that interested distance is the only dignified way I can handle Ted and so I left. During the course of our discussion I found that, as I had feared, the absolute uproar in the class yesterday was due to the fact that my blouse had become unbuttoned, a fact I ruefully noted about halfway through the period. What Ted said was "I would tell you why we were so bad yesterday but I'm afraid you'd get mad."

January 11   Supervisory Report

Today in my mailbox I was greeted by a sheet of paper from an administrative supervisor who observed my class last week. His comments were that (1) I seemed not to have rapport with my class, (2) my voice seemed artificially controlled, (3) one boy didn't have a book, and (4) I should learn to smile in my classroom. I am irritated and annoyed. Of course in some ways this is an accurate report of what he saw, but I feel it most unfair for a judgment of my worth to be made on a single twenty-minute observation of a semi-impossible class. The comment that I should smile struck me as ironic since I was purposely serious and aloof for his benefit, as well as being ill at ease because he was there.

I spoke to Joan about my discomfiture, but she suggested that (1) this man is a fool and (2) my recommendations came from the department school staff and not the administration, so I suppose I won't do anything about it. It seems somehow degrading to try to answer his charges.

January 16   (Mass Adolescent Behavior)

This morning there was an assembly by the Thespian Group. They had worked arduously to present a very well-put-together program about the history of the theater. I was shocked and angry at the audience's reaction. This is not the first time an audience of students has been really nasty. There was even uproarious laughter when someone on stage mentioned *Moby Dick*. After the assembly I said something to Miss Zachary, with whom I've become much friendlier, about my anger. Her response: "Well, I've always felt we should get rid of the scum, but you need someone to change your tires." The frightening thing about this is that I found myself agreeing. I wonder if only a year of teaching is enough to knock out all one's idealism.

As I walked into my fourth-period class after assembly, someone hit me on the rear end with a rubber band. This was one of those moments when you have to make a decision quickly. I chose to ignore it, but this was at some cost. Several of the boys persisted in accusing each other for the rest of the period. I think I figured correctly that making a big issue of it, seeing as I had no idea who had done it, would have merely served to amuse everyone.

The English Faculty meeting this afternoon was good, as usual. Joan, the department head, explained that the grouping for next year would be done only by the English Department with no recourse to Guidance or parents. We will all meet with lists, I.Q.'s, reading scores, and the results of a standarized test we're giving next week, and the grouping will be done there with everyone present so that individual lists can be discussed. Joan made it quite clear that her policy on this is that a kid should be in a group which represents his ability, not his achievement, on the principle that nice, slow kids aren't helped by being pushed up and fast, lazy kids are likely to do better if put in a good class. We talked some about the factors, emotional problems, kids who have failed, etc. I seem to have amassed the reputation of fiery young dissenter; everyone sits around waiting for me to dissent in meetings. I'm beginning to do it simply because it's expected.

January 17 and 18 (How We Lose Good Teachers)

These have been two of the most unpleasant days of my life. I am ready to quit teaching at the end of the month. I told Joan this and she advised me to wait until Monday at least, adding that this feeling is not unusual, especially around this time of year.

Yesterday was merely bad. I started out by getting very annoyed at kids for being late. Of course it hasn't just started, but it's just started to bother me. So I told quite a few kids to come back after school and that got each class off to a roaring start. My slow juniors and messy seniors were so high and so terrible that I was literally at my wit's end all day long. In addition, only one of the kids I told to come back came.

Today was much worse. Again I started badly because, partly, I was still disgruntled by yesterday and partly because there was an extremely icy road on the way to school and I damn near killed myself. My car went off the road, brakes wouldn't hold, etc., and I finally arrived in one piece, but very shaky. My first-period class was O.K. I've just about given up on *The Hidden Persuaders,* and I'm having the kids do an advertising project. Make up a product and a sales campaign. Second period, slow juniors, and again three people arrived sans books. I was irritated, but I was also determined not to have a repeat of yesterday's irritation. Billie started acting up; I sent him to the office. Belda Joe starts humming the Mexican Hat Dance. I tell her to stop and then mention the fact that she didn't show up yesterday after school. She starts this really sly business: "Aw you didn't tell me nothin' ... I ain't comin' nowhere ... you call my mother." I sent her to the office. I started to teach but there was a steady undertone, so I stopped the whole thing, refused to teach, and had absolute quiet for the whole period.

Third-period study was annoying, as usual on Friday, and took constant policing. Then came messy-senior time. It all started when I handed back a test which almost everyone failed—bedlam, real chaos. All of them were attacking me, my grading, etc. I became very defensive and angry and made much noise—I wasn't called on to defend myself, I would answer individual questions after class. John, who has been angelic for two months, but who started up again this week, really raised hell. He dared me to send him to the office. I realized he wanted to go because he wanted to get his class changed. I sent him along with a note stating that I didn't think he should be changed. At the end of the period some of the boys pointed out what really seems an inequity in my system on this test. I consented to take the two parts as separate tests. About five have already thrown theirs away. I can't do it again. I sit down on a tack someone has placed on my seat. I don't let on. John comes back with a note from Little Nap asking me to a conference during the seventh period.

January 23

A huge snow storm is predicted for tomorrow, so today was more than frenetic. Everyone, students and teachers, had nothing on the mind except the possibility of a "snow day."

In messy seniors, I attempted to prepare everyone for a "re-do" of the test they messed up so badly last week. In desperation I asked one of the girls, out of about four who understand about objects and nominatives, to explain it to the class. It was rather interesting to see her struggle with the same blank faces I've struggled with for about a month. I specifically chose her because I see on her face, occasionally, a look of contempt for me—"Why the hell can't she make it clear to them?" After she tried it, she came up to me and said, "I see what you mean!" Ah, vindication.

There have been a series of fights in the cafeteria. Every time there is an unusual noise, all the men teachers swarm out of the teachers' lunch room. The fear is not so much of an individual fight as it is fear of a total riot, and this is a very real fear. The situation in the cafeteria is intolerable. Teachers are genuinely afraid of being on duty. One has the feeling that one is walking into a snake pit. Still no action has come down from the administration, although Little Nap has gone on a suspension kick and approximately five or six boys a day are suspended from school. They consider it a pleasant five-day vacation.

In general I've had the feeling for the past two weeks that I am desperately boring myself and my students. Teaching seems a matter of control, a negative rather than a positive thing. I feel it badly but I have inertia in equal measure. Joan assures me that this is not unusual, especially at this time of year, and reassures me that I'm not evil, just tired.

January 24

Today I had one of those experiences every teacher awaits with anguish—the moment you tell a student to do something and he says, "No." In my slow senior class there are two girls, Violet and Peggy, who are real flip little chicks, very stupid, very annoying, and subtly nasty. They have, with constant chatter, laughing, note passing, flirting, annoyed me for a long time. Today the rest of the class was silently doing some work I had assigned and Peggy and Violet, alone, were being obnoxious, creating a terrible disturbance. I did something I rarely do. I told them both to just stand up and keep standing, saying that if they wanted so much attention they could have it. I don't like that kind of nonsense but I now understand why everyone resorts to it sooner or later. Anyway they both flatly refused. I had no choice. I sent them both to Little Napoleon. I didn't want to send them, but the rest of the class was hanging on every word and I couldn't back down. As usual I got no notification of what happened.

February 4   The Arbitrary Placement

Today, a bleak Monday, I was greeted with a little note from Guidance adding the 34th member to my slow senior class, a class which was supposed to have been closed at 28. I was livid. I stormed up to Joan, figuring that if I went to the incompetent guidance counselor myself, I'd murder her. As I suspected, Joan had not been consulted. She was furious too, because she had been vehement on the subject of placing students in classes without the teacher's consent. When I calmed down, I went to the counselor and informed her flatly that I would not take anyone else until someone was removed. She pussyfooted around, said she meant to consult me, etc., and suggested that I send her a list of people I thought could transfer. When the girl arrived during the first period, I explained the situation to her and sent her off to parts unknown. . . .

February 11

In my slow senior class, which was going fairly badly, or at least loosely, Rita, a rather nudnick-type kid but a talker, was talking continuously. I asked her several times in a rather reasonable tone of voice to stop. Finally I moved her seat, where she proceeded to lounge horizontally on the chair and talk to her nearest cohort. Again I said, and still not nastily, "Rita, perhaps you'd better sit up and do the work in front of you." She looked me straight in the eye and said, "Perhaps I don't feel like it." The class collapsed; they were really quite as surprised as I was. As I saw it I had no choice, so I just sent her down, with as little fanfare as possible, to Little Nap. Naturally, of course, nothing was done, nor am I sure what should have been done. I had to get rid of her or lose face, especially since the other kids in the room also felt that Rita had gone beyond the pale.

Several things occur to me. This kind of direct defiance has only happened twice before and then, too, it was with girls in class—and girls are not usually offenders around here. I wonder if it is jealousy. After all, I'm only four years older than they and yet I have complete authority. Also, I suppose, there is also a certain amount of flirtatious underplay between me and some of the boys in the room, which I guess they resent.

February 14   Mass Pandemonium

Hell broke loose today. Some raw eggs were thrown in the cafeteria, apparently not for the first time although I didn't know about it before. Little Nap decided the time had come, so he kept the whole cafeteria, about 500 kids, locked in until someone would confess or inform. He kept all of them for two and a half hours, then he released the girls for no specific reason. Then about a half-hour later he began releasing selected boys. Approximately 50 boys were kept until 5:30. Little Nap and several other male teachers instigated an inquisition which Mr. D. proudly asserts used physical violence as well. The whole school was in a terrible uproar. I felt the thing was handled very badly. The kids thought Little Nap was an idiot and they thoroughly enjoyed the cafeteria scene, at least much more than they enjoyed classes.

February 19   Evaluation. Based on What?
(Ambivalence about Learning)

I had my evaluative conference with the principal today. I had no idea what to expect. What it turned out to be was a rather general discussion about the value of college boards and a slightly more detailed discussion of the state of the English Department. I sang Joan's praises sincerely, and the principal echoed them. He really had very little to say about me, as he has neither seen me teach nor has he spoken to me more than a "Hello" all year. At any event he said "they" were pleased with my teaching and wanted me to come back. I hedged. I am almost certain that I won't come back, and I did indicate to him that I am doubtful. I felt like something of an imposter: I do not feel that I have done a good job at all, hardly even an adequate one. Maybe this is a little harsh and maybe it is a result of the fierce alter-ego instilled in us by the Harvard Graduate School of Education, but I do not feel at all satisfied with what I have done, and the principal's little speech, made in however much ignorance, embarrassed me.

After I talked with the principal I went to see Joan and told her what he had said. She all but offered me two fast junior classes if I came back. I told her quite honestly that it didn't seem likely that I would. If there is one thing which will make me sad about leaving it will be not being able to work under someone like her.

February 20   English and Sex Education
(Sex Education via English)

An incredible thing happened today—in my messy senior class I taught Freud, successfully.

We are starting on *The Hidden Persuaders* and I decided, at Joan's suggestion, to begin with some definition. I embarked with the subconscious and the unconscious. Someone asked precisely what the difference was. I mentioned the id and said something about sexual desires and aggression.

Mike snickered and I lit into him—I embarrassed him. Everyone was pretty quiet and then all of a sudden Mike said "Why sex and aggression (I had used this term) together? Sex is birth and the other is death." I damn near dropped my teeth. From there on in I had such rapport with that class as I have never had with any class—strange twist of Kismet. I went on to explain, briefly, about the Oedipus complex. The questions I got were interesting. Mike, whose father is dead, asked, "What happens if a father dies?" Others asked about stepfathers. One kid asked whether people who were still in love with their mothers were queer. I attempted to explain that the incest taboo is so strong that sometimes men who still felt this kind of love for their mothers tried to get as far away from it as possible by loving another man. Don, a prime hood, asked why, if someone who loved his mother felt hatred or suspicion or rivalry (not his word) with his father, he could love another man. Magnificent question, and one I couldn't really answer. This kind of questioning went on very freely and seriously, with me being very careful not to make judgments about the cases they were bringing up, obviously their own. Finally, the acme of the period, Sarah, a sweet little girl in the last row, asked what masturbation was. It was one of those moments! I decided to give a rather general answer—I don't remember, or have suppressed, what I said—rather than to not answer, figuring that would only make a big case out of it. To my astonishment, although there was a measure of discomfort on the part of some of the boys who obviously knew, there was no outbreak at all, and I merely went on with the discussion. Ah, triumph was very sweet indeed after such a struggle.

February 26

A bad day today; everything went wrong. I had planned in my slow senior class, which is studying *Animal Farm,* to have the class plan a utopian school along with some commandments. Eventually I planned to have them rewrite the commandments in accordance with the destruction of a utopia. I thought they would enjoy it, but no. There was grumbling.

My slow junior class fell apart and, beside myself, I sent two of the worst trouble-makers to the office in a rage, and having raged, I was disgruntled for the rest of the day. My messy seniors were even worse. They have been reading *On the Beach,* and I decided to have them write a diary as if we were all going to die of radiation sickness in two weeks. Again I thought this would be fun, and what I got was much noise, numerous ridiculous questions designed to annoy me, and a few papers thrown every time I turned around. I became even more enraged, out of control. With my last two classes, which are better behaved, I was merely boring about Emerson and Thoreau.

February 27

More troubles—first of all there was a great deal more bitching about the diary by my messy seniors. John, who has gotten bad AGAIN, started sounding off about it—so much so that it became a "thing" and I was forced to pull an "I'm the teacher and that's it" bit. I also wrote a letter to his father, explaining about John's constant annoyances. I did the same for Ted, who spent most of today whistling barely audibly and then waiting for me to react. All this interspersed with frequent verbal and chalk battles with Dick.

In addition I was most disturbed to receive a most pathological, sinister, and sex-obsessed diary assignment from Saul, two of whose papers I have already mentioned, because I thought they were pretty sick.

February 28

An even worse day than before.

Mrs. M., a parent, showed up today, wanting to see me, so an appointment was set up with her and Little Nap. She started by sounding off about my diary assignment, saying she thought it stupid and unreasonable. Little Nap came to my defense, somewhat belligerently. I tried to explain my purpose, but the whole thing degenerated into an argument about what to do in case of atomic attack. Finally Mrs. M. got to the point. She didn't mean it was my fault, but "John never had no trouble before, John's a good boy," so she wanted him taken out of my class. Little Nap said, "No," and Mrs. M. started noises about people with other names getting things done (implying that her minority status put her in a futile position). Little Nap got very angry and the two of them battled. I was shrinking in my chair. Eventually Little Nap called John in; he was embarrassed, angry, and defensive. He maintained he couldn't stand me, my class, and, in addition, no one in the class could stand it either. I found it very difficult to take, and I had to control myself in order not to end up in a childish sort of quarrel. The upshot was that Little Nap finally capitulated and said he would move John to another class, but that if John didn't prove himself in two weeks he would be removed from English altogether. Both Mrs. M. and John assumed it was a trick, that Little Nap would put him in a fast class where he couldn't possibly keep up. Little Nap's reaction: "Our teachers wouldn't even let him in a fast class." My reaction—real horror.

Finally, with much backing and filling—John refused to give Little Nap his schedule, thereby mortifying his mother— John was placed in another normal class, Miss Appel's, to my (I confess it) pleasure. Miss Appel is a real old-time disciplinarian biddy; John may have his difficulties with her.

March 4

I started teaching *My Ántonia* in my first class today. I like the book very much and was anxious to teach it. I wanted to teach it from the point of view of loss of innocence, alienation from the natural world, etc. I came into class with a great deal of enthusiasm. I was met with absolute blankness; no one had any opinion about anything. This is one thing they never told us, that there would be times when there was no response. I even tried to badger them into a discussion, but no luck. I felt like such an idiot, as if I were talking to myself. I talked to Joan this afternoon, and her class had an excellent discussion on the same material. I can't imagine why mine didn't.

March 11 (Teacher Definition of Role—How Far and When)

Today I told my whole eighth-period class to wait when the bell rang. It rang and Charles made for the door; I told him to stay. Charles is a very bright (Otis Score is 128) and quite crazy kid who will give you a correct answer clothed in the most colloquial English and incorrect grammar he can muster. He is something of a problem in class but not too bad.

I started talking to him, but he wouldn't look at me or even turn around. Finally I got him to do that and launched into the typical bit about capabilities and uses thereof. The thing I notice most about him is his diffidence; he just doesn't seem to care about anything. He allowed as how he got into trouble in other classes, but didn't know why he did things: "Aw, maybe I need a psychiatrist." I asked if there were anything he liked. "Yes." He liked to destroy things. In fact, he was in trouble with the police because he was accused of arranging to derail a train. I asked if he'd done it, but he said, "No." He'd also thrown things at cars and swindled a dumb kid in the neighborhood. But his father found out about the swindle: "You know, when my old man found out, he didn't even care." I asked what he wanted his father to do. He wanted his father to stop him from doing these things, but got no real response. Anyway, then I got scared because I felt I was getting in over my head, and I didn't really know what I was doing, so I just let him go.

March 20

My senior class, messy, had me practically on the verge of tears today. I simply can't handle them. Like mercury, you stop it one place and its pops out someplace else. I became furious—screamed—great amusement—frustration—

really could murder some of them, but I can't. I was literally shaking when the class left. My fast junior group comes next. I nearly decapitated them, and then felt awful because they are so good. It took me a good half-hour to calm down enough to teach my good class. At lunch I was ranting and raving that I had had enough. Some of the older teachers were terribly nice and tried to give suggestions, but I've tried everything they suggest. I will not teach next year; I'm not equipped for this much irritation.

March 25   (Use of Groups)

My normal juniors have been reading *Arrowsmith,* undoubtedly the longest book many of them have ever read. This was the first day on the book, but they were so full of questions that I just opened it up for general discussions and was amazed and pleased at the response. Today I tried something with them I've never tried before, group work. I divided them into four groups and gave every group a topic, such as the relationship between Martin and women, and let them go. It is indeed heartwarming to wander around the room and hear them at each other's throats about issues in the novel. It seemed to go pretty well.

March 27   (Crisis Teacher Needed)

I was teaching my slow, slow junior class which, at the moment, was amazingly quiet. All of a sudden I heard what sounded like a fight in the hall. I went with all deliberate speed to the door, prepared to untangle two young hoods, and there was Alfred, a very nice, easy-going teacher, beating hell out of a kid in the hall. I quickly closed the door and tried to divert my class, which was naturally interested. Two things about this are interesting. First, my reaction was shock and then it was something approximate to "Good for Alfred." A year ago I would have been stupefied by this, now I not only understand but empathize. There are times that I would like nothing better than to really maul one of these impossible monsters. The other thing is that I saw Alfred later and he was rather embarrassed, explaining that he had been pushed to blindness, beyond endurance. I said I envied him; he seemed relieved.

April 8

I expected great restlessness since we get out on Wednesday, but everyone was surprisingly calm, in the student body that is. Teachers' contracts came out in our mailboxes today. A few people got the axe, which caused much uproar, as this was the first notification and it is late now to look for teaching jobs elsewhere. There was also some embarrassment, since Ned, one of the new young teachers, didn't get his contract. No one is quite sure why.

Mine was for $6,500 and it hurts to give that up, but I'm turning in my letter of resignation tomorrow.

April 9

An interesting thing today. Because of Passover, my very best, fast students were absent. I decided to try an experiment, to give some fairly complex stuff and bully some of the shyer kids into taking a verbal chance. I figure they are intimidated by the extraordinary, bright, verbal ones.

I taught better than I have ever taught—pure dynamism—encouraging, eliciting, bullying, and I was physically exhausted at the end, but it was worth it. I got a fine response, and I managed to get them to examine poetry, "Chicago" in this case. I'm sorry vacation will intervene, because I think the sweet smell of success might have carried some of the shy ones into more response even in the face of the more verbal absentees.

April 23   Shock Treatment Teaching

I started *Old Man and the Sea* in one section and was disappointed. I don't know why I have such trouble teaching books I like a great deal, maybe because I expect too

much. The discussion was desultory, except for my brightest
kids who objected to my attempt to make religious analogies.
The only thing that made me feel good was that I think I did
get across some idea of the term "symbol." I pointed at the
flag and said something like, "Why salute a red, white, and
blue rag?" The shock was visible, and someone laughingly
said he'd report me to the authorities. I asked why and he
said I'd insulted the U.S.A., so there we had it. I did some
stuff with crosses, Stars of David, and "2 plus 2 equals," and
it went over well.

Messy seniors are even being relatively good because we're
reading *Journey's End* and they like it very much.

I'm also doing a play, *R.U.R.*, in my slow senior class. The
play is excellent, the kids like it, but they truly cannot read.
I hadn't realized how bad the situation is.

April 30   A   Two-and-a-Half-Year-Old   Teenager and What to Do

Today the school elections got into full swing
and very imaginatively too. There are three parties, each with
its own organization, symbol, and slogan. It is almost frightening to see how good kids are at mass appeal. I have two of the
three candidates in my class, so I have to maintain impartial-
ity.

In messy seniors today I was in desperation—what to do
with Mike? He is driving me slowly nuts. First of all I walked
into the room and everyone laughed. I was stern. "What are
you laughing at?" At this time, Mike jumps out of my coat
closet—bedlam. You don't want to squelch him nastily, because he really is not vicious, but he simply cannot sit still
and shut up. I more or less ignored his leap and went on with
the class. I figured I'd fix him by having him read; we're doing
Journey's End. To my shock and pleasure, he read well and
he likes to do it. I should have guessed it would be a good idea
to appeal to the ham in him. Anyway, I know what I'll do
with him for the next week.

(Leave-Taking—the Hard Part)

Some of the kids have found out that I'm leaving. Some of the reactions are interesting. Several kids asked me, in a rather embarrassed way, if their classes were responsible for my leaving. After school Pat, one of my fine, fast juniors, asked me if it were true that I was leaving. I told him it was and he said very simply: "That is a real loss." I almost cried. In fact, the closer it gets to the end, the more unhappy I become. I do like my kids, even Mike. I just do not think I could take the group harassment for another year. Anyway, I'm sad.

(An Evaluative Summary from Our Diarist)
My Magic Genie Paper

Once upon a time ... there was a small blonde teacher who had an arbitrary spell over 140 assorted adolescents. Some of them were very evil indeed; others even cared about what the little blonde teacher said, a fact which never ceased to amaze the teacher. One day, or rather one night, after the teacher had fallen into a coma, having just corrected many, many, bad, bad term papers, a Genie, in the disguise of Dr. Conant, appeared to her. He said, "Since you have tried very hard to be a good teacher, I will grant you any three wishes which will help you to improve your lot."

The teacher thought and thought. She had to work very hard to restrain herself from wasting her wishes on small potatoes. First she thought she would ask the Genie to annihilate her whole messy senior class; then she thought she might wish something slightly obscene for the big bad assistant principal. When she had overcome all these temptations, she came up with three very constructive wishes:

1. An adequate guidance department: if it were possible to consult with someone who really knew something about the kids, someone for whom the kids had respect, it would be much easier for the teacher. A non-disciplinary official with an understanding both of the student and the problems of

handling a large classroom would make it possible to have remedial, rather than judgmental, recourse when a student was impossible in class.

2. An effective method of discipline: it is difficult to elaborate on this, because I'm not at all sure what would go into creating effective discipline. There were times when I was sure that only a horsewhip would be effective, but now, with a vacation perspective, I return to my more gentle self. It would seem to me that discipline is a matter of attitude. If the prevailing attitude in the school were of mutual respect between student and teacher, if the mores didn't prescribe "getting away with something," then at least the groundwork could be laid. I am also convinced that discipline in a school has to be consistent. If more teachers were better, if more cared to make things fun and exciting, especially in the grade schools, then the students would, presumably, come to the high school with enthusiasm rather than antagonism. This utopia being purely a figment, something must be done to control behavior in the school. Whatever it is should be quick, effective, but not inflexible. Student courts for discipline might be some kind of an answer, but I doubt that the teen-age code could handle it.

3. The elimination of pettiness: This is a pretty general wish that needs elaboration. Under this rubric comes all the minutiae which students and teachers put up with. I must have signed about twenty-five useless pieces of paper a day— go to the bathroom, go into the hall to get a book, take a test during study hall, etc. This is a tremendous drain on teacher time and it simply creates a whole continuum of minor regulations for the students to fight back against. Can't read magazines in study hall, can't leave the school for lunch, can't have a room in which students may smoke—all these can'ts force the teacher to expend unbelievable amounts of energy enforcing something she can't even see the reason for herself, which in itself is rather demoralizing.

This elimination of pettiness goes further too. It covers all the silly teachers' meetings; the numberless pieces of paper which are sent home, signed, returned, alphabetized, turned into the office for no good reason; the ridiculous duties—three quarters of an hour after school to make sure students get on the late bus in an orderly fashion, one hour in the hall to make sure that everyone in the hall has a hall pass—silly, arbitrary trivia, all of which serves to frustrate student and teacher.

Of course, this little blonde teacher was lucky in many ways, because she was an English teacher, and she had a very good department. Had she not, she might have made many more wishes about books, professional guidance, open files of past units and tests, exchange of ideas, profitable relationships with other teachers, an experimental attitude—but she had all this, so the Genie didn't have to worry.

Appendix B

The Life Space Interview

The Life Space Interview technique has been referred to often in this book. The term was coined by Dr. Fritz Redl after having discarded the term Marginal Interview, which was deemed to be less descriptive, since the more the technique was used, the less marginal and the more intrinsic to treatment it appeared. The concept and strategy were developed by him and workers under him first at Pioneer House in Detroit, then at the Child Research Branch of the National Institute of Mental Health. It grew out of the need for therapeutic intervention at the very moment of a crisis, rather than when the feelings have been lost and even the memory of the event is hard to recall. In time, these ideas, first defined in treatment settings, were applied in schools where there are children with pressing problems as well as children who, suffering through an upsetting period, occasionally run into difficulties requiring the immediate intervention of an adult. For the intervention to be therapeutic, it takes skill and experience in interviewing, timing, waiting, use of silences, and interpretations. These interviews have a strategy and purpose of their own aside from, or in addition to, any type of therapy a child may be undergoing. The technique can be used by a trained therapist who is on the spot for this purpose, by a teacher, a principal, a counselor, or a crisis teacher, if they have been trained in its uses and varieties.

The excerpts that follow come from a pamphlet published by the Washington School of Psychiatry entitled *The School Centered Life Space Interview*. It includes a series of papers on the theory and practice of the technique and its application to school. It also includes Dr. Redl's original paper on the subject given at a workshop of the American Association of Orthopsychiatry in 1957. The excerpts given here come from his papers and one by Dr. Marcella Bernstein (Brenner), who was then principal of an elementary school.

The Concept of the Life
Space Interview*
by Dr. Fritz Redl

It is our contention that life space interviewing plays an important part in the lives of all children. All adults in an educational role in children's lives find themselves in many situations which could correctly be thus labeled.

It is our contention that the life space interview assumes a mediating role between the child and what life holds for him, which becomes just as important as the interviewing that goes on within the pressurized cabin [of the psychiatric interview].

It is our contention that in work with seriously disturbed children, even if they are not exposed to the special type of pressurized cabin therapy over and beyond their exposure to milieu therapy, the strategically wise use and the technically correct handling of the life space interviews held with the children are of foremost clinical importance.

It is our contention that even where children are exposed to clear-cut pressurized cabin therapy, for special therapy of one phase of their problem, the wisdom of strategy and technique used by their natural home or school life personnel in mediating life experiences for them is of major strategic relevance in its own right.

It is, before all, our contention that what goes on in a life space

* *The School Centered Life Space Interview*, pp. 60, 61.

interview, even though held with the child by somebody not his therapist, in the stricter interpretation of the term, involves as subtle and important issues of strategy and technique as the decisions the psychoanalyst has to make during the course of a therapeutic hour.

It is our contention, last and not least, that any application of total life milieu therapy as supportive to individual therapy, or undertaken in its own right, will stand or fall with the wisdom and skill with which the protectors, teachers, and interpreters in the children's lives carry out their life space interview tasks.

First Aid and Ego Support for the Healthy Child in Moments of Unusual Strain*

The idea that normal and healthy children don't need any therapy is basically correct. The further assumption that being normal and healthy also means freedom from the danger of being overwhelmed by the complexities of life is a naïve illusion. Most healthy and normal kids are equipped with a considerable amount of resilience. They can handle a lot of experiences in their stride which would send their more disturbed compatriots into fits of psychotic blow-ups or neurotic convulsions. This, however, does not mean they can manage all of them. Take any child, no matter how well endowed, how healthy, how wonderful, even in the best conceivable classroom. At some time, during some phase of his life, he will find himself in two kinds of predicaments in which he will need the adult at hand to stand by. Indeed, during such a time it will make a lot of difference just how well this adult handles himself in this task.

Predicament No. 1: Child Overwhelmed by Internal Confusion or Conflict from Within

Even well-put-together children have moments when they are suddenly filled with rage, fear, shame, fury, embarrassment, anger, or fear of consequences. They may be disgusted with what adults did or did not do. They may experience a flare-up of an impulse to do or say something which they would not ordinarily consider acceptable. The moods of most normal children

* *Ibid.,* Introduction.

will sometimes swing from depressed to elated, from apathetic and bored to "high" and overexcited.... In short, sometimes kids need to be given some immediate ego support by an adult who is in an important role in their lives, regardless of therapy hour schedules which they may neither have nor need.

Predicament No. 2:   Child Overwhelmed by Experiences and Events from Without

All children find themselves, from time to time, overwhelmed by life situations which are unusual. They may not be prepared for such events. Indeed, such events may be more than anyone could expect even a well-developed and healthy ego to cope with. Consider the degrees of regression one may find even in perfectly healthy children when they suddenly get a new little brother, lose an old friend, experience the traumas of divorce or death in the family. Consider what contortions of behavior even well-brought-up kids may get into when they suddenly have to cope with the pressure of a group manipulator. In a bored classroom where the manipulator is working hard to get the other kids to clown, a self-respecting normal child might well feel he has to take the dare. Recall what occurs when a child meets with his first disappointment—a friend who betrays him, an admired hero who ridicules him. In such a case a child might well fall apart temporarily. Recall children's reactions to that painful period of suspended time before an exam, or right after an exam, or before a performance in front of an audience. Certainly it is usual for children to be exposed to all these experiences. While much of this kind of stress and strain can well be taken in stride, destiny does not use clinical judgment about how much a given child can manage on his own at a given time. Just as in our own lives, in theirs, too, things sometimes pile up. The point is, if the pile-up comes to a certain child at a certain age, it is important that an adult be near by to help the child cope with these overwhelming experiences.

Regardless of how basically healthy or normal the youngster is, during the onslaught of some experiences—just as in times of confusion and conflict from within—at such crises times, normal youngsters are much more similar to the legitimately disturbed ones than to their own normal selves. The same child who can listen respectfully to preaching and teaching under ordinary circumstances may be hard to reach while in tears, in a sulk, or under the impact of an excited flare-up. The same words and gestures that may be ordinarily used for his benefit won't do the trick in crises. To talk with a child in moments of strain necessitates an approach more similar to that of the clinician, therapist, psychiatrist, than to the usual civilian task of a classroom teacher.

In summary, there are moments in every child's life when he needs something that is very close to what we call "psychiatric interview technique," if only he were sick enough to need therapy. In this case, emergency depth-oriented interviewing may have to be done right then and there by the adult at hand. One cannot always wait until the doctor comes, and often a doctor is not what is actually needed.

Life Space Interview in the School Setting*
by Dr. Marcella Bernstein

By definition it is apparent that in most school situations the classroom teacher has limited opportunity to conduct a life space interview. Rarely is she free to conduct such an interview at the moment of trouble. Often the best she can do is to take the child out of the room and talk with him for a few moments in the hall. When more talk or time or privacy is needed, and the teacher cannot leave her class, she must be able to find help elsewhere.

At the time of the provocation the teacher may be excited, angry, or guilty, because the child's behavior is a response to something she has said or done. It is difficult for a teacher to be helpful, to give emotional first aid, when she herself is wounded. She may be angry because the lesson is interrupted or spoiled for the other children. Frequently she feels altogether ineffective at the moment and is in no condition to be supportive. Moreover, she is aware of thirty pairs of eyes watching her to see what she is going to do to the miscreant. She may be threatened at an open challenge to her authority and status. She worries about what the others will think if Johnny "gets away" with this. . . .

Fritz Redl suggests that all schools should have a person to assist with individual problems at the moment of flare-up. However, teachers will have to be taken into partnership with this person. For this discussion let us call him the principal. [He could be the

* *Ibid.,* pp. 35, 36, 37, 43, 44.

counselor or crisis teacher as well.] He must understand some of the unspoken elements in teachers' requests for help. The teacher is conflicted. She likes to think of herself as independently competent. She resents having to ask for it, yet she wants help when she wants it. Sometimes a teacher feels that the only way she can prove that she has problems is to unload them on the principal—"I failed with this kid, now you fail for a while"—not a particularly good referral spirit. Obviously, shuffling children back and forth from teacher to administrator in order to teach each other lessons is an unfortunate example of thoroughly bad staff relationships. The teacher, in turn, must understand that the principal cannot be expected to mete out observable punishments. She must know what he is trying to accomplish so that she doesn't feel, "It's no use to send a kid to the office. The principal doesn't do anything."

When an interview is indicated, it goes without saying that some amount of background knowledge is necessary. The teacher seems to have the advantage because she knows the child. However, if knowing the child and his past misdemeanors makes it difficult for the teacher to keep the interview focused on the immediate situation, it can be a disadvantage. Thus, her knowledge of Jane leads the teacher to the temptation to remind her that, in addition to the present incident in which she used four-letter Anglo-Saxon words, she didn't do her homework yesterday, she was late the day before, and she was reported by the School Patrol last week. In any case, regardless of the built-in temptation, the teacher does know the child. Also, she usually knows the facts of the altercation, and if it occurred in her presence, she knows—to some degree anyway—what happened.

The principal, on the other hand, may know very little about a child who is sent to him. He knows very little about the blow-up. At best, he may have a hasty note from the teacher describing the misbehavior. . . . In most cases, however, the child comes to the principal with a brief note or nothing more than an unhappy, "She sent me to the office." . . . It is hard to view the repeater with a fresh eye each time he appears in the office and, of course, impossible for the principal to pretend that he—and the culprit—don't realize that this is the third visit this week. But the principal can use what he knows so that he does not destroy, at the very outset, all possibility of affirmative movement.

The principal does know the teacher—or thinks he does. He

knows her level of tolerance for different kinds of misbehavior; he would know if a teacher were under some special strain for any of a hundred reasons, professional or personal; he knows the teacher's competencies and vulnerabilities. If he knows that the teacher herself was part of the problem, he has some sense of the aspects of the situation which the child cannot possibly report. . . .

How is the Return to Class Managed?

The return to class is important. It is only sensible to get children back to their rooms in a fashion that does not destroy all your hard work in the interview. The child may return to the classroom before the teacher has had enough time to swallow her anger. The child has had a chance to talk out his bad feelings but the teacher has not. It can be very frustrating to a teacher who still feels like beating the culprit—or wishes the principal would do it for her—to be confronted by a smiling Bill, relieved of his anger, or by a too benign principal or counselor. Here, of course, are the components of another life space interview—one which often must be conducted with haste and largely by means of non-verbal communication between the adults. Its effectiveness will rest heavily on the degree of rapport already established between them. A child must know on what terms he is brought back and so must the teacher. If you can accompany a child back to his room, it will prevent a triumphant re-entry, often an irresistible temptation to a fourteen-year-old. If you cannot take a child back to his room, a note to the teacher is imperative. You write it—not the child. Ask him to help you if it is appropriate. Let him dictate part of the message. Read it to him or let him read it for himself. Say exactly what you mean and don't dress the message up in educational jargon or a sophisticated code which the child can't understand. Don't expect the note to take the place of a necessary follow-up conference with the teacher. It is very difficult, at least for me, to find enough time for this follow-up, but it is none the less imperative.

Appendix C

A Note on Method

Before consultation was actually under way, our project staff set up a set of hypotheses concerning process, procedure, interaction, and conclusions. We agreed on a system of narrative logs, or reports, to be written within twenty-four hours of each consultation by every consultant. Although we scrupulously kept to the logs, it became apparent through the material we collected that a priori hypotheses were not only too inflexible for our material but would eliminate some of the depth, nuance, and breadth which we were getting. We wanted a tool which could show us how any one consultation with one individual had gone over a period of time. We also wanted information on cross-currents within a setting as well as how, let us say, the first sessions, or last session, or critical sessions had gone. Therefore, believing that in this pilot action-research we would derive more meaning from descriptive material than purely numerical analysis, we hit upon a kind of contextual analysis of our logs in which, from the material, we derived categories under which various aspects of the material would fall. By using a modified critical incident technique, by coding subcategories, we were able to see what we had done and what had happened both vertically and horizontally. That is to say, we could take any one interaction, or any one series of consultations with an individual, or we could take a glance at the fifth consultation at one setting or across the board at all settings. Along with questionnaires which we gave to all consultees, and which were also coded according to our contextually derived categories, we put all our material from the logs and all the teachers' diaries under this type of scrutiny. We did compile figures and tables from this material where we believed they would help clarify issues. Because of space, we have not included these in this book, although they were submitted to the National Institute of Mental Health as part of our report. At this point, having gone through this experience, we feel we could (or others could) make a far better controlled statistical kind of analysis of material gained through such a study. However, we did not want to miss out on the meaning by a too early rigidity in research framework. We found our categories useful and believe it is a helpful method for pilot projects of this sort.

Index